David Iredale and John Barrett

Discovering
Your Family Tree

D1076606

A Shire book

British Library Cataloguing in Publication Data: Iredale, David. Discovering your family tree. – 5th ed. 1. Genealogy – Popular works. 2. Great Britain – Genealogy – Popular works. I. Title II. Barrett, John. 929.1'072041. ISBN 0 7478 0535 0.

ACKNOWLEDGEMENTS

The line drawings and original artwork on pages 11, 16, 69, 87, 98, 147, 171 and back cover are by Christine Clerk.

Photographs are acknowledged as follows: John Barrett, pages 5, 6, 18, 45, 52, 67, 69, 74, 88, 91, 111 (both), 129, 136, 139, 183; David Iredale, pages 10, 35, 86 (both), 96, 130, 174, 183 (top and middle); Essex Record Ofice, page 39.

Published in 2002 by Shire Publications Ltd, Cromwell House, Church Street, Princes Risborough, Buckinghamshire HP27 9AA, UK. (Website: www.shirebooks.co.uk)
Copyright © 2002 by David Iredale and John Barrett. First published 1970; second edition 1973, reprinted 1975, 1976; third edition 1977, reprinted 1979, 1980, 1981, 1983. Fourth edition, completely revised, updated and rewritten by David Iredale and John Barrett, first published 1985, reprinted 1987, 1989, 1991, 1993, 1995 and 1998. Fifth edition, also rewritten and further expanded and published in a larger format, 2002. Number 93 in the Discovering series. ISBN 0 7478 0535 0.
David Iredale and John Barrett are hereby identified as the authors of this work in accordance with Section 77 of the Copyright, Designs and Patents Act, 1988.

Printed in Malta by Gutenberg Press Ltd, Gudja Road, Tarxien PLA 19, Malta.

Contents

1
Family history and genealogy

'Tinker, tailor, soldier, sailor, rich man …' – the start of the child's chant might list the people to be found in your family history, or, just as likely '… poor man, beggar man, thief'. Discovering ancestors is an absorbing pursuit. The old technologies of the printed book and pen-and-paper or ink-and-parchment archives trace ancestors in their hundreds. The new technologies of the internet and personal computer organise the crowds of predecessors into disciplined files and happy families. An optimistic handful of researchers takes the ancestral trail in the hope of uncovering an entitlement to an unclaimed fortune or a dormant peerage, though usually this is the road to disappointment. For most people, the search for ancestors is an adventure into the past, perhaps discovering along the way some explanation of the family's present situation. Tracks for future travel might also be signposted.

Ancestry has been important throughout history. Civil war may result when there is a disputed succession to the throne. Old English kings, aware that they held power precariously by armed force, made strenuous appeals to ancestry to legitimise their rule. The writers of the *Anglo-Saxon Chronicle*, initiated by Alfred the Great, were at pains to trace that Wessex monarch's descent from the fifth-century Germanic warlords Cerdic and Cynric, whose own descent was recited as follows:

> That Cerdic was the son of Elesa, the son of Esla, the son of Gewis, the son of Wig, the son of Freawine, the son of Frithugar, the son of Brand, the son of Bældæg, the son of [the god] Woden.

Ancestors are, technically, the people from whom the researcher biologically descends. An ancestor is also known as a forebear. During the sixteenth century, this word was written *forebeer*, a spelling that makes the meaning clearer: literally, a forebear is a person who is said to have *been before* – a 'before-beer'. The term *forefather* is also employed, though apparently not *foremother*. Western society has for some thousands of years been on the whole patriarchal, with descent conventionally traced through the male line. Traditionally, the male or father's line is known as the 'spear side' because a thrusting weapon has particularly masculine connotations. Following the female line offers the surest chance of a pedigree containing the true biological family, with the added interest of a new surname in each generation. The female line is known as the 'distaff side', named for an implement used in the womanly activity of spinning. The distaff, a rod used to hold the hank of carded wool from which a thread was drawn, was cleft and splayed and so thought to epitomise feminine characteristics.

A researcher's ancestors or, from another point of view, an ancestor's descendants can be arranged on a chart

The Maiden Stone, Aberdeenshire, carved with Pictish symbols indicating marital alliances.

4

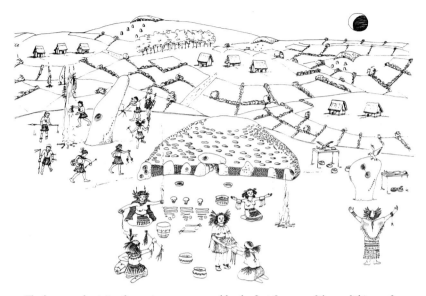

The bones and spirits of ancestors were revered by the first farmers of the neolithic era from around 4000 BC.

known as a *family tree*. This is a diagram that connects individuals and generations to show who married whom and which children resulted, how people were linked or related, where families lived, when individuals were born and when they died. Biological ancestors are, naturally, limited to just two parents, four grandparents, eight great-grandparents, and so on. An ancestor's direct descendants or progeny may be legion. A man and woman might easily have a dozen children. If every boy child went on to father twelve children and if every girl bore twelve babies then the original couple could be proud of 144 grandchildren. If matters proceeded unchecked there would, in due course, be 1728 great-grandchildren. By the ninth generation, perhaps less than 300 years later, the original couple would be the ancestors of nearly six billion descendants! In practice, of course, human beings do not multiply like cockroaches.

This neolithic ritual chamber at Ballykeel, County Armagh, was constructed before 3000 BC to house the bones and spirits of the ancestors of a prosperous Stone Age farming community.

5

This wedded pair of Bronze Age standing stones in Strathspey, Inverness-shire, epitomises the masculine and feminine characteristics of god-like forebears who ensured the fertility of crops and stock and from whom the community claimed descent.

Some individuals die young or are infertile; others choose not to have children or deliberately limit their family size. None the less a researcher in 1911 was able to prove that by the beginning of the twentieth century some tens of thousands of individuals could claim descent from the virile fourteenth-century English king Edward III. In such a descendant family tree, numerous uncles, aunts and cousins are included in each generation. Most of these people are probably someone's ancestors, though not the researcher's.

A family tree is like a woodland tree. Rooted in the past, it has a trunk from which major limbs branch out. These branches in turn sprout side shoots. So progeny proliferates from a forebear, the generations spreading upwards and continually budding new offshoots. The metaphor of a tree to represent the connection between ancestor and descendants is ancient, found in the Bible. Among the prophesies of Isaiah (11: 1), written in the eighth century BC, we find the words: 'And there shall come forth a rod out of the stem of Jesse, and a Branch shall grow out of his root.' The gospel writers Matthew and Luke, in the first century AD, traced the family tree of Jesus back to Jesse, the father of King David, and

The tree of Jesse from Christchurch Priory church, Dorset: a stem springs from the loins of King David's father, Jesse (below), and the nativity of Jesus is shown amid foliage (above); the intervening twenty-seven generations of the biblical family tree are omitted.

thus to the complex ancestor-lists of the first Book of Chronicles. The tree of Jesse, carved in stone or depicted in stained glass, was a familiar motif in medieval parish churches. An Old English word for tree stump, *stoc*, became the medieval *stock* referring to a family line from the earliest recorded ancestor. People might proudly claim descent from Norman, yeoman or good Welsh *stock*. A tree trunk sprouts new shoots, giving *stock* a meaning of 'store', as in a *stock* of memorable family stories. Inventories took *stock* of household goods while, for the daily soup, the *stock* pot was continually refilled with meat, vegetables and kitchen scraps. A forebear may have owned *stock* (cattle) or *stocks* (government bonds), worn *stock*ings, been *stock*y, hopefully not a laughing-*stock* – all associated with the one original root.

The word *pedigree* is sometimes used instead of *family tree*. This derives from the medieval *pedegru*, an expression coined by Anglo-French heralds who marked the names of heirs in a line of family descent with a spidery mark resembling a crane's foot, in French *pié de gru*. The branching shape of a family tree was also thought to resemble a crane's foot. A person boasting a known line of descent, in effect everyone on a pedigree chart, is said to be 'pedigreed'. The word, however, is usually reserved for people with a special, perhaps aristocratic, ancestry – and for cats, dogs and herds of cattle with a well-documented and untainted bloodline. The crucial word *genealogy* is adapted from the Greek. The first half of the word means 'people, race, family'; the second half means 'study of'. A genealogist is a person who studies families.

The first stage in this study is the compilation of a tabular pedigree or family tree, a bare skeleton of names, places and dates. The genealogist then proceeds by gathering biographical documentation relating to each individual itemised on the pedigree. The information is analysed and collated into a comprehensive family history. This narrative typically traces the relationships and life stories of family members, generation by generation, against a background of regional and national history.

Family genealogy and history should eventually be traceable through ten or twelve generations, perhaps covering three centuries. The family tree for such a period might contain a thousand personal names, or more if in-laws are included. It may be possible to discover links with renowned historical figures, not necessarily direct ancestors, who appear among the outlying branches. King Edward III is a favourite guest on the periphery of a pedigree. Some people like to find connections with the blue blood of the aristocracy. (The Spanish term *sangre azul*, 'blue blood', is derived from the Persian blue mineral lapis lazuli, whose rare rich hue was regarded as the colour of heaven.) Such families may proudly link themselves, legitimately or otherwise, with William the Conqueror, legendary Gaelic kings, Anglo-Saxon heroes, the god Woden and the biblical progenitors Adam and Eve.

The genealogist brings particular skills to the task of compiling a family history. Patience is called for when reading printed sources and old documents. Care and application are essential when compiling a pedigree. Self-discipline is required in adhering to the task in hand, leaving sidetracks for future generations. An interest in, and some knowledge of, regional and national history is a distinct advantage. Economic, social and political circumstances may be crucial to family fortunes. Housing conditions, leisure pursuits, job opportunities, sexual mores, church attendance, diet, morality, education and personal health are important influences in the lives of people listed on a genealogical chart.

The attributes of ancestors may be transmitted down the generations. Intelligence, academic ability, musical and artistic gifts are sometimes thought to result from such factors as wealth, encouragement by elders or family traditions. Physical attributes such as hair colour, facial features, blood groups, general stature and susceptibility to particular diseases may be congenital, written into the individual's genes and transmitted inescapably from parent to child. The science of genetics including DNA analysis promises a revolution in genealogy. Proverbially it

7

is a wise father who knows his own child. Family trees typically show the names of husbands and wives and their children. The genealogist appreciates, however, that a husband is not always the father of his wife's children and so there are strong arguments in favour of pedigrees traced through the female line. Occasionally even the wife is thought not to be the mother. Mary of Modena, wife of James II and VII, produced a son and heir, later the Old Pretender, who was said by Protestant opponents of the Stuarts to have been a stranger's child smuggled into the palace in a warming-pan.

Genealogical research can be pursued for practical advantage and financial gain. An accurate family tree, fully authenticated by archival documents, is usually essential for proving rights to disputed land, money or titles of nobility. A will cannot normally be contested without proof of descent. An heir is recognised in law only if a pedigree supports the claim. A genealogist could authenticate the relationship of a mother and child separated for decades by family circumstances. It is little wonder that lawyers demand substantial fees for conducting genealogical research. A client saves the cost of providing evidence for litigation by gathering his or her own information. Expertise comes with experience. But not everyone has the time or the aptitude for genealogical research, involving long hours in the public library and archives or surfing sessions on the Internet. An expert genealogist may therefore earn a comfortable subsistence compiling pedigrees for other people.

From the middle of the twentieth century, numerous genealogical sources have been opened to researchers. Once the privileged preserve of academics, lawyers and administrators, today even the most esoteric archives may be available to ordinary people pursuing an ancestral trail. Archive offices have been established by national government, county councils, commercial and industrial organisations, universities and churches. Public libraries have energetically embraced heritage and history, offering documentary sources crucial to genealogical research. The progressive computerisation of records and finding aids speeds up and simplifies research. Databases of hundreds of archive and research institutions are now accessible through the Internet (see pages 47–9). A pedigree can be compiled on a personal computer in the comfort of the home. The trail is followed along the easy path of the digital database and CD-ROM. Parents, grandparents, second cousins and great-great-aunts nestle comfortably together on the disks or hard drive of the researcher's own home computer. Past generations are recalled and individuals reunited into families at the click of a mouse. Digital records lead into less familiar but well travelled territories.

It should be possible to progress beyond a bare pedigree to research a short history of the family. This might require looking at the recorded events of each individual's life. One of the popularisers of the pursuit of family history in recent decades was the black American Alex Haley, whose book *Roots* (1976) – an instructive exemplar of the delights (and pitfalls) of genealogy – inspired television adaptations and documentaries and fixed *roots* in its modern sense of 'family history'. A firm grounding in national and regional history is an advantage here. History will seem far from tedious when related to particular individuals with whom the researcher has established a personal sympathy and family connection. Information on educational achievements invites broader research on school regimes in the past. Sources that reveal an individual's lifestyle, employment experiences, domestic arrangements and relationships beg the reading of a general social history. The discovery of an individual's financial situation and political affiliations demands a setting in a wider economic environment. Military service, whether as a private soldier or a celebrated admiral, and foreign travel, as migrant or holidaymaker, put the family on the world stage. Moral lapses and criminal activity add spice to the story, perhaps as surprising and uncharacteristic aberrations that require explanation through psychological insight, but sometimes within a pattern of deviancy that pervades the history down to generations still living. There are skeletons in the tidiest closets. On the whole, though, the pursuit of family history is relatively painless – a harmless personal endeavour that seldom receives academic plaudits or financial gain. Perseverance is amply rewarded by a growing intimacy with generations long departed, even though the entrancing humdrum variety of ordinary lives may sometimes lead to an exasperated expletive, a raised eyebrow or a sentimental tear.

Genealogical societies

A family history society offers the company of like-minded enthusiasts as well as a pool of experienced genealogists happy to offer advice and constructive criticism. Fellow genealogists have probably encountered, and surmounted, the whole gamut of challenges arising from a growing family tree. Society membership gives access to workshops and seminars led by guest speakers as well as convivial joint expeditions to research centres. Specialist library resources, archival catalogues, indexes, transcribed documents, pedigrees and computer software may be available to members. The address of your nearest society is obtainable at the public library. Particularly useful is the Federation of Family History Societies (referred to as FFHS), formed in 1974. From a succession of headquarters the FFHS has published a variety of finding aids describing and locating genealogical sources. These booklets are updated as new information emerges on the availability and location of archives. In citing FFHS guides in subsequent chapters, only the date of first publication is given, with a recommendation to consult the latest edition. FFHS produces standard forms for recording family connections and archive searches. A register of societies and individuals working in particular genealogical fields is also maintained. In Scotland the equivalent grouping, the Scottish Association of Family History Societies, was founded in 1986. For researchers concentrating upon just one surname, there is usually a Guild of One-Name Studies. Membership establishes contact with other researchers and avoids duplication of work on a particular family. No limit is set on the number of one-name societies that can be applied to.

The Society of Genealogists in London maintains an advice service for members. The society's centre of operations offers an extensive library of heraldry books, periodicals, databases of surnames and sources on microfilm and microfiche. The society is noted for its collection of printed parish registers as well as indexes of wills, marriage licences, monumental inscriptions and family histories. Also available are the International Genealogical Index (IGI), the Bernau index to Chancery proceedings and Boyd's indexes of London inhabitants and of marriages. Society publications include the series entitled *My Ancestor was a Baptist/Jewish/Methodist/Merchant Seaman/Migrant (in England and Wales) ... how can I find out more about him?* The society's *National Index of Parish Registers* discusses the whereabouts of original parish registers, transcripts, bishops' transcripts and related documents. Genealogical records in the regions are set out in the series *County Sources at the Society of Genealogists*. Another useful source is the Institute of Heraldic and Genealogical Studies, Canterbury, and its journal *Family History*. The academic study of families and communities is promoted by the Cambridge Group for the History of Population and Social Structure. Contributions are welcomed from regional historians, genealogists and social scientists. Information is collected from archive sources on the name, age, occupation, marital status, children and residence of each inhabitant of a parish from the sixteenth century onwards. This data makes possible the reconstitution of families, the academic analysis of occupational structure, the study of social groupings and research into the population of a community.

Family history centres, funded by the Church of Jesus Christ of Latter-day Saints (LDS), and associated with the Genealogical Society of Utah, are open to researchers of any faith, normally without charge. Addresses can be found via the public library, the Internet and the telephone directory under *Church of Jesus*

Christ. Facilities include genealogical reference books, boxed files on particular families and surnames, copies of parish registers, indexes of wills and microfilms of selected public archives. Computers are set to the proprietary software known as *FamilySearch*, accessing information on archives, books, catalogues and finding aids. Members of the LDS church are popularly known as Mormons, from the author of the scriptural text the *Book of Mormon*. The existence of this sacred record was revealed by a divine messenger named Moroni to a young man, Joseph Smith, in New England in 1823. The sect expanded in a climate of religious revivalism in the 1830s. Smith himself was lynched by zealots in 1844 and his followers migrated west to the Utah desert, where Salt Lake City was established. The family was central to the Mormon way of life and continued into eternity. In the hereafter individual spirits awaited resurrection. Promises (covenants) made in temples by parents and offspring might unite families, including deceased ancestors, who choose (or not) to accept these covenants. In order to covenant on behalf of the deceased, Mormons must first research the family tree and identify each individual. When a pedigree is satisfactorily completed, all identified progenitors may be baptised and ceremonially sealed as posthumous church members. To assist members' genealogical research, LDS authorities have sent specialist teams around the world to locate and copy existing genealogical records. Copies of documents from many parts of the world, though with a strong emphasis on the readily accessible archives of Britain and Western Europe, are collected at considerable expense into a central archive. This repository is located in chambers hollowed out of Granite Mountain, Utah, where storage areas are designed to withstand natural disasters and nuclear strikes. Security arrangements, physical storage and air-conditioning systems are the envy of archivists working for old-world public bodies. This is the collection made available to researchers worldwide through microfilm, microfiche, CD-ROM, database and website.

The religious and administrative centres of the Church of Jesus Christ of Latter-Day Saints (Mormons) in Salt Lake City, Utah; God's messenger Moroni trumpets from the temple spire.

2
Family stories

Each member of a family has a story to tell. Reminiscences should be collected and preserved because the entertaining anecdotes, character-forming episodes, secret hopes and fears of everyday life are rarely recorded in documentary sources. An elderly relative, telling a tale learned as a child at his own grandfather's knee, spans a century or more of the family history. Younger relatives, including parents, aunts and uncles, are a rich fund of family jokes, secrets and legends. Friends may contribute surprising or contradictory supplements to a family story as well as offering different perspectives upon the attitudes, tastes, temper, physical appearance and intellectual abilities of people living and dead. Listening patiently to people talking by the fireside or in the pub is a natural means of gaining information. Songs, poems, proverbs, prayers and family histories were in the old days normally passed down by word of mouth – until writing arrived to fix oral traditions in ink on a page. As a conscientious newspaperman, Charles Dickens interviewed residents of the Fleet Street district of London. He was a keen devotee of oral history. He based the characters of his novel *Oliver Twist* upon real people of the generation before 1834, though changing their names for dramatic effect. We can imagine Fagin, the disreputable trainer of thieves, maintaining good records of income and expenditure, enforcing performance indicators in respect of the productivity of his young protégés. On the other hand, Dickens could not expect Bill Sikes to open his books for inspection. Instead he relied on oral testimony in respect of Sikes's branch of the business. Nancy's trade as a prostitute might be documented through court records, directories and the memoirs of clients. Her enterprise was underground but not illegal, though the secrets of pimps, rent-boys, streetwalkers, gigolos, courtesans, madams and clients could be discovered only by the most adventurous and persistent of hands-on oral history techniques.

Human memory is deplorably fallible. We lament today that our grandmother as a child did not pay proper attention when her grandfather related episodes of his

What did you do in the 1960s, Mummy? It is not always easy to persuade parents and grandparents to discuss their youthful activities and enthusiasm or to visualise the teenage antics of respected elders.

youth. We regret that Granny, careless of the value of such information to family historians of the future, was only half listening, fidgeting to go out to play, wondering what cakes would be on the tea table, smiling politely but inwardly bored by her Grandpa's incomprehensible circumlocution. The process of remembering is sometimes more creative than truthful. The ignorant or forgetful informant conjures from imagination facts, faces and figures to fill gaps in a threadbare story, generously adding here and there new elements to please the interrogator. Thus the bare facts of a legend, preserved orally through several generations, are thickly encrusted with the embellishments of each retelling. The skilful interviewer soon learns to pick the threads of truth from the embroidery of fiction and to know when, through some affected niceness, an episode of illegitimacy, divorce, crime or poverty is being avoided or concealed. Academics early appreciated the richness of oral culture, particularly in districts where literate habits had not yet taken root. Expeditions were mounted to note down such traditions. Arguably, this intervention accelerated rather than prevented extinction! A pioneer of the personal approach to history was George Ewart Evans, whose interviews made fascinating books. Techniques were formalised through the writings of Paul Thompson of Essex University's oral history unit and in publications of the Ruskin College History Workshop. The journal *Oral History* keeps the genealogist abreast of developments.

For recording interviews a portable cassette-recorder or tripod-mounted camcorder preserves the maximum information with the least trouble and expense. Shorthand notes cannot keep pace with the gush of reminiscences from an enthusiastic informant. Nor can written notes reproduce an individual's quirks of emphasis and inflexion. The interviewer should be familiar with the equipment – which ought to be in good order, set up without fuss or delay. Microphones are placed appropriately to pick up the words of interviewer and interviewee. A sensible researcher carries a supply of adaptors, fuses, extension leads, spare tapes and batteries. At the beginning of each tape is recorded the name of the interviewer and informant, with the date, place and time of the conversation. This information is also written on the cassette and cassette box. The first task of the interviewer is to persuade the subject to speak, and to speak naturally. Even voluble people become irretrievably tongue-tied when faced with a microphone. The interviewer establishes a rapport through ordinary conversation, not minding the amount of tape used to obtain one fragment of family history. An informal setting, a comfortable chair and a warm fire in the subject's own home put both parties at ease. A pot of tea or a stiff drink will further help to settle nerves on both sides and lubricate the memory. A family photograph album starts the reminiscences flowing. Informants may be old, frail in body and weak in mind. They may be tedious, evasive, abusive, obscene, obtuse, enigmatic, ironic, vindictive or rude. They may tell lies. The interviewer accepts this, knowing that there are nuggets of family history in the matrix of memory. Informants will be disconcerted by severe questioning and unlikely to recall incidents and dates with forensic precision. The researcher is not in any position to apply the thumbscrews to extract the truth, the whole truth and nothing but the truth.

Questions should be carefully framed, suited to the interviewee's personality and intellect: comprehensible but not patronising, penetrating but not impertinent. A structured interview requires the preparation in advance of a questionnaire. Questions arranged in a logical, perhaps chronological, sequence provide the maximum information, making the most of an opportunity (perhaps the last) of speaking with an aged relative. The structure should never be so rigid as to make the conversation impersonal and the interviewee uncomfortable; nor should the programme be so pedantically followed as to prevent digression into potentially interesting unforeseen areas.

A STRUCTURED QUESTIONNAIRE
childhood
date and place of birth

parentage, brothers and sisters

earliest memories

unpleasant episodes: death, illness, accidents, scandals, mischief, punishment

pleasant episodes: holidays, birthdays, Christmas, trips and treats, pocket money

home: address, description, contents, garden, street, moving house

religion: Sunday school, church activities, nativity plays, picnics, ministers

hobbies and pastimes, fashions and fads, games, food, clothing

school: subjects, interests, awards, friends, teachers, school dinners, pranks, punishments

youth groups: Cubs, Scouts, Brownies, Guides, Boy's Brigade, sports clubs, dancing classes, collectors' clubs

crushes, girl/boy friends, puberty, first period, sexual experimentation

young adult
first date, first love, virginity, masturbation, sexual activity, contraception, abortion

college: subjects (why chosen), awards, friends (names, social status), teachers

recreation: sports, societies, pastimes, politics, drink, drugs, travel, music, art, theatre, music hall

voluntary service

military service: stations, combat, rank, exploits, discipline, comrades, officers

apprenticeship, vocational and other training

career
childhood ambitions

jobs: dates, firms, types of work, wages, peculation, promotion, colleagues, bosses, working conditions, travel, accidents, sackings

trade union: membership, office, strikes

retirement

marriage
fiancés/fiancées, love affairs, liaisons, homosexuality

spouse: first impressions, subsequent impression, developing relationship

in-laws: first impression, subsequent relationship

wedding: place, guests, reception, speeches, finances

honeymoon, adultery, divorce

family
home: house, flat, garden, mortgage, rent, evictions and flittings

furniture and possessions: consumer goods, bicycles, car

children: names, birthdays, infant deaths, character, first words, hobbies, education

daily routine: food, clothing, bedtime, meal times

activities: games, walks, outings, pets, pastimes

holidays and travel

community involvement
church: denomination, offices

politics: membership of party, offices, activities, pressure groups, demonstrations and direct action

friends: name, social class, gender, fallings out

enemies: name, social class, reason for enmity, consequences, reconciliations

clubs and societies

culture: arts, theatre, amateur dramatics

personality
religion: views on God, life, death and other religions or sects, conversion, loss of faith

politics: views on class, economics, race, ecology

health: injuries, disease, treatment

prosperity: good times, bad times, achievements, disappointments

aspirations

The interviewee may choose to speak frankly. The interviewer then listens patiently without appearing shocked or embarrassed if other family members are abused, awful secrets revealed or unconventional opinions aired. No hint of impatience should be expressed if the subject strays from the strict confines of the family history. There cannot, of course, be any outright contradiction of the story being told – if there are hopes of being invited back for a second visit. Usually it is difficult to persuade a subject to speak candidly about the intimate and visceral details of everyday life, and all the more so when interviewing a near relative such as a parent or grandparent. There are, in most families, large areas of life that are simply not spoken of. Divorce, death, crime and wartime experiences may all be off limits. In such cases the researcher must accept the boundaries drawn and seek some other avenue of enquiry. Despite its fundamental role in projecting the family into the future, sex is an especially difficult area. Occasionally a relative will be psychologically driven to speak of traumatic experiences such as abortion, incest and paedophilia. Ordinary sexuality including homosexual relationships, adultery, pornography and the humdrum intimacies of the marriage bed remain close secrets – blank pages in the family history unless an intimate diary or secret correspondence emerges from the archives to fill the gap.

Oral information is quite often all the genealogist has to rely on, at least in the first instance. On 7th November 1940 a Whitley bomber crashed on houses in the burgh of Forres, Moray, killing all on board. Wartime censorship ensured that the incident was not reported in the newspaper or in town council minutes. Families were advised 'Like Dad, keep Mum' because, in wartime, they were told, 'careless talk costs lives'. An anodyne legend was started, declaring that the pilot had heroically spurned a temptation to land his crippled plane on the school field where children were playing, thus selflessly sacrificing his own life and the lives of his five crewmen. Numerous people were happy to theorise otherwise:

> There was an almighty bang. It shook all the windows … When we got to Fern Villa Mrs Bethune was throwing her clothes, fur coats and best clothes and other items out of the window. We could see the flames and smoke from the plane. Mr Miel, an Italian who owned a fish and chip shop, was the hero of that night. I can still see to this day the men taking the stretchers out with 'heaps' on the stretchers. It really made us sick … During that time there was an awful lot of planes crashing and the local people were saying 'It's sabotage. The Irish are putting sugar in the petrol' and we all believed that.

> (Jeanie Ross, 110 Anderson Crescent, 25th September 1978)

Other witnesses concentrated on the more unsettling aspects of the story. One of these emphasised the memory that the plane struck the garden of Fern Villa just as old Mrs Bethune was climbing out of (or perhaps into) her bath. Another regaled hearers with lurid accounts of how each victim died: the pilot decapitated, the rear gunner impaled on his guns, and so forth. A board of inquiry also took oral testimony from all concerned. The board's investigation ignored as irrelevant the alarming frequency with which planes from the nearby airfield plummeted from the skies. The blame was placed squarely on the dead pilot. He had, it alleged, disobeyed orders and overflown the town to buzz the house where his wife of six weeks was lodging. The genealogist sifts all the evidence, written and oral, before tentatively deciding what really happened and who was responsible. The crash will be alluded to again (page 179) in another connection.

While the interview is still fresh in the researcher's mind the tape may be accurately transcribed and typed. The typescript can be annotated to reproduce nuances of emphasis and inflexion. The account may then be carefully checked for any inconsistencies of place and time. These ambiguities could be resolved during a second interview. A typed synopsis of each transcribed tape may prove useful

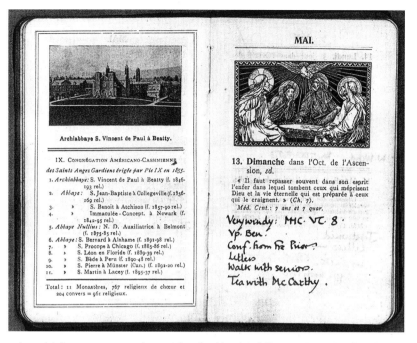

An oral informant uses even the most heavily abbreviated diary entries to jog the memory about people and events.

when collating and analysing the information. The tape should not be edited. The significance of an apparent irrelevance or error will probably emerge later. All of a relative's thoughts, words and significant silences are useful as indicative of character and attitude. Information should not be deleted or improved: not the infelicities of language and syntax that pepper ordinary speech, not the colourful expletives of an old soldier, nor the malicious insinuations of an embittered divorcee. Even a mistaken, false, indecorous or obscene statement adds to the historian's appreciation of an ancestor's character and influence upon the rest of the family.

3
Family papers

Family archives may be reverently preserved by parents to pass on to their children, or prudently lodged with the family lawyer. Sometimes the archive is difficult to recognise as such, consisting of a jumble of unsorted papers and photographs in an old suitcase under the bed. Some of the papers could be duplicated in archives of church or central government. But official files on individual citizens, such as adults serving in the armed forces or children in care, are not always retained permanently. Destruction through weeding of 'particular instance' papers is a prime function of government archivists, and documentation in the family's own keeping is of crucial importance.

Family papers require careful preservation and systematic organisation. Advice may be sought from archivists and conservationists at the town or county archives. Commercial firms offering conservation services will recommend the most appropriate treatment for any damaged item. Careful storage and an embargo on handling usually suffice to ensure the survival of precious papers. Where positive action is called for, bookbinding and paper-repair services are available, for instance from Cedric Chivers in Bath or Riley, Dunn & Wilson in Falkirk. Original documents such as photographs, title deeds, wills, birth certificates, letters, bills and receipts are best stored flat rather than folded, in manilla folders and strong cardboard boxes. A shoebox lined with acid-free paper is quite adequate if archive boxes of professional quality are unavailable. The fugitive inks and wood-pulp papers of the past two or three centuries may deteriorate if exposed to ultra-violet light. These, and indeed all documents, benefit from being kept away from daylight and fluorescent light in a relatively dry atmosphere at a cool 16°C (60°F). The attic may meet these requirements. Fragile items may be photocopied so that the originals are spared excessive handling. Reproductions of favourite items, enlarged, reduced, sepia-

Attic archives and artefacts in the family home are the starting point for genealogical research.

16

toned or otherwise enhanced, are eminently suitable for framing. It is also feasible to scan family papers onto disk for ready reference on the family personal computer.

An annotated family **Bible** is the treasure that heads a genealogist's wish list. As soon as the holy text was widely available in print during the seventeenth century, most families acquired a copy for home study and family devotion. It became traditional to record signal family events on the blank leaves, or end-papers, at the front and back of the book. Usually this was restricted to notes of births, marriages and deaths, though other information also occasionally appeared. A Bible was handed down, each new generation adding to the record. Additional end-papers, pasted in as required, survived the wear and tear of household upheavals better than loose sheets simply interleaved.

A Bible belonging to the Cogger family begins with this inscription: 'Alfred Cogger And Margaret Watson Was Mared On the 15th Day of April 1857 this Boock Was Made A present to Me ... by My Mother Elizabeth Cogger.' Other entries follow: 'Charles James Cogger Was lost in the Schoonar Viscount McDuff ... on a Voige from Sidney to ... bay of Bengall ... 1882'. Information was diligently recorded over the decades. The Bible eventually came to rest in the public library, held for five years but then destroyed to save space – a lesson perhaps for genealogists.

A prayer book, hymnal, psalter, missal or other religious manual was in the past purchased for recording family history, or perhaps a sturdy volume of Bunyan's *Pilgrim's Progress*, revered even if unread. Isaac and Ann Skelton, who set up home in the prosperous fishing town of Whitehaven after their marriage in 1759, preferred a Book of Common Prayer. Their children were born between 1760 and 1778. The youngest daughter, named Ann or Nancy, married in 1802 Richard Woosnam, recently arrived, perhaps with the Montgomeryshire regiment. As the youngest daughter, Ann nursed her parents in their final illnesses and inherited the prayer book. The Woosnams carried the volume to their new home on thriving Merseyside, and then to prosperous Birmingham.

Family **portraits** show individuals, posed and primped for the occasion. The sitters are surrounded by a selection of props and possessions. Through an open window the artist offers a distant glimpse of

Formal Victorian photographs often commemorate important events in the life of the family – here the acquisition of a bicycle.

17

'Carte-de-visite' photographic portraits were a notable craze during the 1860s and 1870s. These examples show friends and relations of Captain William Thom RN.

a well-heeled family's reeking factories and rolling acres. Outdoor portraits are posed in improbably romantic landscapes and impossibly tidy gardens. Nor was it only the landed gentry and comfortable industrialists who commissioned portraits. Professional but provincial artists painted shopkeepers, farmers and public officials. Among even the humblest households may be discovered sketches and caricatures of parents and siblings as revealing of character and pretensions as the most accomplished studio portrait.

A **photograph album** is a prized possession, offering immediate portrayals of people and places associated with the family over a period of perhaps 150 years, though pictures in albums are very often uncaptioned and undated. Photography was popularised during the 1840s. Within a generation, most towns supported a professional photographer. Their sharp early pictures from glass-plate negatives profit from study with the aid of a magnifying glass. During the 1860s all but the poorest people posed for studio portraits that were reproduced and mounted as cartes-de-visite. These photographic visiting cards were distributed among relatives and left with the servant when making a courtesy call. As the craze continued, people collected scores of cartes-de-visite, annotated with names, dates and personal messages, preserving a record of family resemblances. The photographer's own address printed on the mounting card may provide a helpful clue to the subject's place of residence. Photography as a hobby attracted people with money, who usually recruited a servant to assist with the ponderous early paraphernalia. In the absence of any social convention forbidding involvement, women excelled in the new art form. One such was Julia Cameron, who at the age of fifty emerged as an outstandingly skilful photographer with the collodion wet-plate process of the 1860s. From the 1880s improved film and affordable portable cameras permitted ordinary people to take pictures.

Indoor photographs were taken to commemorate signal events in the family history, especially rites of passage such as christenings, confirmations, a boy's graduation from skirts to trousers (breeching), weddings and first birthdays. Victorian sentimentality also required portraits of the recently departed laid out ready for the grave. People were usually carefully posed, in formal dress, perhaps with a few studio props and a painted backdrop as insubstantial as the sitter's pretensions. Families were also pictured outdoors, against a background typically of the family home. In the foreground may be a first bicycle or a newly shot stag. Informal snaps show people taking tea, playing tennis, tending the garden or paddling at the seaside. Photographs may speak volumes if sensitively scrutinised, perhaps freezing a particular mannerism that has been transmitted down the generations to the present. Much can be inferred from the body language of individuals within a group picture: an uncle standing close to his daughter but aloof from his wife; a teenager sulking on the margin of the group; a husband smiling at his wife's sister while his spouse scowls. Researchers may be able to determine whether the family are dressed in the latest fashion or obliged to wear unfashionable coats and hand-me-down frocks. Shoes may be carefully polished or scuffed and scruffy, cravats arranged with due precision or carelessly knotted. Jewellery such as brooches, watch chains and necklaces may be recognised as items still worn by family members. A pedigree gains added interest if a copied picture of each ancestor or relative is pasted onto the chart or perhaps scanned into the computer file relating to each individual. Old pictures can be copied and indeed digitally enhanced at modest cost by high-street photographers. Negatives, slides and prints can be transformed into Photo-CDs. Software is readily available for accessing and manipulating the images on a home computer.

Home movies were popular from about 1925 onwards. Middle-class families could afford the popular Kodak and Pathéscope cameras and projectors. These systems used either 9.5 or 16 mm, then 8 or Super 8 film, initially only black-and-white. Colour film became widely available from the 1950s. Serviceable projectors are not easy to find nowadays, hence the popularity of home movies copied on videotape. The introduction of practicable home-video equipment from the 1970s onwards has resulted in a burgeoning film coverage of family life. Family holidays, outings, weddings, christenings, birthdays, Christmases, bar mitzvahs, Diwalis and Ramadans are copiously recorded. Bath-times and the birth of babies are familiar video subjects – carefully preserved as archives of the future.

Correspondence may survive, particularly from the period of improved postal services at home and abroad after 1840. Letters addressed to family members and, more rarely, copies of letters despatched may be found neatly filed or simply dumped in an old tin trunk. A first task is to sort the letters into date order or to create subject files such as *Letters from Australia, 1847–53*, or *Correspondence over Bert Aynsley's lost will, 1888*. Careful thought will be needed before breaking up any original bundles of papers. Clearly a collection of love letters tied with ribbon makes a sentimental plea not to be separated. Other bundles may seem to contain unrelated items accidentally thrown together, but some future revelation in the emerging family history may prove they were put together for some good reason. There was some concern in correspondence among members of the Mather family in Derby in 1861 when a favourite and aged uncle, Robert Bates, disappeared. Modern genealogists were quickly on the case searching death certificates for the period 1857–61. But no death was recorded. Robert's fate seemed likely to remain a mystery until the papers of a certain Charles Mather came to light. These included a letter written on 23rd December 1861 by a friend, William Atkinson of Laurel Cottage, Kedleston Road, Derby. Atkinson had tramped the streets enquiring after the old reprobate, at last finding him at 147 Abbey Street, 'looking hale and well and as he states not quite stumped up yet we had a Pot together ... he is very Jolly'. This happy ending provides the fullest picture available of Bates. There is no photograph of him, no indication of his character beyond these few phrases in a family letter.

Horatio, son of the above Charles Mather, was born in 1835 and married Jane Roberts, from the borders of Wales. The couple opened a beershop in a room of

A family letter from Pitlochry, Perthshire, with a view of Dunkeld, 1879.

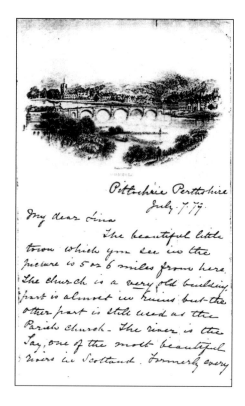

their home in Liverpool. On 18th September 1873 Horatio wrote in despair to his father:

> I am sorry to say that Jane as not been sober only three days since the time you ware hear breaking Glasses refuseing to leave the bar night or day. She will neather be advised nor forced out … I cannot bare with it eney longer what her temper and the drink one day after another i should come over but cant leave the bar or the rughts might healp themselfs … no servant will stay with her so if you will get a smal wooden box I will try to do better things one way or other if it was not for the children i would have left long since. I have about £20 in cash and that will take me to some place …

Horatio was a competent penman, though spelling was not his strongest point. The word *rughts* may be a misspelling of 'roughs'. He perhaps intended the Manx-Liverpool dialect *rughts*, for which dictionaries offer the definition 'hags, scoundrels'. Horatio carried out his threat. He packed a few essential possessions into his 'smal wooden box' and took ship for America. When he next wrote to his father in 1875, the letter was headed 'Duncurk 480 Miles from N York June 10th 9pm' and reported that he and a companion 'went to Central Park New York 9½ Miles round the nices place I ever saw but the most part of New York is a stinking place … we payed 75 cents for the bed'. Having received a reply from his father, which has not been located but may survive among American family papers, Horatio wrote again in July, this time from Columbus, Ohio:

> you say Jane in her letter wants to know what I intend to do about the children you

may tell her that unless she helps to suport them I intend to put them in the workhouse and get marred again … thir as been a deal of rain hear …

True to his word, Horatio did indeed remarry, bigamously, after giving his alcoholic wife permission to do likewise. His children were initially brought up by their grandparents. A letter from Horatio, by now a merchant in Columbus, was preserved by his sister Charlotte Woosnam. It is dated 27th October 1895. Horatio and Jane's daughter Louisa, the child of a broken home, was now herself suffering a failed marriage. Horatio announced that Louisa 'as not lived with her husband for about three years … am sorry to say she as some of her Mothers temper and looks like her but not so large'. Horatio, or perhaps we should call him 'Oratio, dropped his aitches and retained a Liverpool accent in speech and writing to the end of his life. Horatio's son William also turned his back on things Liverpudlian. According to the Groton and Ryegate edition of *The Times* (Vermont) newspaper in 1901, William became secretary of the United Mine Workers Association. With money so earned he paid for a course at the Ohio Central Normal School and was ordained a Methodist minister in 1894. He married a doctor's daughter and moved east in 1899 to a charge in the fashionable community of Groton – to where his two sisters had already escaped from dreary family quarrels in Liverpool.

Correspondence was a crucial means of maintaining family links even between continents. From the seventeenth century onwards emigration was an attractive proposition. The prospects of religious freedom, virgin land and commercial opportunities attracted enterprising individuals and younger members of large families. Immigration controls were minimal and boat fares affordable. Peasants cleared from highland estates might even obtain a passage for the new world paid for by their landlord, laird or clan chief. These migrations sometimes resulted in children disappearing without trace, leaving a tantalising bare branch in the family tree. In 1879, William and Charlotte Woosnam decided to migrate with their seven children to Townsville in Queensland. This region of north-eastern Australia was being vigorously promoted in the newspapers and shipping offices. Evidence for the family's decision takes two forms: a wooden box and a bundle of correspondence. William, a carpenter by trade, made a cabin trunk for the family's luggage. For each female in the party, Charlotte was advised to pack:

> 6 Chimeses, 6 pair of Drawers, 3 Night Dresses, 2 Petticoats, 2 white cotton Skirts not for the voyage, 6 pairs of Stocking, 2 pair of Boots 3 Dresses warm one thin one for the Different Climate Best one to land in, bring an Ulster, 2 hats, 3 or 4 Bars of soap

In the event, the parents sent two of their older daughters ahead to spy out the land. The girls travelled alone under the auspices of an emigration society with a vicar's certificate that their former surname Wolstenholme was now written (as it had long been spoken) Woosnam. In letters home, Lina and Cissie reported that the family's passes for settlement were ready. But by 1881 father and mother had still not made a move. They were both now over forty years old, the cut-off age for emigration to Townsville. The difficulty was not insurmountable. Cissie wrote on 21st June 1882 promising to say 'you both are not 40 years yet we will send you word what we will say your age is may get the pass in october'. Lina concocted a family age list for the authorities and urged her parents to put a 'couple Dozen Lemons at the bottom of your Box' as preservatives. Parents and box, however, stayed put on Merseyside. A final, afterthought child was born in 1883. The family, separated by half the globe, remained united by mail.

Correspondence during wartime kept people in touch with family events. Military personnel recounted their experiences in letters home that may be more immediate and informative than memoirs and oral accounts compiled years after the event.

Christmas greetings to the family, from T236836 Corporal Freddy Macpherson, 1944.

Censorship could be a hindrance to the free exchange of news. Servicemen might be restricted to printed cards stating 'I am well' from 'somewhere in the Mediterranean'. Prisoners of war fared better through the Red Cross. Their communications might be numerous and lengthy, arriving in batches at long intervals. Children evacuated from cities to escape bombing wrote letters home that do not always describe a rural idyll. On the outbreak of war in 1939, William Eckford, aged thirteen, and his little brother John were evacuated from Edinburgh to the bleak coastal burgh of Buckie in Banffshire. Their fisher-wife guardian seemed an ogress. On 14th September 1939, William wrote to his mother, asking for clothes for himself and John: 'A pair of trousers, he has only one pair, shoes he needs as well, his Wellingtons are all ripped and his plimplsoles are trough at the toes.' It was not unknown for belongings of evacuees to be shared out among the host's children, or simply taken and sold. William concluded: 'My Faverite comic-book is the champion. BEANO for John.' After the letter had passed their landlady's

A telegram often brought bad news.

An employment opportunity as rural postman, 1897.

official censorship, the boys added a postscript:

> I suppose you heard about Hitler's threat to bomb all British harbours. Every night John goes to bed at 10pm. because the boarder is in the front room until then Mrs Gunn is always Grumblying, last night John WAS ASLEEP ON THE floor. TUESDAY he WAS CRYING because of the cold and She would not let him in all letters read inc: this but only overleaf every time you send me a letter I find it opened

With the introduction of the telegraph in the nineteenth century, brief messages could be exchanged within hours, though often, especially in wartime, the delivery boy was dreaded as a harbinger of bad news. The telephone followed hard on the heels of the telegraph, offering instant communication for those who could afford to subscribe. Ordinary families might have a home telephone by the 1960s. Since the 1990s, email has rescued the written word, though not everyone goes to the trouble of preserving a printout for posterity.

Careers may be documented in correspondence containing job applications and testimonials, accompanied perhaps by job descriptions, records of service and 'situations vacant' columns clipped from the newspapers. Apprenticeship agreements from the early eighteenth century and army records from the 1780s onwards were preserved among family papers, because the authorities insisted that no duplicates could be obtained if the parchment original was lost. The information is difficult and sometimes impossible to recover from official archives. The military were notably keen on printed forms, for instance B128, 2077A, C311, D402, 426,

When Baptised 1866 May 1 2841 | C. Name Lawrence | Page 356 Arnold & Jane | Mather | Abode Overton | by whom A.J. Tomlin curate | When born 1866

29th August 1897
J. Douglas Lord Curate for Canon Stewart

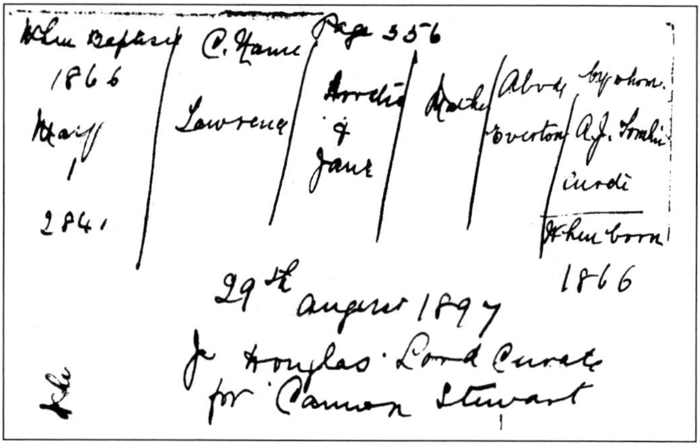

Certified copy of baptism in 1866, required for a job application in 1897.

439, 444, E528 and 663, together with the crucial pay book, narrate an individual's service, physical appearance, education and family background. Service records for Private John Mather referred to eight years of peacetime service completed in Hong Kong in 1894. Peace, of course, yielded few opportunities for heroism and he was discharged, undecorated, but in 1898 was called up from the reserve to fight the Boers in South Africa. It was a busy engagement as attested by the soldier's letters home. And this time there was a sizeable clutch of medals. An employment

One of the many army forms that offer a physical description of an ancestor, 1902.

Civil Employment.

A Register for Civil employment is kept at the Hd. Qrs. of Regimental Districts, in which are entered the names of men of good character discharged, or transferred to the Army Reserve, who reside in the Regimental District. Applications for registry should be made to the Officer Commanding the Regimental District within one year of Discharge or transfer to the Reserve.

Re-enlistment in the Militia.

Men discharged from the Army with not less than three years' service can re-enlist in the Militia of the County in which they reside on advantageous conditions, which will be communicated to them by the Adjutant on application.

NOTICE.—Recruits for Army or Militia.

Pamphlets showing the conditions and advantages of the Army or Militia are supplied gratis at every Post Office.

Any man wishing to enlist into any arm of the service, should apply personally, or by letter, to the Officer Commanding the Regimental District in which he resides, or to any Volunteer Serjeant Instructor or other Recruiter.

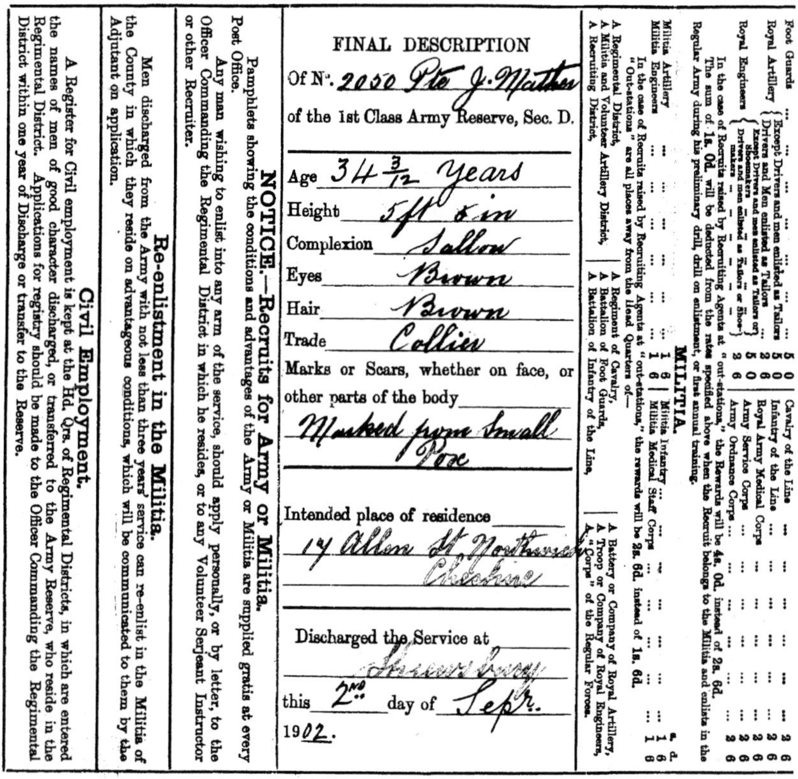

FINAL DESCRIPTION

Of No. 2050 Pte J. Mather

of the 1st Class Army Reserve, Sec. D.

Age 34 3/12 Years

Height 5ft 8in

Complexion Sallow

Eyes Brown

Hair Brown

Trade Collier

Marks or Scars, whether on face, or other parts of the body Marked from Small Pox

Intended place of residence 17 Allen St, Northwich Cheshire

Discharged the Service at Shrewsbury

this 2nd day of Sept. 1902.

	s. d.		s. d.
Foot Guards	2 6	Cavalry of the Line	2 6
Royal Artillery { Except Drivers and men enlisted as Tailors	5 0	Infantry of the Line	2 6
{ Drivers and Men enlisted as Tailors	2 6	Royal Army Medical Corps	2 6
Royal Engineers { Except Drivers and men enlisted as Tailors or Shoemakers	5 0	Army Service Corps	2 6
{ Drivers and men enlisted as Tailors or Shoemakers	2 6	Army Ordnance Corps	2 6

In the case of Recruits raised by Recruiting Agents at "out-stations," the Rewards will be 4s. 0d. instead of 2s. 6d.

The sum of 1s. 0d. will be deducted from the rates specified above when the Recruit belongs to the Militia and enlists in the Regular Army during his preliminary drill, drill on enlistment, or first annual training.

MILITIA.

	s. d.		s. d.
Militia Artillery	1 6	Militia Infantry	1 6
Militia Engineers	1 6	Militia Medical Staff Corps	1 6

In the case of Recruits raised by Recruiting Agents at "out-stations," the rewards will be 2s. 6d. instead of 1s. 6d.

"Out-stations" are all places away from the Head Quarters of—

A Regimental District,	A Regiment of Cavalry,	A Battery or Company of Royal Artillery,
A Militia and Volunteer Artillery District,	A Battalion of Foot Guards,	A Troop or Company of Royal Engineers,
A Recruiting District.	A Battalion of Infantry of the Line,	A "Corps" of the Regular Forces.

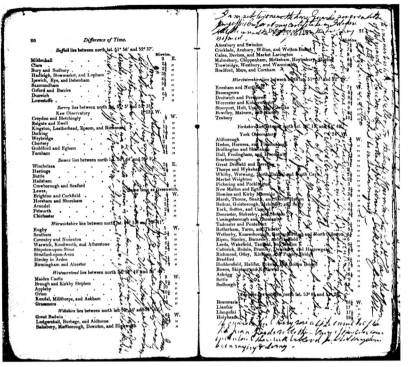

A lunatic in the family: the owner of this almanac for 1831 filled its pages with rambling notes on numerous obsessions, including astronomy, spirits, angels, fiends, sodomy, the French, the Russians and British government ministers.

association for retired military personnel shifted men around the country in search of work. John Mather was despatched from Llangollen in Denbighshire to Northwich in Cheshire. This former collier and soldier became a postman, covering 15 miles (24 km) a day with a horse and trap he provided for himself.

Posterity appreciates an ancestor who took the time to write down memories from younger days, a kind of autobiography. The record may cover any of the incidents of daily experience: work, marriage, friends, travel, emotions, ambitions, religious duties. These writings normally remain in manuscript among the family papers. A **diary** is usually written up daily, recording incidents and emotions with a raw immediacy. The contents may be diverse, the syntax unsophisticated and the tone unsettling if spared the emollient touch of subsequent expurgation. Once an individual establishes a diary habit it may become a lifelong addiction, no day seeming complete until its main events have been recorded. A journal was often kept for specific purposes such as a holiday journey, concerning places visited and people encountered, perhaps enlivened with notes of prices, food, condition of bedclothes, bouts of sickness. The writer's personality can scarcely fail to shine through, though the unfamiliar activity of writing may lead to a self-conscious or affected literary style larded with bombast and bathos. In the seventeenth century, journals were kept to record spiritual experiences and to note divine providence dealing with an individual's sinful nature. In the twentieth century, the recording of dreams was not uncommon, especially among intellectuals with Freudian interests. Trade union investigators ask members to compile daily records of bullying, abuse and harassment by colleagues and supervisors. **Memoirs** are written from notes or memory some time after the events described and are thus measured, analytical and with the benefit of hindsight. Incidents and opinions of youth viewed through the eyes of respectable old age seem banal and are glossed over. It seems unnecessary to assault the sensibilities of an aged spouse or a grown-up child with lurid descriptions of immature yearnings and adolescent fumblings. First loves are thus edited out of the account or cloaked in euphemism. All is decently veiled that was once stripped bare. The creative urge is irresistible in certain middle-class people. Family papers may include a bundle of notebooks or a ream of typescript containing the manuscript of a novel or a collection of verse. These texts, some crude, some affected, others surprisingly polished, are sharply revealing of the author's personality and opinions. Books and articles written by an ancestor that are available in print from the library also shed light upon individual interests, circumstances, opinions and prejudices. Collections of scribbled drafts expose substrata of sentiments too idiosyncratic or outrageous for acceptance by a publisher.

Legal and **court** papers concerning debt, divorce, drunkenness and furious driving, not to mention bigamy, burglary, blasphemy and bankruptcy, are commonly preserved but reluctantly produced for perusal even (or especially) within the family. Black sheep tend to be better documented than meek lambs. Unaccountably, a conviction for sheep stealing is celebrated as a badge of pride in some genealogies.

Character assassination is a normal activity in court circles. Even the most innocent actions seem nefarious when subjected to the wheedling of lawyers. The dismemberment of families through divorce requires statements from both sides and copious evidence of fault and general misery. Parties usually emerge from the process in a light much murkier than the clear black and white of smiling wedding portraits. The comings and goings of spouses, their absences, inexplicable telephone calls and trivial indiscretions are magnified by the distorting lens of marital rancour:

> A. went to Manchester (I presume) came home 1 a.m.
> (3rd September 1938)

> A. nagging because Wendy was crying while nursed. A. went to pictures
> (1st October 1938)

> A. came in late nagging as usual. never empties water after washing. A. went
> to pictures
>
> (8th October 1938)

The court required sworn affidavits showing the respondent in the worst light:

> some special outside evidence should be obtained in support of your application, which evidence will, of course, be by Affidavit and one of the parties who can, I think, assist us will be your Doctor supplemented by some person who can swear as to your husband's violent temper, such as your friend who was present when David was snatched from your custody (1st February 1940)

A **scrapbook** of newspaper cuttings, drawings, picture postcards, railway tickets, menu cards and other documentary keepsakes is a tantalising source. Doubtless each item was preserved because of its special significance to someone. The researcher, though, is taxed to the limit to discover this significance from other family records and oral histories. A scrapbook, unfortunately, is a prime candidate for the refuse collector when a home is cleared before a removal or following a death. Ephemera accumulated in cupboards and crannies, denied the dignity of a book, are the first family papers to hit the bin in a clearout. A birthday book was a usual means of recording and remembering the names and birthdays of friends and family, useful too for the modern genealogist in complementing official records. An autograph book may contain a signature and a wise or witty epithet from each family member. The

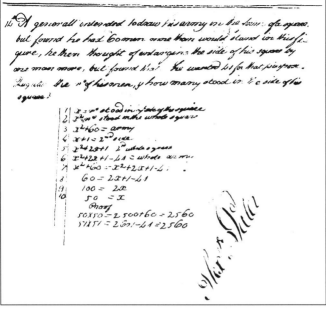

Mathematical equations in the exercise book of Alexander Paterson, an undergraduate at King's College, Aberdeen, 1788.

handwriting samples in this record may prove useful for identifying the date and authorship of anonymous manuscripts among the family papers.

Educational diplomas, school reports, exercise books, examination papers, lecture notes, prizes, trophies, leaving certificates and university degrees may all be retained as evidence of ability and achievement. It is surprising, though, how the lack of academic qualifications – or even the ability to read and write – was no bar to advancement for individuals with useful connections. The genealogist will be intrigued by the psychological effect of scathing elementary school reports and fascinated by a forebear who achieved a string of 'letters after the name' and a top job despite being branded as a dunce at the age of seven.

Certificates of birth, baptism, vaccination, inoculation, marriage, naturalisation, death and burial were kept among family papers for legal reasons such as applying for a driving licence and claiming a pension or inheritance. These documents are usually treated with considerable reverence even though copies may readily be obtained from official sources, albeit at a price:

Samuel Mather of the Parish of Langley and Hannah Bakewell of the same Parish were married in this Church by

Certificates among family papers testify to an ancestor's talents and achievements.

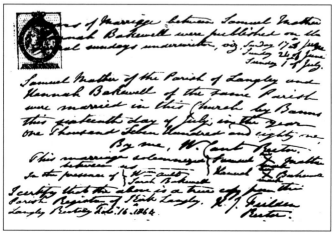

Vaccination against smallpox was widespread in the nineteenth century; a certificate proved that the individual had been successfully treated.

Banns this sixteenth day of July in the year One Thousand Seven Hundred and eighty one By me, W. Cant Rector
X Mark of S M *X* Mark of H B
Certified a true copy H.J. Feilden, Rector, Kirk Langley, Feb 16 1864

Oral sources may contradict the official record. When the Post Office accepted former Private John Mather as a rural delivery man, army records showed his year of birth as 1868. Mather's baptismal record, however, stated he was born in 1866 and christened Lawrence. In practice, neither John nor Lawrence signified because he was always known as Jack. His mother-in-law, Charlotte Emily Woosnam, was advised in 1909 to authenticate her age of seventy years in order to qualify for the old age pension introduced in that year. This was not easy. Her father, a gardener moving from estate to estate, apparently did not report Charlotte's birth to the registrar. No baptism entry was ever found. The place-name Deauville in her father's garden notebook suggests the family may have been abroad that year. Charlotte

Certified copy, dated 1864, of a marriage in 1781.

Certificate of registry of birth, 1900; failure to register a birth was an offence.

always claimed she was 'born on the German ocean'.

Documents for overseas **travel** were obtained before 1914 in the form of a letter of recommendation or *laissez passer* from a government official, academic employer, minister of religion and other upright person. Passports in blue-covered booklet form containing a photograph of the holder were introduced only in 1921, when certification of birth or marriage was required. Pages of entry and exit stamps preserved a record of the actual route. Affleck MacIntyre, who ran a general store in the Banffshire village of Aberlour, retained brochures relating to holidays enjoyed with the Blue Cars coach company. The tour operator promised 'EUROPE – in armchair comfort'. In 1938, MacIntyre took the nineteen-day tour of Mussolini's Italy. For 1939, undeterred, or perhaps encouraged, by the Anschluss, he highlighted a £21 jaunt through Brussels, Bonn, Würzburg, Landshut, Vienna ('second capital of GREATER GERMANY') and Budapest ('the gayest city in Europe'). Blue Cars tours departed every fortnight from May to October, though in September 1939 operations were suspended and MacIntyre's holiday was cancelled due to circumstances beyond the company's control. MacIntyre kept no diary of his trips. Brochures apart, the only record of his European travels was a slim volume of pornographic photographs purchased in France.

An ancestor's holiday would not be complete without a guide book. For descendants the interest arises from scraps of paper inserted and revealing annotations that suggest the traveller's itinerary and reactions to places visited. In 1893, Emily Woosnam met Jose Serra Y Front in Paris. The dashing *Señor* invited Emily to visit him in Barcelona when next on her travels, though his directions were not altogether specific (illustrated below). Emily arrived in Paris armed with Karl Baedeker's 1876 handbook for travellers. She diligently ticked off each monument visited and each work of art appreciated, sometimes adding her own comments. She went to the *Hammam* in Rue Neuve des Mathurins for a warm bath. Of all the theatres and *folies*, she judged the 'Hippodrome is much the best of the lot', well worth 5 francs. Of the Colonne Vendôme she wrote: 'the most splendid view from the top but an awful bother to go up'. After this she did not risk the Eiffel Tower, perhaps because that attraction was too recent to appear in her Baedeker guide.

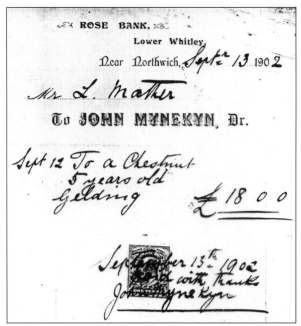

A postman buys a horse to carry him on his rounds.

Present or previous family homes are documented in **title deeds**, leases and insurance policies. Deed bundles may include records of the loans and mortgages that facilitated the purchase and erection of property. Guides to understanding the legal language of deeds are in the list of further reading. A whole chapter in the family history may be filled with investigations into the houses the family occupied down the centuries. Sometimes a family moved house every few years. Each flitting might represent a movement up or down the social scale as the father chased employment opportunities, kept ahead of the bailiffs or sought improved accommodation in prosperous times.

Financial papers are among the most voluminous in a family collection. People tend to retain bills, receipts, insurance payment cards, post-office savings books, land tax and rate demands, lair (grave) certificates and housekeeping books. The following account, dated 10th September 1776, was raised by Isobel Edie, servant to Janet Falconer in Darkless, Moray, following her mistress's death. Isobel's wages were fixed in Scots money at a time when one shilling Scots was worth one penny sterling:

To Ballance of old wages due before I went to Peter Thomson in Dyke	11s 0d
Return'd from Peter Thomsons Service to Darkless again and Continued for the space of four full & compleat years at the rate of ten Pound Scots each year is	£3 6s 8d
To an Apron each year at Sh1 6d each is	6s 0d
To an half yard linnen each half year makes four yards at Sh1 each yard is	4s 0d
To two pair shoes due of the whole time at Sh1 6 pr pair is	3s 0d

Families transmitted furniture, crockery, cutlery, needlework and jewellery as **heirlooms** down the generations. Men carved love offerings for their fiancées, made

30

The temperance movement was popular from the mid nineteenth century.

toys for their children or constructed items of furniture for the home. Housewives engaged in craftwork and practical needlework, especially sewing and knitting everyday clothing for the family. A sampler, an embroidered panel, displayed a girl's skill, perhaps depicting a family member, coat of arms, house or garden.

Death and burial created copious documentation, including death certificates, obituaries, condolence cards, accounts recording the purchase of cemetery lairs or plots, *post mortem* reports and copies of coroners' papers. Probate, inheritance and subsequent squabbles all generated paperwork. Perhaps a more intimate relic of an ancestor survives: a lock of hair in a brooch; a baby's tooth 'left for the fairies'; a death mask; a plaster cast of an infant's foot; an urn of ashes on the mantelpiece. Some of these mawkish artefacts are suitable for DNA analysis. Physical remains survive in greater quantities than supposed, because some soils have remarkable preservative properties. Studying human bodies has become acceptable in the interests of research, particularly after skeletons from abandoned cemeteries are excavated during building works. Archaeologists and police want to know the date of such remains. Perhaps there is a coffin plate, inscribed finger ring

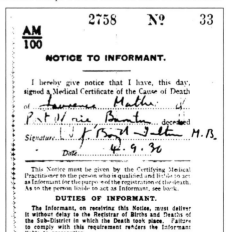

A doctor's notice to an individual qualified to report a death to the registrar, 1930.

31

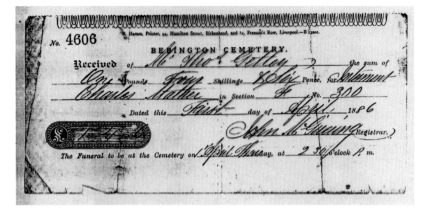

Payment for a grave (lair) in a public cemetery, 1886.

or identification tag. Detailed scientific examination of bones, teeth and tissue may provide some evidence of disease, diet, deformities, injuries, lifestyle and cause of death – and in some way help our understanding of our ancestors' problems. The bodies of John Torrington and his comrades, ordinary seamen of the nineteenth century buried in the Greenland permafrost, were excavated and investigated. Some church crypts and graveyards have been studied in advance of essential redevelopment, while unexpected burials have been discovered during building works. Museums thus hold collections of skulls and bones from archaeological excavations, some confidently identified as belonging to a particular individual. Institutions accumulate and preserve samples of tissue and whole bodies of some people's ancestors for medical purposes. There are numerous commercial organisations offering DNA analysis in Britain and the United States. A list can be obtained by searching the Internet with the words 'DNA testing'. On payment of a fee, the researcher receives a kit including instructions and containers for samples. The DNA test procedure, used chiefly to establish paternity by comparing genetic patterns, can also be applied genealogically to establish whether a supposed ancestor was indeed the progenitor of a particular line. The evidence is unambiguous. The genealogist expects to be surprised, though not disconcerted, by genetic evidence of adulteries: a wife passing off children fathered elsewhere as her

An undertaker's invoice, 1912.

32

Black-edged family mourning stationery, 1872.

husband's legitimate offspring; a husband willingly or ignorantly accepting his wife's bastards as his own.

Reproductive science adds complications that will tax genealogists for generations. Surrogate mothers, donor eggs, anonymous sperm and frozen embryos may create convolutions and genetic dead ends in the family tree. There may be genetic implications concerning accidental incest and inbreeding. For example, during the year 2000 it was reported that all donated sperm used in Glasgow clinics came from one generous donor. Problems arise when test tubes are mixed up and samples mislabelled by busy staff. On the other hand, there has always been a good deal of informal surrogacy. Couples happily adopted orphans or took on the surplus progeny of near relatives and unrelated acquaintances. By quietly seeking impregnation elsewhere, dutiful wives might spare their husbands the shame of being thought infertile and the legal implications of failing to produce an heir. Husbands of infertile spouses might follow the biblical precedent of Abram, who fathered a son, Ishmael, by his wife's Egyptian servant Hagar.

4
Surcoats and surnames

Surcoats

The medieval science of heraldry remains relevant in the new millennium, partly because its motifs and mottoes offer clues to family histories and relationships. On the medieval battlefield the identification of individuals might be a problem. A knight was clad in chain-mail or plate armour, the face hidden by a helmet with an iron visor. A shield was carried, usually on the left arm, with sword, dagger, lance, poleaxe and mace. As a protection against the sun, especially on crusade in the east, over his armour a knight wore a flowing cloth surcoat, while a mantle or lambrequin fell from the helm to cover his shoulder. A personal emblem emblazoned on the knight's shield helped to distinguish friend from foe. This colourful device was duplicated on the surcoat. This is an origin of the coat of arms, strictly applied only to the display on the shield. To make assurance doubly sure, the helmet was topped with a distinctive sprig of vegetation, a plume or crest.

From the fifteenth century, royal heralds or forerunners conducted visitations to investigate who might rightly and hereditarily bear coats of arms and with what devices. The science of heraldry thus recorded a complete display of armorial bearings for numerous individuals and their direct descendants. This achievement of arms consisted basically of a shield. Families commissioned painted and carved representations of the shield, supported by real or mythical beasts, with a crest above. The lambrequin swirled around like some fine fabric sword-slashed in a mêlée. A panel or parchment inscribed with the family motto completed the picture. Registers of arms are known as armorials. Burke's standard *General Armory* was first published by Edward Churton in 1842.

Sir Geoffrey Luttrell, a fourteenth-century knight: his shield, helmet, horse, wife and daughter-in-law are all decorated with the family's heraldic colours and emblems.

The pedigree of the Lambtons of Lambton 'can only be traced from the twelfth century' according to Burke. Unsurprisingly, the family shield exhibits three lambs, the crest a ram's head. The family remained commoners until the radical politician John-George Lambton intrigued for ennoblement as Earl of Durham in 1833. He later gave his name to the report recommending the creation of a united Canada. His memorial is on the hill at Penshaw.

By the 1470s, heraldry was a profitable and regulated profession. The College of Arms, incorporated in 1484, functioned as a heraldic and genealogical authority for England, Ireland and Wales. In the hierarchy there were three kings of arms and six heralds attended by four juniors or pursuivants. The college now preserves grants of arms, armorials, heraldic visitations of 1530–1688, archives of the Court of Chivalry and of Garter King of Arms, papers of individual heralds, as well as estate, family and antiquarian accumulations such as the Arundel and Talbot papers. In Scotland the Court of Chivalry, presided over by the Lyon King of Arms in Edinburgh, exercised jurisdiction under an act of 1672 over the right to arms, the succession of clan chiefs and claims to other clan dignities through registration of arms, bearings and genealogies. The Lord Lyon is assisted by three heralds and three (formerly six) pursuivants. An Ireland King of Arms, first mentioned in 1382, supervised heraldic affairs until 1487, when the office lapsed. In 1553, an Ulster King of Arms was created, primarily concerned with the arms of planter families but with jurisdiction throughout the island until 1943. Ulster heraldry was then added to the remit of Norroy King of Arms, supervisor for the English northern counties. Copies of Irish records in Ireland were lodged with the English college. A Chief Herald of Ireland was instituted in 1943.

Norman French was the language of the court, heraldry and chivalry – the last a mounted knight's code of conduct and morality named from the French *cheval*, 'horse'. The basic unit of a display, the shield, was divided into two vertical sections: the *dexter* and *sinister*, respectively the right and left side from the knight's position, but reversed as we look at a heraldic shield. French terms include colours painted on a shield: *gules*, 'red'; *vert*, 'green'; *azure*, 'blue'; *purpure*, 'purple'; and *sable*, 'black'. The metals *or*, 'gold', and *argent*, 'silver', were also permitted. Furs were represented by conventional colour combinations: *ermine* by black spots on a white

35

Fifteenth-century arms from a manuscript at the College of Arms, including shields invented for legendary Arthurian knights of the Round Table.

background; *ermines*, white spots on black; *erminois*, black spots on gold; *pean*, gold spots on black; and four patterns of *vair*, a squirrel fur, depicted in combinations of blue and white. The slippers worn by Cinderella were of soft *vair*, an appropriately cosy and aristocratic material – preferable to *verre*, 'glass'.

Strict rules governed the use and juxtaposition of colours, metals and furs when

36

Fairbairn's 'Crests of the Families of Great Britain and Ireland' may help to identify the family names associated with crested heirlooms such as tableware, a signet ring or embroidered linen.

PLATE 121.

designing a shield. The earliest patterns on the shield were simple and geometric, such as a cross formed by horizontal and vertical bands. These basic forms are known as ordinaries. A diagonal St Andrew's cross known as a saltire was especially popular in Scotland. A single stripe might divide the shield diagonally, vertically or horizontally into two compartments. A diagonal stripe, slanting from top left (sinister chief) to bottom right (dexter base), technically known as a bend sinister, has often, but incorrectly, been thought to indicate illegitimacy. As demand for coats of arms increased, more complex patterns were devised, borders added and backgrounds elaborated.

The shield was painted with motifs known as charges. These included representations of star-shaped spur rowels known as mullets or molets and barbed arrowheads called pheons. Also popular were roundels, lozenges and crosses in a variety of styles. Inanimate objects such as weapons and even ships appeared. A shield with its full complement of charges was known as an escutcheon from the Latin *scutum*. An incorrect representation on the shield was as unforgivable as a departure from knightly virtue: the former literally and the latter metaphorically a blot on the escutcheon.

The crest fixed to a knight's helmet was a family emblem perhaps of some historic significance. Indeed the term *family crest* is sometimes improperly used to describe an entire achievement. Birds, beasts and mythological monsters were

'Fairbairn's Crests' index of families.

especially popular. The enfield, crest of the O'Kellys, had the head of a fox, chest of an elephant, mane of a horse, forelegs of an eagle, hindquarters of a greyhound and tail of a lion. Crests are engraved on items of cutlery, plate and glassware, incorporated into seals and signet rings, embroidered on napery and represented in stained glass, wall paintings and decorative plasterwork. A single crested teaspoon handed down over the generations may be the vital clue that connects a humble family to a noble house. The definitive dictionary of crests up to the 1880s was J. Fairbairn's *Book of Crests*, edited by A. C. Fox-Davies, now reprinted.

The family motto might originate in a medieval war cry or a worthy prayer in Latin, French, English or Gaelic, sometimes alluding to the surname. Heralds cunningly contrived achievements alluding

Family mottoes from 'Fairbairn's Crests'.

Papworth's 'Ordinary'.

DOVE including Pigeon

Arg. a dove .... with an olive-branch in the beak vert on the top of an ark in water ppr. GEILIE, Blackford.

Arg. a dove rising ppr. out of a tree growing from a mount in base vert. CHAURAN.

Az. on a mount in base vert a pigeon arg. CROP.

Or a dove rising on the top of a tree ppr. growing out of a mount vert. DUPRATT, Middlesex.

DUCK

including Mallard, Seateal, Sheldrake, Shoveller, Smew, Teal, and White Nun.

(? Arg.) a sea-teal gu. winged or. ELCHAM.

Az. a sheldrake arg. LONGFORD.

Az. a smew or white nun ppr. ABNOTT, *Holme, Academy.*

Gu. a sheldrake arg. LANGFORD.

Gu. a shoveller wings close arg. a crescent.... for diff. LANGFORD or LANGEFORD, London and Middlesex.

Quarterly sa. and arg. in the first quarter a teal of the last. BREZZY.

Quarterly per fess dancetty sa. and arg. in the first quarter a teal of the last. BRESSEY.

Quarterly per fess indented sa. and arg. in the first quarter a mallard of the last. BRESCY or BRESSY, Wistaston, co. Chester.

Sa. a shoveller arg. POPLER. POPELLER, *V*.

Surnames

A surname is an identifying addition to a person's given name, originally applied to a particular person, for instance Eric *the Red*. By the thirteenth century some surnames were becoming hereditary. A surname provides interesting, possibly significant, clues to a family's origin, residence, occupation, social status, personal traits and physical characteristics. People with the same surname are not necessarily related, even way back in the past. Various spellings of a name, conversely, do not rule out relationship. Successive generations of one Gerrerd family appear in documents as Garrett, Garret, Jarritt, Gerald, Jerrold, Garard and Jerrard. Families altered spellings to their own taste: Smith to Smythe, Fitch to ffitch. Following the family line through fathers in each generation normally limits the search to one surname, at least back to the sixteenth century. Tracing the line back through mothers raises the stimulating possibility of a different surname every thirty years or so. Researching the present family surname back through hundreds of years may introduce several biological families because unrelated people can adopt a surname, perhaps to inherit a title or property. On the other hand, tracing biological parents generation by generation may entail moving from one surname to another, after adoption, divorce, illegitimacy or change by deed poll.

In the late nineteenth century, H. B. Guppy pioneered the study of the origin of regional surnames and the mobility of population, concentrating on yeoman families traced county by county. This study has been further developed in universities. An important conference was organised in 1975 by Herbert Voitl at the Friedrich-Alexander University of Erlangen-Nürnberg, Germany. Participants examined an impressive database of modern British and Irish surnames traced backwards to suggest earlier homes and original meanings. In Sweden, the University of Lund has long been a centre for the linguistic study of place-names and surnames, particularly of Germanic origin. Early written examples collected from archives and monumental inscriptions are followed forward to present or latest instances. Professor Eilert Ekwall was the principal authority, always willing to discuss names sent in by ordinary researchers. Leicester University, a leading centre for English local history, is responsible for the *English Surnames* series, analysing names county by county.

Among the earliest surnames were **nicknames** describing physical characteristics and personal qualities. A name such as Redhead might be adopted, not inappropriately, if ginger hair or a ruddy complexion ran in the family. The Welsh Gough was formed in this manner from the vernacular word *coch*, 'red'. Nicknames were given ironically: Thynne might attach to a fat person. Characteristics of an ancestor could be read into such names as Bull (headstrong), Lamb (meek), Duff from the Gaelic *dubh*, 'black', Grant from the French *grand*, 'tall/great', and Rowse (red). Sly (cunning) and Gay (pretty) have meanings somewhat different from their most usual modern senses of the words. Fraser from the French *fraise*, 'strawberry', perhaps suggests a birthmark. Affectionate nicknames are evident in, for example, the French-derived Bellamy (*belle ami*, 'good friend'). In districts with a limited number of surnames, nicknames may be useful, as in Jones the Shop. Fisher families of north-east Scotland have hereditary tee names, officially recognised, such as Stripie, Fling, Bobbin, Wockie, King and Carrot. A few names may originate in an individual's annual performance of one role in a medieval pageant or mystery play. The actor famous for the character of Herod or the Egyptian Pharaoh might earn the surname King or Farrar. The role and therefore the name might even become hereditary.

Among the most widespread surnames are those based upon a father's given name. These are known as **patronymics** ('names from fathers'). Metronymics ('names from mothers') are less usual. An alternative classification would be 'font-names'. In their simplest form these surnames are just a parent's name. Thomas the son of John might be Thomas John; or (later) Thomas John's son (Johnson). The 'son' suffix might appear as just a letter 's' as Thomas John*s*. Daughters accepted the 'son' suffix too. Maud's offspring could be Maudson or Mawson; Mary's perhaps Marriott. Surnames derived from female names may indicate an unmarried mother, a legitimate infant born after the father's death or veneration of a female saint.

The origin and meaning of first names, which are the basis of numerous surnames, are set out in standard dictionaries (see 'Further reading'). First names are usually termed Christian or given names because conferred at a child's baptism into the church. A baptismal name is not normally altered, though an individual entering new life as a monk or nun adopts a hallowed name, banishing William for Brother Ignatius, plain Jane for Sister Mary Joseph. Given names, like surnames, may be passed down directly from parents or obliquely from uncles, aunts and godparents. Occasionally, an unusual given name will offer a clue as to remote or alleged ancestry. The New Testament is a favourite source for given names, including Andrew, Luke and Mark. Norman names such as Robert, William, Emma and Richard were introduced from the eleventh century onwards. The Greek name Alexander took root in Scotland, where Queen Margaret named her son in honour of Pope Alexander II, decisively favouring Rome against the Celtic church. Native Gaelic names survived, for instance Duncan, Donald, Dougal, Brendan and Bridget. The religious fervour of the seventeenth century popularised biblical names such as Deborah, Judith, Ebenezer and Obadiah. Christian, the ancestor of Christine, was popular, along with Praise-the-Lord and Joy-in-Sorrow. The nineteenth-century revival of interest in the Anglo-Saxon spurred parents to revive Alfred, Cedric, Wilfred and Osric. The 1960s saw coinings such as Buttercup, Happiness and Jade. Mass communications have allowed cultural cross-fertilisation as given names are exchanged among continents. Wayne, originally an occupational surname meaning 'wagon maker/driver', was introduced to Britain from the USA. Kylie is listed in the vocabulary of an aboriginal tongue of Western Australia as meaning 'curl, curved stick, boomerang'.

In Wales, until the nineteenth century, it was normal to adopt a parent's Christian name as surname, which thus changed in each generation. Evan the son of William Jones was known as Evan Williams or Williamson. The Welsh word *mab* or *ap*, 'son of', was usually preferred, so Evan son of William Jones was known as Evan ap William. To complicate matters (for outsiders), Evan ap William's son Harry might be Harry Evanson, Harry Evans or Harry ap Evan, pronounced and written Bevan. Harry Bevan's son Thomas could be Thomas Harryson or Harries or, more likely, Thomas ap Harry, or Parry. Medieval documents usually recorded names in the form of X son of Y son of Z, as in this translation of an arbitration award made in 1510 settling a family squabble over a property in Caernarfonshire:

> Be it known to all who come henceforth of the making by Griffith son of Meredith son of David of a compromise between Rhys son of Jenkin son of Llewelyn son of Thomas on the one part and Evan son of Rhys son of Llewelyn and Angharad daughter of Griffith son of Evan on the other part on condition that Rhys relinquishes the hay which is in Big Meadow in the hand of John son of Griffith son of Belyn to Evan and to Angharad for the term of six years for the debts of Isabel daughter of Griffith son of Evan.

In Gaelic surnames of Scotland and Ireland, the words *mac*, *mc* or *m'* indicated 'son of'. Native given names provided the basis of early surnames. A son of Connor was Macconchobhair or MacConnor, while a son of Coinneach (the Gaelic form of Kenneth) became Mackenzie. Other surnames formed in this way include Macartney (Art), MacCarthy (Cárthach), Macdonald (Domhnall), Macdougal (Dhubgall) and McKellar (Ealair). Biblical and Christian names were adopted too: Seán (John) in Macshane, Laurence in McLaren, Thomas in Mactavish. Irish surnames are also prefixed with *ua*, *ui*, *ó* or *o'* for 'grandson/descendant of' as in Ó Briain. In the Isle of Man, *q* (Old British *meqq*) represents 'mac': the son of Coinn is Q'Coinn or Quinn.

Anglo-Norman landowners devised patronymic surnames with the prefix *fitz*, 'son of'. These surnames usually contain a Norman, French, Flemish or Breton given name such as Alan, Hugh, Robert, Roger, William, Walter, Gerard or Henry. Even today a *fitz* name has a certain cachet of blue blood with a disproportionate number in the peerage. Fitzalan is the surname of the Dukes of Norfolk, premier peers of England. The Fitzgeralds were Dukes of Leinster; the Fitzmaurices, Marquesses of Lansdowne; the Fitzgibbons, Earls of Clare. Bastard sons of kings were *fitz*: Henry Fitzroy ('son of the king') was Charles II's son by the Duchess of Cleveland; William Fitzclarence, son of William IV, formerly Duke of Clarence. Fitzpatrick, a *fitz* surname of Irish origin, is different, being a form of Macgiollaphádraig or MacKilpatrick, 'son of a devotee of Patrick', perhaps an illegitimate offspring of a priest or nun.

Pet forms of given names employed in everyday medieval speech were put to use as surnames. Robert was familiarly referred to as Rob, Hob, Dob, Nop or Nobb. These forms gave rise to surnames in their own right or as patronymics such as Robson, Robbs, Hobson, Dobson, Dobbs, Nopps and Nobbs. Richard became Dick, hence Dixon. John in the form Han gave Hanson. Isabel as Ibb, Belle or Biby provided Ibson, while Adam as Addy became Aitcheson. Pet names were made even more familiar with a suffix. Anglo-Saxons added *uc* or *oc*. Norman-French speakers preferred *el*, *en*, *et*, *in*, *ot* and *un*. So Richard in its pet form Dick became Docken. Mary as Mall became Mallet. Special fondness might be shown by a double diminutive, for instance *el* + *in*, *el* + *ot* and *in* + *ot*. Jack was a pet form of John. Jack + *el* + *in* gave Jacklin. Medievally, *cock* and *kin* were terms of endearment. Added to a pet name, the words gave rise to such surnames as Hann-cock or Hann-kin.

A surname may reflect a place of (usually) former **residence**. Arriving in London from Rochester, a family might be known as the Rochesters. An individual on the move might have several successive surnames in an active lifetime, each indicating the last place of settlement and none showing a place of birth. Certain place-names and associated surnames are found in several parts of the country, including Easton, Weston, Norton, Sutton, Milton and Newton, as are landscape features, such as Wood, Moore/Muir and Burns. There is also Atwood for one living 'at the wood'; Green for a person dwelling by the village open space; Lee, 'at a woodland clearing'; Underwood, 'below a wooded hillside'; Bottom, 'in a low-lying place'; Nash, from Old English *atten ash*, 'at the ash tree'. It may be difficult to fix the geographical origin of families with such unspecific surnames. From their French homeland, Norman conquerors brought surnames that still retain a hint of gentility, including Sinclair from St Clair, perhaps in La Manche or Calvados, also Bruce, Curzon, Boswell, Quincy, Lacy, Montgomery, Beaumont, Grenfell, Quinton and Conyers. Some families preserved the *de* ('from') element, as in Darcy from Arcy, Dauncey from Anisy (Calvados) and Dando from any French village called Aunou. To exploit the new markets opened up by the conquest, merchants and craftsmen migrated to Britain and Ireland from Flanders, as suggested by the names Fleming and Flanders. Lubbock came from the Hanseatic town of Lübeck; Danvers from Anvers (Antwerp); Brabner, Brebner and Brabazon from Brabant; Jermyn and Germaine from Germany. The surnames Walsh and Wallace identified immigrants from the ancient British territories of Wales, Cumbria and Strathclyde. The word *Welsh* in Old English means 'foreigner, non-English'. The Walsh families of Ireland claim descent from Anglo-Norman landowners in southern Wales who crossed the sea westwards in the late twelfth century. Moving north, these conquerors were progenitors of the Scottish patriot William Wallace.

Surnames derive from positions of responsibility and **status**. Scotland's royal house of Stuart originated in the household official known as a steward, responsible for the supply of necessities. A good steward might be accepted as a confidential adviser. Walter the steward rose in this way and married into the royal Bruce family. Not all Stuarts or Stewarts have royal blood because there were stewards in other substantial households. Similar surnames are Sellar, guardian of the cellar; Butler, keeper of the buttery or food store; Chamberlain, carer of the private apartments. Full-time Christian officials established families with names such as Abbot, Parsons, Dean, Monk, Nun and Prior. This raises a question, if not an eyebrow, because these people were unmarried, supposedly celibate, and bound by solemn vows of chastity. Priests were said to be clerics, a word once associated with casting lots for fates and fortunes, but later describing a person able to read. A cleric's bastards consequently bore the surname Clerk or Clarke. The Gaelic surname Macmillan denotes 'son of a monk or tonsured one'. Macnab is 'abbot's son'; Macpherson 'parson's son'; MacTaggart 'priest's son'.

A surname was coined from an individual's **occupation**, such as Carpenter, Butcher, Slater, Thatcher, Baker, Brewer and Miller. The surname Smith is widespread, because there were many different kinds of smith working different metals in a diverse industry. The Old English word *worhte*, 'work', gave the surname Wright, 'general worker', with specialists Cartwright, Arkwright, Plowright and Wheelwright. Cordwainer or Cordiner indicated a worker in fine Cordova Spanish leather. Female occupations were designated by the suffix *-ster* as in spinster, 'female spinner', or *-steress* as in seamstress, 'female sewer of cloth'. Because surnames were, in the main, formed upon a father's name or occupation there are few female occupations clearly identified in surnames. Baxter and Brewster may be female equivalents of Baker and Brewer. The first Hollister was a female brothel-keeper, from the Old French *huler*, 'whoremonger'. Occupational surnames in Wales, Scotland and Ireland may be expressed in the local language.

Sean Gow uses the Gaelic *gobhan*, 'smith', while John Gough has *gof*, also meaning 'smith'. In 1797, James Gow or Smith was licensed to retail liquors at his inn on the military road at Bridgend of Dulnain in Speyside. He employed both surnames, depending on circumstances, and his children were variously Gow and/or Smith.

Gaelic people were grouped in **clans**, or extended families, many of whom might adopt the same surname as their chief. Andrew Caird, whose surname means 'tinker', used his laird's name Munro when working away from Ross-shire. An Irish act of Parliament of 1465 required natives within the territory or pale around Dublin to adopt an English style of surname. Beyond the pale native forms persisted. Migrants might translate or replace traditional family names: Maciain to Johnson, Maceachrain to Cochrane, Ó hEalaighthe ('clever') to Healy, Macfhionnáin ('son of the fair one') to McKenna or more simply Fair.

It has always been possible to alter a surname with very little trouble, for example by a legal announcement in a newspaper or the *London Gazette.* People have adopted a new surname with no more formality than a note to some local official. Women have for centuries done this upon marriage, adopting their husband's surname, and even expecting to be addressed by their husband's given name as, for example, Mrs John Smith. In Scotland, by contrast, it was not unusual for married women to retain their maiden names, being known as Jane Smith, wife of John Brown; Jane Smith or Brown; or Jane Smith alias Brown. Changes of name before 1901 are in Fry and Phillimore's *Index.*

In the isle of Barra supplementary occupational surnames distinguish different people bearing the clan name McNeil, here identifying a dynasty of postal workers: Neil J. MacNeil 'Niall a Phosta', John McNeil 'postman' and Roderick J. MacNeil 'Ruairidh a Phosta'.

5
A world of information

Collecting and organising information is key to a successful family history investigation. Copious paperwork remains at present the basic element. Correspondence files, research notebooks, photographs, reference pamphlets, photocopied documents and pedigree charts can be efficiently and neatly stored in files and folders. Each file, clearly labelled, is stored in a logical order in a filing cabinet or a carton of suitable size. Paperwork could be filed day by day in a simple date-order sequence as research progresses. Alternatively, arrangement could be dictated by provenance, according to the person or place where the information was found. Thus folder 1 might contain notes and photocopies garnered in the public library; folder 2 from the county archives; folder 3 from the public record office; folder 4 from family interviews. Over the years these files will require reorganising as sources snowball. A popular filing system allocates separate folders to each surname or individual in the pedigree, arranging files alphabetically or in family groups. In taking notes from documents or compiling family trees, there are advantages in writing words in full without abbreviation. This could avoid problems in the future from ambiguous abbreviations, for instance when an enigmatic *B* might mean baptism, birth, brother, buried, or something else entirely. In practice, though, life is too short and time in the archives too limited for counsels of perfection. Consistency is important, for instance the three-letter codes for county names devised by the genealogist C. R. Chapman. Another useful organisational system is a register of research visits and projects, as tabulated below.

REGISTER

Number	date	source	documents
1	12th May 1981	Cumbria Record Office, Carlisle	Wills of Ann Skelton, 1719 (1/1), and Richard Skelton, 1656 (1/2)
2	13th May 1981	John Woosnam, Solihull	Prayer book, Skelton & Woosnam, 1760–1839
3	14th May 1981	National Library of Wales, Aberystwyth	Will of Francis Woosnam, 1731 (3/1)
4	16th May 1981	Derby Central Library	International Genealogical Index, 1981 (4/1) Parish register Littleover, with census 1811 (4/2)
5	18th May 1981	Allan J. Williams, Birkenhead	Family tree, Woosnam & Mather, 1780–1959 (5/1) Census extracts, Woosnam, Cheshire, 1871 (5/2)

Information from the register and folders is indexed by person, place and subject, as shown in the example below.

INDEX

WOOSNAM, William Skelton	1839–1932	
married Charlotte Mather, Liverpool	1859	5/1
carpenter, Birkenhead	1871	5/2
baptism, Liverpool	1839	2/1, 5/1
mother, Mary Ann Richardson	1801	4/1

The index next provides the beginnings of a family group sheet.

sources of information ....

man's name .... wife's maiden name ....
    residence ....   residence ....
    birth (baptism) ....   birth (baptism) ....
    at ....   at ....
    marriage ....   other marriages to ....
    at ....
    death (burial) ....   death (burial) ....
    at ....   at ....
    other marriages to ....
    father's name ....   father's name ....
    mother's maiden name ....   mother's maiden name ....

children	date born (baptised) at	date married at	date died (buried) at	married to	chart
1					
2					
3					
4					
5					
6					
7					
8					
9					
10					
11					
12					
13					
14					

notes
name of compiler   address   date

Personal computer (PC)

The personal computer (PC) is an information processor. Facts and figures can be entered, stored, arranged, rearranged, processed and retrieved. Processed information, readily available, is exactly what the genealogist requires from scores of archival documents recording hundreds of people and thousands of events. The modern computer sits comfortably on a desk at home. Formal instruction, if required, is generally available near at hand, accessed in the first instance through council adult-education services. By the end of the first session the beginner should be familiar with the desktop equipment ('hardware'), processing programs ('software') and computer jargon: keyboard, mouse, visual display unit (VDU), disk drive, compact disk read only memory (CD-ROM). The basics of entering information, making and saving a document, are acquired in two or three sessions. Practice increases typing speed, keyboard skills and dexterity in using the mouse to click commands on screen. Guides and manuals are available in disconcerting numbers. Research away from home is facilitated with a portable laptop computer, which may be carried nearly everywhere, even, with permission, into the library and archives. Data and extracts can be typed directly into the computer.

For home use, it might be advisable to consider acquiring a machine working at a speed in excess of 600 megahertz (MHz) with at least 64 megabytes random access memory (RAM). This normally comes with a word-processing software package. This in turn permits the user to type in ('input') information from documents, edit texts, design pedigree charts and produce a family history for distribution. Paper copies in black and white or colour are produced with a printer. Photographs and manuscripts can be scanned and stored in the machine and retrieved on command. Text, research notes, family trees, correspondence and copies of documents are preserved on inexpensive $3^1/2$ -inch floppy disks, which can be labelled and stored in a small box. For security, disks can easily be copied or information printed out to avoid the despair of a system crash or of losing a disk. The Society of Genealogists, Charterhouse Buildings, London EC1, publishes a quarterly newsletter, *Computers in Genealogy*, for members of the Genealogists Computer Interest Group as well as a *Computers in Genealogy Beginner's Pack*. *Family Tree Computer Magazine* offers advice on new developments.

Genealogical database software **programs** multiply the variety and quality of projects the family historian can undertake by basically converting raw genealogical data into family trees and biographies. Programs are usually reviewed in publications of any family history society. Each program offers standard forms for completion, which have to be filled in by the researcher. A personal record form might begin:

First names..…..
Surname..…..
Birth
    date...
    place..
    notes..
    source..
Baptism
    date...
    place..
    notes..
    source..

If every ancestor is entered, the computer can then arrange people by, say, age at death, alphabetically by surname, husband with wife, parents with offspring, and so forth. Footnotes, bibliographies, scanned copies of photographs and archival documents may all be inserted into a family tree under the guidance of the program.

Popular programs include *Brother's Keeper*, *Family Origins*, *Generations Family Tree*, *Legacy*, *Master Genealogist*, *Pedigree*, *Personal Ancestral File*, *Reunion*, *Trees* and *Ultimate Family Tree*. A program likely to be found on the shelves of a computer superstore is *Family Tree Maker* (FTM), first released by Brøderbund in 1989, with a range of facilities enlarged and refined in subsequent versions. A comprehensive guide by M. V. Gormley, available through agents, is *Prima's Official Companion to Family Tree Maker Version 5* (Prima Publishing, Rocklin, California, 1988). M. L. & A. L. Helm's *Family Tree Maker for Dummies* (IDG Books, Foster City, California, 2000) provides further guidance. FTM automatically sets up a scrapbook for each individual and marriage. A family group sheet is produced for each set of parents, with individuals neatly numbered and pedigrees set out in standard formats. The FTM search engine, known as Internet FamilyFinder, seeks surnames worldwide.

The **Internet** is a means of retrieving millions of pages of information, including guidance on genealogical research, family trees, the addresses of archive offices, thousands of catalogues, indexes, transcripts and images of documents – a kind of universal encyclopedia. The information is stored electronically in a collection of linked pages – the world wide web (www) founded in 1991 – and is available through the PC screen and Internet at the cost of a local phone call (*on-line*), occasionally also on a pay-per-view basis. The Internet is available at public libraries, community centres and cyber cafés – and, of course, at home. Internet awareness courses are offered in public libraries and through community education outlets. Commercial genealogy programs usually connect to relevant Internet sites and also assist in compiling individual web pages through which a family history is shared with genealogists worldwide.

A starting point could be one of the Internet directories known as *portals* setting out resources required by various categories of researchers from alchemists to zoologists. Genealogical sites and records are accessed through the national archives FamilyRecords portal at **<http://www.familyrecords.gov.uk>**. The UK & Ireland Genealogical Service 'virtual reference library' at **<http://www.genuki.org.uk>** is a comprehensive collection of on-line information, particularly about primary (original) documentation. A *gateway* is a directory to one particular subject, for instance genealogy, such as the international Cyndi's List at **<http://www.cyndislist.com>** maintained by Cyndi Howells. Directories of general information include Yahoo at **<http://www.yahoo.co.uk>**.

Exemplary websites of archival information include:
English and Scots origins **<http://www.origins.net/>**
Latter-Day Saints (LDS) **<http://www.familysearch.org>**
National Archives of Ireland **<http://www.nationalarchives.ie>**
Public Record Office **<http://www.pro.gov.uk>**
Registry of family trees on personal websites **<http://www.gendex.com>**
Scottish civil registration **<http://www.gro-scotland.gov.uk>**
Society of Genealogists data **<http://www.sog.org.uk>**
Tupman's links in British and Canadian genealogy with births, marriages, deaths, title deeds and passenger lists **<http://freespace.virgin.net/alan.tupman>**

Specific information about a person, family, place or event can most efficiently be sought through a *search engine*, combining an index to the web and a means to search for specific words or phrases. Examples of sites are:

AltaVista **<http://www.altavista.co.uk>**
FAST Search **<http://www.alltheweb.com>**
Google **<http://www.google.com>**
Hotbot **<http://www.hotbot.lycos.co.uk>**
Lycos **<http://www.lycos.co.uk>**

Because the engine searches millions of pages, the researcher's choice of keywords is important. A request for even an uncommon surname such as Slasor can produce hundreds of results (*hits*) whereas a search for the whole phrase 'James Slasor Gateshead' is limited to five.

Internet Bulletin Board Systems (BBS), also known as Message Boards or Usenet, are organised by topic. The genealogist who reads or posts messages on the BBS is communicating publicly with the whole world of Internet users. Information can be downloaded from the bulletin board. The genealogist may publish pedigrees and family history for all to see on a personal website. This helpful sharing of information may attract advice and information from other researchers working on related pedigrees. It may generate whole new branches and uncover unknown relatives perhaps on the other side of the globe. Internet access allows personal electronic mail (email) communication with family members, societies and fellow genealogists worldwide. Email addresses for research institutions, archives and societies may be found through the Internet itself. The researcher's oral history informants may enjoy participating in a talking family tree. Family stories, legends, regional ballads and samples of secret languages may be preserved as sound clips for a computerised pedigree using a proprietary database to give an authentic voice to each individual's digital scrapbook.

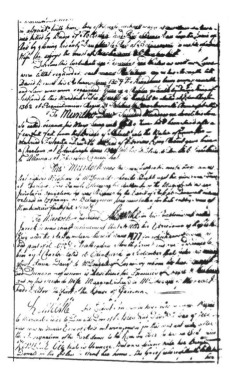

A narrative pedigree of the Mackenzies.

Setting out a family tree

There are various methods of setting out a family tree. A traditional **narrative** follows eldest sons with just a few sentences on each individual and spouse.

A **descendant tree** begins with an individual in the past, spreading thence to children, grandchildren, and so on. Heralds recorded the results of their visitations in this manner from the fifteenth century. A descendant tree may be followed from the top of the page downwards or from the left margin rightwards. This style of pedigree can grow to enormous dimensions, particularly if marriages produce a dozen children who are equally prolific. Excluding peripheral individuals is a normal means of keeping the growth of the tree to within manageable limits, as in the example of the Skeltons of Lowcarrig (illustrated on page 51). This species of tree is often termed a line pedigree because marriages and children are connected in a straight line. The pedigree can be extended into the future without revision simply by drawing further lines for

An ancestor tree

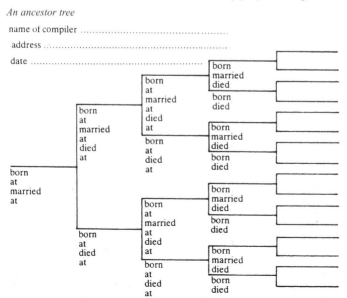

name of compiler ....

address ....

date ....

subsequent marriages. The descendant tree is perhaps the most popular because it is simply set out and easily understood. Each generation lies on the same horizontal plane, though in the Skelton tree the rule is bent to highlight the vital direct progenitor. Lines of descent spring from the marriage symbol (=). Each name is written above personal details. Children are recorded in order of birth regardless of gender. Pedigree lines do not intersect. Gaps indicate unauthenticated data.

A descendant tree

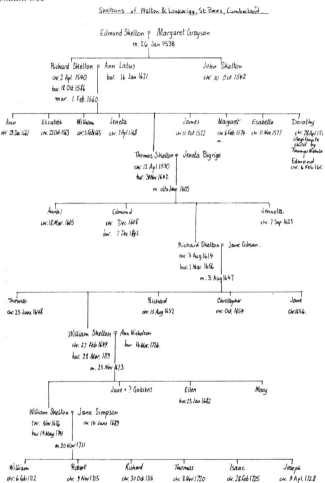

An **ancestor tree** commences with the latest person still living, typically the researcher, and displays generations of parents, grandparents, and so on. This pedigree may be termed a birth brief, because the headline evidences are births. The example on page 50 has been simplified for the sake of clarity by omitting names and dates. This approach is of little merit for researchers pursuing just one line of male ancestors, because, as can be seen, by the fifth generation there are sixteen surnames involved. In ten generations there would be 512 names.

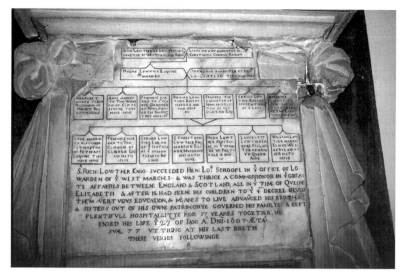

Family tree on a monument at Askham church, Cumbria.

Professional researchers recommend a chart with generations indented in a variety of ways. Employed by Burke, Fox-Davis and Debrett for pedigrees of landed gentry and nobility, this is termed a **narrative indented pedigree**. The indents show children and grandchildren of each generation. Space may be allowed for the insertion of biographical details because there is no set form for completion. A combination of roman and arabic numerals clarifies matters, though different individuals may still bear the same identification numbers. The use of a PC can assist by dignifying different individuals and generations with particular typefaces and print sizes. The indented pedigree advantageously continues for page after page in chronological order with no widely spreading branches of collaterals. The genealogist compiling an indented pedigree is, in practice, limited to detailing descendants of a genealogically irrelevant marriage to just three or four generations before the main line is resumed.

BOWEN of TYDDYN

I EVAN BOWEN, Pen-y-castell, purchased Tyddyn, parish Llanidloes, about 1691; two sons, wife survived him, he died 1734, buried Llanidloes
   1. Thomas Bowen II
   2. Richard Bowen, Kerry, died 1722, buried Llanidloes
II THOMAS BOWEN, Tyddyn, married about 1720, six children
   1. Elizabeth Bowen, born 1721
   2. Evan Bowen, born and died 1723
   3. Thomas Bowen III
   4. Anne Bowen, born 1725, married Richard Woosnam of Tymawr Trefeglwys, four sons, died and buried at Llanidloes 1809
      i Evan Woosnam, Badaioch, died leaving two children
      ii Richard Woosnam, USA
      iii Thomas Woosnam, Builth
      iv Bowen Woosnam, Glandwr, solicitor, married Elizabeth daughter of Charles Cole, four children, died 3 Sep 1841 aged 70
         1. Charles Thomas Woosnam, Newtown, born 1804, solicitor, married Harriet daughter of Joshua Peele, Shrewsbury, no issue, died 28 Jan 1869

  2. Elizabeth Alicia Woosnam, born 1808, married Rev George Fisher, Greenwich Hospital, three children, died 1846

  3. James Bowen Woosnam, born 28 Jan 1812, Inspector-General of Ordnance, Bombay Artillery, served Afghan campaign 1839, married Agnes fifth daughter of William Bell, Bellview, Queen's County, eight children.

    4. Richard Woosnam, born 9 Apr 1815, diplomat, married Margaret third daughter of William Bell, Bellview, Queen's County, six children

 5. Sarah Bowen, born 1727, married 1755 Simon Lloyd, Bala, six children, she died 1804

 6. Hanna Bowen, born 1729

III THOMAS BOWEN, Tyddyn, born 8 Jan 1724, married Eliza daughter of Mr Baxter, Newtown, five children

 1. Elizabeth Bowen, born 1755

 2. Elizabeth Bowen, born 1757, died unmarried

 3. Thomas Bowen, born 1759

 4. James Bowen IV

 5. Mary Bowen, born 1767, married 1790 William Teece, Shrewsbury

  i Mary Teece, born 1792, married Robert Wilkinson, Shrewsbury, six children

  ii Charles Teece, born 1802, married Jane Brown, Wrexham

  iii Thomas Teece, born 1803, died unmarried

  iv Josiah Teece, born 1805, died unmarried

 6. Jane Bowen, born 1769, married 1794 Thomas Colley, Cefngwifed

IV JAMES BOWEN, Tyddyn, born 1760, married Anna Maria daughter of George Matthews. Llanwnog, five children, he died 1833

When the New England Historical and Genealogical Society commenced publication of its periodical *Register* in 1874, the editor A. H. Hoyt (1826–1915) devised a form for recording a pedigree. This was known as the **register plan**. The method was refined in 1912 by the National Genealogical Society's quarterly journal and so may be referred to as the **NGSQ system**. The system is suitable for published pedigrees because the rules are internationally approved and followed. In the simplified **modified register system** (MRS) the progenitor or earliest known ancestor is placed at the top of the page. Each individual bears a personal arabic numeral (1, 2, 3, 4). Roman lower-case numerals (i, ii, iii, iv) assigned to each child of each set of parents begin at i on each occasion. The marginal + denotes an individual appearing with further details later in the list.

MODIFIED REGISTER SYSTEM

1.		Charles Mather, born 1812, Derbyshire, gardener
		known children of Charles Mather and wife Harriet Bennett were:
+	2 i	Horatio, born 1835
	3 ii	Herbert, born 1839
+	4 iii	Charlotte Emily, born 1840
	5 iv	Charles, born 1843
	6 v	Elizabeth Jane, born 1847
2.		Horatio Mather married Jane daughter of William and Jane Roberts of Chirk, Denbighshire, 1859, known children were:
	7 i	Charles, born 1860
	8 ii	William, born 1862
	9 iii	Lawrence John, born 1866
	10 iv	Louisa, born 1868
	11 v	Lavinia, born 1871
4.		Charlotte Emily Mather married William Skelton Woosnam, 1859, waggonmaker known children were:
	12 i	Horatio, born 1859

	13 ii	Mary Harriet, born 1861
	14 iii	Emma, born 1864
	15 iv	Selina, born 1866
	16 v	Emily, born 1868
+	17 vi	Charles Isaac, born 1870
	18 vii	Annie Gertrude, born 1872
	19 viii	William Frank, born 1875
	20 ix	Alfred, born 1879
	21 x	Wilfred James, born 1883
16.		Emily Woosnam married Laurence Mather (9 above), her cousin, in 1899

The chart of a **collateral pedigree** includes direct ancestors as well as side-shoots grafted on to accommodate cousins, uncles, siblings and second spouses. The chart is conventionally drawn up painstakingly across page after page, cobbled together in an ever-expanding patchwork. The collateral pedigree usually places the earliest ancestors at the top of the page. Descendants cascade downwards through the generations to arrive in the present at the foot of the page. The pedigree can equally well flow from left to right.

The **Ahnentafel** (German for 'ancestral chart') is popular in the USA. The system was employed by the Spanish genealogist Jerome de Sosa in 1676 and publicised by S. K. von Stradonitz in 1896. Each person bears a number, which is doubled to indicate a father, plus one for a mother. Males are even-numbered, females odd-numbered. The present or latest individual is numbered 1. Names are listed numerically. Each generation appears in turn. Gaps in the sequence represent the absence of information. Reference numbers following a surname relate to biographical files held on disk or in the filing cabinet.

Generation 1
    1 Doris Mather (1) 1904
Generation 2
    2 Lawrence Mather (2) 1866–1930
    3 Emily Woosnam (3) 1868–1969
Generation 3
    4 Horatio Mather (15) 1835–1906
    5 Jane Roberts (91) 1834–
    6 William Skelton Woosnam (124) 1839–1932
    7 Charlotte Emily Mather (180) 1840–1924
Generation 4
    8 Charles Mather (21) 1812–1886
    9 Harriet Bennett (87) 1805–1885
    10 William Roberts (18) 1804–
    11 Jane Jones (18) 1807–
    12 Isaac Woosnam (106) 1803–1854
    13 Mary Ann Richardson (122) 1801–
    14 Charles Mather (21) 1812–1886
    15 Harriet Bennett (87) 1805–1885
NB. 4 & 7 are brother and sister; 8 & 9 are the same individuals as 14 & 15; 2 & 3 are cousins

6
The public library

At the public library the professional librarian is a knowledgeable and free resource whose advice and guidance could be invaluable. Researchers browse the library's catalogue of printed books and special collections. This may take the form of a card index, microfiche or computerised database. Books not in stock can usually be borrowed from other libraries at a modest cost through an inter-library loan system. Library stock is arranged by subject. Each book bears a class number typically derived using the Dewey decimal classification system. The public library usually holds the British Library's *General Catalogue of Printed Books to 1955*, with supplements to 1975. This is available on the Internet at <**http://blpc.bl.uk**>, listing most books published in Britain and Ireland, including obscure and out-of-print regional publications. Books may be traced by author, title or subject through the *British National Bibliography*, available in print or CD-ROM formats and containing books published since 1950. The library may offer access to co-operative cataloguing databases that share information among libraries nationwide. Particular books for genealogy and family history are identified from guides issued by the Historical Association and Society of Genealogists. Sources on CD-ROM may be cheaper and easier to use than printed books. For example the full text of the Oxford English Dictionary, an invaluable and encyclopedic source for the obscure, technical and defunct terms encountered in archives, can be accessed at home. Each book consulted offers its own list for further reading.

Four volumes on sources and methods were published by the Open University in connection with the course *Studying Family and Community History: 19th and 20th Centuries*. British pedigrees and family histories in print are listed in guides by G. W. Marshall, J. B. Whitmore and G. B. Barrow. Genealogical magazines may be taken by the public library or ordered from newsagents, for example *Family Tree Magazine* and *Practical Family History* <**http://www.family-tree.co.uk**>, *Family History Monthly* (Diamond Publishing Group, 45 St Mary's Road, London W5 5RQ) and the Public Record Office magazine *Ancestors* <**http://www.spub.co.uk/ancestors.html**>. Articles in journals of historical and antiquarian societies explore particular families and genealogical topics. For example, the Catholic Record Society published a census of Oxburgh Catholics, 1790–1804; a list of convicted recusants, 1671; boys at Liège academy, 1773–91. The Lancashire and Cheshire Record Society offered Talbot deeds with a pedigree of the Domvilles of Brimstage and Oxton before 1400. The Historical Society of West Wales issued genealogies of Cardiganshire, Carmarthenshire and Pembrokeshire families and accounts of Quaker emigrants to Pennsylvania.

As the family tree is extended into the past, the genealogist naturally seeks information on the social, political and religious environment of the times through such textbooks as the *Edinburgh History of Scotland*, *New History of Ireland*, *New History of Scotland* and *Oxford History of England*. Regional histories offer genealogies particularly of families of social, political or economic prominence. England (except Northumberland) is covered by the Victoria County History (VCH). The disconcertingly infertile lords of the manor of Almshoe in St Ippolyts parish were investigated in VCH for Hertfordshire:

> Sir Richard Spencer at his death in 1624 was succeeded by his son, John … who was made a baronet in 1627, held the manor until his death in 1633, when he left an only child Alice, so that the property passed to Sir Brockett Spencer. The manor eventually passed through Brockett's eldest daughter, Elizabeth, wife of Sir Humphrey Gore … to

their only child Elizabeth, who married Sir Henry Penrice. They left an only child, Anna Marie, wife of Sir Thomas Salusbury. He died in 1773 leaving the property to his second wife Sarah, who at her death bequeathed the manor to a distant cousin, Sir Robert Salusbury, bart. … Mr H.G. Salusbury is the present owner.

VCH noted that the house at Almshoe, 'now a farm, is built on the site of the old manor-house', failing to observe thirteenth-century roof beams and other medieval features that allow more recent historians to claim the building as one of the oldest continuously inhabited family homes in Britain. In his monumental history of Cheshire, George Ormerod noted the descent of the family of Massey from Hamo, Lord of Dunham Massey, recorded in the Domesday Book of 1086. William Rufus granted the family the town of Puddington 'with bounds and limits of Heaven above and Hell beneath'. Edward Massey was visited by heralds in 1663 who checked his pedigree. His grandson William,

> last representative of the Masseys of Puddington was a zealous catholic … traditionally said to have fled home after the battle of Preston, and to have effected his escape to Wirral by … swimming his horse over the Mersey below Hooton … He was … imprisoned in the castle of Chester, and died shortly afterwards, having bequeathed his estates to his godson Thomas Stanley, fourth son of sir William Stanley, of Hooton, bart. who assumed the name of Massey … which he afterwards assigned to his elder brother John Stanley, esq. who also assumed the name Massey. On the death of sir William Stanley of Hooton, bart. in 1792, the baronetcy and estates devolved to his uncle … and are now [1816] vested with the estates of the Masseys in his grandson sir Thomas Stanley Massey Stanley, bart. from whom the Puddington and some few other estates … descended to the last heir male … Sir John Stanley Massey Stanley-Errington, bart. of Puddington, whose heir presumptive, his sister's son, sir R. Williams-Bulkeley, bart. of Baron Hill, is next in succession

Ormerod reminded readers (volume 2, part 2, page 560 of the 1882 edition) that surnames might be assumed and altered according to whim or to facilitate succession to money and land. This practice lays snares for genealogists who incautiously assume that people with the same family name must be closely related.

Economic surveys of an ancestor's native region usually refer to prominent families. From 1793 the Board of Agriculture sponsored county surveys. These *General Views* were revised and republished in 1805–17, complementing the unofficial *Annals of Agriculture* of 1784–1815. Scottish parishes are surveyed in *Statistical Accounts* of the 1790s, 1840s and 1950s.

> A wise Providence … sent among them Mr Aneas Sage, a man of undaunted spirit … The people were so barbarous, that they attempted to set fire to the house he boarded in … There was a wicked fellow in Tofgag, who kept a mistress in the same house with his lawful married wife. When Mr Sage went to see him, Malcolm Roy drew a dirk; Mr Sage drew his sword; and the consequence was, that Malcolm Roy turned his mistress off
> (*A Statistical Account of Scotland*, volume XIII, Ross & Cromarty, parish of Lochcarron)

Histories of towns and villages are constructed with a myriad of biographical building blocks as researchers uncover the commonplace or eccentric life stories of landowners, farmers, peasants, householders, merchants, officials and clergymen. Descriptions may seem unfair and unflattering. The genealogist will probably wish to reprise the sources and make an objective assessment. The antiquarian Richard Gough takes his readers on a tour of his Shropshire parish church in his *Antiquities and Memoryes of the Parish of Myddle* and *Observations concerning the Seates in*

Myddle and the Familyes to which they belong, compiled 1701–2, giving as much information about each person as archives and his own long memory could provide:

> … Humphry Reynolds who was Churchwarden … One William Cleaton married a daughter of this Reynolds … Hee lived in good repute, and served severall offices in this parish. Hee had 4 sons. 1. Francis who displeased his father in marrying with Margaret Vaughan, a Welsh woman … 2. Isaac who married a daughter of one White of Meriton, and had a good portion with her. The widow Lloyd, of Leaton, who is very rich in land and money, is a daughter of this Isaac … 4. Richard, an untowardly person. Hee married Annie, the daughter of William Tyller, a woman as infamous as himself … Richard Cleaton soone out ran his wife, and left his wife bigge with child. Shee had a daughter, which was brought up by Allen Challoner (the smith) of Myddle; for his wife was related to William Tyler.

(D. Hey's Penguin edition, 1981, pages 92–3)

Published reminiscences, **autobiographies**, memoirs and correspondence offer descriptions of people and places. Classics of the genre include Reverend J. C. Atkinson's *Forty Years in a Moorland Parish: Reminiscences and Researches in Danby in Cleveland* (second edition, Macmillan, 1891), E. M. Sneyd-Kynnersley's *H. M. I.: Some Paragraphs in the Life of one of H. M. Inspectors of Schools* (Macmillan, 1908) and R. Roberts's *The Classic Slum: Salford Life in the First Quarter of the [twentieth] Century* (Manchester University Press, 1971). Published diaries are revealing, if the editor has exercised restraint in the use of his censorious pencil. The schoolmaster Amhlaoibh Ó Súilleabháin (1780–1838) of Callainn, County Kilkenny, kept a diary during the years 1827–35. Humphrey O'Sullivan, as he was known for official purposes, a linen draper by trade, assisted his father in the teaching of up to 120 children in the hamlet of Crossroads. The schoolhouse, a cabin erected in just three days, was a slight improvement on open-air classes, but not enough to spare Humphrey the title hedge-school teacher. Selections from the journal, now at the Royal Irish Academy, were published as *Cín Lae Amhlaoibh* (An Clóchomhar Teoranta, Dublin, 1970). A translation by Tomás de Bhaldraithe appeared from the Mercier Press, Dublin, in 1979. The journal

Oliver & Boyd's directory for 1842 showing the names of industrialists and officials of societies in Inverness.

demonstrates Celtic veneration for family and forebears:

> At ten o'clock this morning my mother, Máire Ní Bhuachalla Ní Shúilleabháin, wife of Donncha Ó Súilleabháin, my father, died having received Extreme Unction, by the Grace of Almighty God. She was close to eighty years of age. Her husband, my father, died in the year of Christ 1808, the year of the big snow. He was buried in Cill Bhride, beside Áth an Iúir a mile from Callan, although the family's burial place is Iriolach Monastery at Mucros beside Loch Léin in Killarney, Co. Kerry. But the pressures of life sent us a long way from our people, sixteen and twenty years ago … While I was digging my mother's grave my mind was troubled by many sad thoughts. The bones of my brother who died thirty-one years ago in 1796 were there mingled … with those of my three children, two of them called Anastáisin and the third Amhlaoibh.

(16th–17th August 1827)

Travel writers leave engaging glimpses of people and place. A chief source here is G. E. Fussell's *The Exploration of England: a Select Bibliography of Travel and Topography, 1570–1815* (Mitre Press, 1935). Examples of the genre include the complementary accounts by James Boswell and Samuel Johnson of their Scottish expedition of 1773, the *Torrington Diaries* of John Byng, Viscount Torrington (1743–1813) and *Wynne Diaries* covering Elizabeth Freemantle's journeys during the period 1789–1820. Gazetteers combined parish histories, statistics and deferential nods at families of importance. In this example from the *National Gazetteer of Great Britain and Ireland* (Virtue & Co, 1875) the editor, N. E. S. A. Hamilton, unfortunately confuses Herefordshire and Hertfordshire:

TEWIN, a par. in the hund. and co. of Hereford, 4½ miles W. of Hertford, its post town, and 2½ S.E. of the Welwyn station on the Great Northern railway. The village is situated on the river Naran. The manor was formerly held by St. Alban's Abbey, the Tywinges, St. Bartholomew's Priory, Cooks of Broxbourne, the Cecils, and Lord May … In the churchyard is the tomb of Lady Ann Grimston, which in the course of a century has been gradually displaced by seven ash trees and sycamores. There are also monuments to Lady Cathcart and her second husband, General Sabine, who rebuilt Tewin House

Printed **directories**, arranged by county, town or parish, appeared from the seventeenth century onwards, listing the names and addresses of merchants, craftsmen, landowners and professional men. Officials

George Collier	Hon. T. Murray	J. E. Lewis	H. Hamilton
Wm. Brumell	Cha. Winter	H. D. Griffith	Dugald M'Neill
F. R. Phayre	J.M.Kennedy,pm.	J. S. Atkinson	H. J. White
William Hore	S. B. Ross, adj.	T. Buckland	J. W. Collins
Jas. Brabazon	J.W.Preston,qm	H.Mackenzie,pa.	pm.
R. Pri. Puston	Peter Smith,sur.	M. F. Steele, adj.	J. E. N. Bull, adj.
Francis Ellis	A.Fergusson,M.D.	J. Powell, q. m.	Wm Gunn, q. m.
T.H.Doyle,paym.	a. s.	Cha. Dealey, sur.	D.Henderson,sur.
Wm. Sutton, adj.	Facing s red.	J. P. Munro, as.	W.Robertson, as.
Rich. Berry, q. m.	Greenwood & Co.	Wm. G. Byrne	Jas. Young
E.S.Graham,M.D.	Agents.	Facing s yellow.	Facing s buff.
sur.	Armit, Borough,	Lace geld.	Mr Brent, agent.
J. L. Tighe, a. s.	& Co. Ir. ag.	Greenwood & Co.	
John Caw. m.d.		Armit & Co.Ir.a.	
Facing s yellow.			LXXIX.
Greenwood & Co.			(or Cameron
	LXXVII.		Highlanders.)
	(East Middlesex.)	LXXVIII.	Egmont-op-Zee
	The Plume of the	(Highland, or	Egypt
LXXVI.	Prince of Wales.	Ross-shire Buffs.)	Fuentes d'Onor
The Elephant	Seringapatam	Cuidich'n Rhi.	Salamanca
Hindoostan	Ciudad Rodrigo	Elephant	Pyrenees
Peninsula	Badajoz	Assaye	Nivelle Nive
Colonel,	Peninsula	Maida Java	Toulouse
Cha. Chowne, g.	Colonel,	Colonel,	Peninsula
Lt Col.	Sir G. Cooke, lg	Sir E. Barnes,lg	Waterloo
Hen. Gillman	Lt Col.	Lt Col.	Colonel,
Majors,	G. P. Bradshaw	Martin Lindsay	SirR. Ferguson,g
John Clarke	Majors,	Majors,	Lt Col.
W.N.Hutchinson	Edward Jones	H. N. Douglass	Sir N. Douglas, c
Captains,	Nich. Wilson	Benj. Adams	Majors,
Joseph Clarke	Captains,	Captains,	D.M'Dougall, lc.
J. H. Grubbe	James Algeo	M. M'Gregor	Rob. Ferguson
R. F. Martin	Rich. Tatton	Arth. O'Keeffe	Captains,
P. Le P. Trench	G. A. Ramsay	M. G. T. Lindsay	K. Cameron
Aug. Hotham	J. R. Raines	Jonath. Forbes	J. C. Young
W.L.P.Moriarty	Charles Barry	E. Twopeny	A. Forbes
George Varlo	A. Buchan	T. H. Hemmans	W. A. Riach
F. Martin	G. F. Paschal	R. J. P. Vassall	Geo. Mathias
HEBHutchinson	James Mason	E. M'Pherson	Jer. Robinson
R. A. Gossett	G. P. Clarke	Hen. Holyoake	Tho. L. Butler
Lieuts.	J. P. Nelley	T. J.Taylor	A. Macdonell
S. B. Ross			Andrew Brown
Rob. Shepperd	P.W.A.Bradshaw	Lieuts.	Tho. Crombie
J. Montgomerie	T. L. Butler	W. Beales	Lieu's.
W.W.J.Cockcraft	E. Sutherland	Geo. Mitchell	D. Matheson
G. P. Pickard	Anth. Dillon	W. Hamilton	D.M'Douga:l
S. C. Hilton	W. N. Persse	W. B. M'Alpin	Wm. Cartan
Walter Ray	Wm. J. Clerk's	R. M'Beath	T. C. Cameron
Rob. Lloyd	B. C. Bordes	W. H. Pickthorn	Jas. Macdonald
G. F. C. Scott	Wm. Galway	J. E. N. Bull	Geo. Johnston
R. J. Ireland	D. Herbert	E. W. W. Pawsey	M. Fi z Gera'd
Robert Bruce	Charles Lee	J. Macleod	Hon. R. Boyle
Harr. Trevelyan	Mat. F. Steele	F. Montgomery	W. H. Lance
R. Le P. Trench	W. T. Servantes	Thomas Wingate	Rob. Manners
Ensigns,	John Powell	John Shields	John S. Smyth
T. W. Fountaine	Ensigns,	Ensigns,	Thomas Isham
F. S. Prittie	D. Cameron	Wm. Alvares	W. L. Scobell
E. H. Smith	R. J. Straton	John Burns	Ensigns,
Bert. Wodehouse	George Bell	Wm. Fisher	A. W. Browne
J. B. Flanagan	George Dixon	A. W. Browne	J. Cockburne

478

Army list from the 'Edinburgh Almanack', 1833.

connected with churches, schools and public institutions as well as ordinary townsfolk are recorded in comprehensive directories produced by Baines, White, Pigot, Slater, Bagshaw, Holden, Kelly (*Post Office London Directory*) and Oliver & Boyd (*Edinburgh Almanack*). Ancestors are traced from year to year and from house to house. Directories are listed in P. J. Atkins (London 1677–1977), J. E. Norton (national before 1856) and G. Shaw and A. Tipper (England and Wales from 1850, Scotland from 1773). Researchers sometimes study the other residents of an ancestor's street to note the people who were neighbours and social equals. Specific directories were published for the army, navy, clergy, surgeons, physicians, lawyers, architects and even prostitutes. It is possible to follow an ancestor through a career, rising through the ranks of the military or moving from backstreet premises to high-street offices as reputation and clientele increase. Biographical dictionaries, arranged alphabetically by surname, describe the careers of prominent individuals and their family backgrounds. The *Dictionary of National Biography* with supplements and the *Dictionary of Labour History* follow men and women of renown. The annual *Who's Who* from 1897 is supplemented with *Who Was Who*.

The careers of ships that ancestors owned, shared, skippered or manned are documented in *Lloyd's List* (a newspaper issued from 1741 onwards), the annual *Lloyd's Register* from 1764, *Mercantile Navy List* of 1857–1976, and Lloyd's casualty books for war losses from 1914. Names of owners were published by entrepreneurs such as Marwood, Christie and Turnbull. The National Maritime Museum maintains indexed resources for following the histories of individual ships.

The first register of the **peerage** was the brainchild of the Whig journalist and bookseller John Almon (1737–1805). The project passed in 1781 to John Debrett, who advertised a modest compilation entitled the *New Peerage* in 1784. The famous *Debrett's Peerage of England, Scotland, and Ireland* appeared in two volumes in May 1802 under the author's own imprint. Debrett provided family descents, names and mottoes with notes of collaterals and extinct branches. Debrett's *The Baronetage of England* (1808) included British subjects holding foreign knighthoods. Debrett died in 1822, but his work lived on in periodic revisions. John Burke (1787–1848) improved on Debrett by listing peers and baronets alphabetically. His *Peerage and Baronetage* appeared in 1826–37. Burke then compiled *A Genealogical and Heraldic History of the Commoners of Great Britain and Ireland, Enjoying Territorial Possessions, or High Official Rank* (1833–8),

Burke's 'Peerage and Baronetage'.

BECKETT.

BECKETT, SIR THOMAS, of Somerby Park, co. Lincoln, *b.* in 1779; *m.* 3 March, 1825, Caroline, dau. of Joseph Beckett, Esq. of Barnsley, and has issue. His dau. Elizabeth *m.* 17 March, 1853, Henry Hickman Bacon, Esq.

Lineage.

I. JOHN BECKETT, Esq. of Leeds, co. York, and of Somerby Park, co. Lincoln, grandson of Gervase Beckett, Esq. of Barnsley, was created a Baronet, 2 Nov. 1813. He *m.* in 1774, Mary, dau. of the Right Rev. Christopher Wilson, Bishop of Bristol, and had issue,

JOHN, 2nd baronet. Christopher, *b.* in 1777.
THOMAS, present baronet.
Richard, capt. in the guards, slain at Talavera, in 1809.
William, banker at Leeds, *b.* 3 March, 1784, *m.* 20 Nov. 1841, Frances-Adelina, sister of Hugo-Meynell Ingram, Esq., of Temple Newsham, co. York.
Edmund, M.P. for the W. R. of Yorkshire, *b.* 29 Jan. 1787; *m.* 14 Dec. 1814, Maria, dau. of William Beverley, of Beverley, Esq., and great-niece of the wife of Sir Thomas Denison, Knt., judge of the Common Pleas, and has issue. (See BURKE's *Landed Gentry*, p. 324.) Mr. Edmund Beckett assumed the surname and arms of DENISON, in 1810.
Henry, *b.* 11 April, 1791.
George, in holy orders, prebend of Lincoln, rector of Epsworth, and vicar of Gainsborough, *b.* 10 Feb. 1793, *d.* 13 April, 1843.

Sir John *d.* 18 Sept. 1826, and was *s.* by his eldest son,

II. THE RIGHT HON. SIR JOHN BECKETT, F.R.S., M.P., &c., *b.* in 1775; who *m.* 20 Jan. 1817, Lady Anne Lowther, dau. of William, Earl of Lonsdale, K.G.; but dying *s. p.* 31 May, 1847, was *s.* by his next surviving brother, the present SIR THOMAS BECKETT.

Creation—2 Nov. 1813.
Arms—Gu., a fesse, between three boars' heads, couped, erminois.
Crest—A boar's head, couped, or, pierced by a cross patée-fitchée, erect, sa.
Seat—Somerby Park, Lincolnshire.

ASHBROOK

VISCOUNTCY [I.] 1. HENRY (FLOWER), BARON CASTLE-DURROW [I.],
I. 1751. was only surv. s. and h. of William, 1st BARON
CASTLE-DURROW [I.], by Edith, da. of the Hon. Toby
CAULFEILD, of Clone, co. Kilkenny. In Aug. 1710, he was cornet of a troop
of Horse, and, soon after, a captain. On 29 Apr. 1746, he suc. his father
as LORD CASTLE-DURROW [I.] and took his seat in the House 28 Oct. 1747.
On 30 Sep. 1751, he was cr. VISCOUNT ASHBROOK [I.], and took
his seat, as such, on 8 Oct. following. He m., 9 Mar. 1740/1, at St. Paul's,
London, Elizabeth, sister of Col. Nevill TATTON, da. of William TATTON,
of Hillingdon, Midx., Lieut. Gen. in the army. He d. at St. Stephen's
Green, Dublin, 27 June 1752, and was bur. at Finglas, near Dublin. Will,
in which, calling his cons insane, he devised the reversion of all his estates
to his wife absolutely, dat. 25 June, pr. 31 July 1752, in Dublin, and June
1753, in London. His widow d. 10, and was bur. 13 Feb. 1759, (with
her father) at Hillingdon. Will dat. 27 Nov. 1757, pr. Feb. 1759.

II. 1752. 2. WILLIAM (FLOWER), VISCOUNT ASHBROOK, &c. [I.],
only s. and h. s [4 June 1744, at Castle-Durrow, co.
Kilkenny. Matric. Oxford (Ch. Ch.) 29 Nov. 1762. He m., 9 Mar.
1766, Elizabeth [*] da. of Thomas RIDGE, of co. Oxford. He d. 30 Aug.
1780,[†] at Shillingford, Berks, and was bur. there, aged 36. M.I.
Will pr. Oct. 1780. His widow, who was b. 18 July 1746, m., 20 Jan.
1790, the Rev. John JONES, D.D., and d. 22 Feb. 1808, at Shipston
upon Stour, co. Worcester, and was bur. at Shillingford afsd. Will pr.
May 1808.

III. 1780. 3. WILLIAM (FLOWER), VISCOUNT ASHBROOK, &c. [I.],
s. and h., b. 16 Nov. 1767. Ed. at Eton. Matric.
Oxford (Trin. Coll.), 13 July 1785. He d. unm., 6 Jan. 1802, at Wadley
House, Berks, aged 34. Will pr. Feb. 1802.

IV. 1802. 4. HENRY JEFFERY (FLOWER), VISCOUNT ASHBROOK, &c.
[*] only br. and h., b. 16 Nov. 1776. Sometime Capt.
fifth Foot. Claim to Peerage allowed 25 Aug. 1871. Lord of the Bedchamber 1835-37. He m. 1stly, by spec. lic. 26 May 1812, at St. Geo.,
Han. Sq., Deborah Susanna, (fortune £19,999) only da. and h. of the Rev.
William Mansfield FREIND, F—ow of Chaister, co. Chester, by Deborah, da.
and h. of Thomas WALKER, of —ew Woodstock in that co. She d. 24 Mar.
1810, aged 30, and was bur. at Hurley, Berks. M.I. Admon. July 1812.
He m., 2ndly, 22 June 1812, by spec. lic., at St. Geo., Han. Sq., Emily

[*] According to his marriage, writing in 1766 to Horace Walpole, she was
"a waterman's daughter, near Oxford." V.G.

[†] There is an abusive acco t of him, purporting for an epitaph, which
refers to his insignificance, boorishness, stupidity, &c., in The Abbey of Kilkhampton, by
Sir Herbert Croft, 1780, part ii.

G. E. Cokayne's 'Complete Peerage'.

Births, marriages, deaths and household goods for sale in the 'North British Advertiser', 7th April 1855.

Argyllshire; also Mr Dougall, gunmaker, 23, Gordon Street, Glasgow.

BIRTHS, MARRIAGE, AND DEATHS.

BIRTHS.

GARDINER.—At Calcutta, on the 13th February, the wife of the Rev. Thomas Gardiner, of a daughter.

MACKAY.—At 11, Danube Street, Edinburgh, on the 6th instant, Mrs John Mackay, of a son.

MENELAWS.—At 187, Canongate, Edinburgh, on the 31st ultimo, Mrs Menelaws, of a daughter.

POPLE.—At King's Place, Perth, on the 28th ult., Mrs J. B. Pople, of a son.

PRINGLE.—At 1, Grove Street, Edinburgh, on the 6th instant, Mrs Alexander Pringle, of a son.

SMITH.—At 24, Nicolson Street, Edinburgh, on the 5th instant, Mrs John Smith, of a son.

WHITE.—At Kipplaw House, Roxburghshire, on the 3d instant, the wife of Robert White, Esq., of a daughter.

MARRIAGE.

GRIEVE, NESS.—At 15, Leith Walk, Edinburgh, on the 4th inst., by the Rev. Dr Glover of Greenside, Patrick David Grieve, Esq., Brighton Place, Portobello, to Jessie, daughter of the late David Ness, Esq.

DEATHS.

ANDERSON.—At Edinburgh, on the 3d instant, Mrs Margaret Anderson, at No. 2, Queen Street.

ANDERSON.—At Elgin, on the 30th ultimo, Janet Watt, wife of Alexander Anderson, Esq., and daughter of the late Mr James Steuart Watt, farrier, Edinburgh.

CUNNINGHAM.—At West Mills, Colinton, on the 28th ultimo, Isabella Lawson, relict of Mr Laurence Cunningham, farmer, Rosebank, Currie, aged 72.

CURRIE.—At Dalkeith, on the 5th instant, while on duty with the Edinburgh County Militia, of typhus fever, Charles Russell Currie, younger of Linthill. Friends will please accept of this intimation.

FEA.—At No. 4, Ratcliffe Terrace, Newington, Edinburgh, on the 3d instant, Elizabeth Carrick Fea, third daughter of Mr Magnus Fea, of Hull.

GALBRAITH.—At 2, Melville Street, Edinburgh, on the 3d instant, Mr Colin Galbraith, writer.

LEE.—At No. 16. Windmill Street, Edinburgh, on the 3d instant, Mr Hamlin Warren Lee, surgeon, late Conservator of the Royal College of Surgeons, Edinburgh. Friends will please accept of this intimation.

MACKINNON.—At Edge-hill, Dean, on the 6th instant, Charles Richards, infant son of Charles MacKinnon, Esq.

DAVIDSON.—At Christian Bank, Trinity, on the 5th instant, aged 88, Janet, daughter of the late Rev. Dr George Moir, of Peterhead, and relict of Christopher Norton, Esq. of Penkridge, Stafford-shire, and of John Davidson, Esq., Gottenburg.

RADCLIFF.—At Moulmein, Burmah, on the 22d January, Frances Susan, wife of Captain Radcliff, H.M. 84th Regiment, daughter of the late Captain Murray, Barrack Master, Edinburgh Castle. Friends are requested to accept this intimation.

YOUNG.—At Enfield House, Southampton, on the 1st instant, aged 31 years, David Young, Esq., of Dharwar, India, youngest son of the late Mr David Young, teacher, Edinburgh. Friends will please accept of this intimation.

Birth.

At Goulburn, on the 6th instant Mrs. W. Richardson, of a daughter.

Deaths.

At his residence, Bathurst, on Thursday morning, the 16th inst, Mr. W. N. Kuble, innkeeper. Mr. K. has left a wife and large family to deplore his loss; his death was occasioned by a fall down the stairs of his house, the head coming in contact with some sharp substance, which caused a fracture of the skull.

On the 18th inst, at his residence upper Castlereagh-street in the 41st year of his age, Captain E. H. Cliffe, after a lingering illness which he bore with christian fortitude. Captain Cliffe was for several years an active and enterprising trader between this Colony and India, and enjoyed the reputation of a strictly upright Man.

An ordinary birth followed by extraordinary and exemplary deaths in the 'Sydney Monitor', 20th November 1837.

ancestor of Burke's *Landed Gentry*, which John's son, Sir J. B. Burke (1814–92), continually revised. The elder Burke also wrote *A Genealogical and Heraldic History of the Extinct and Dormant Baronetcies of England* (1838) and *A Genealogical and Heraldic Dictionary of the Peerages of England, Ireland and Scotland, Extinct, Dormant and in Abeyance* (second edition 1840). In 1887–98 G. E. Cokayne issued *The Complete Peerage of England, Scotland, Ireland, Great Britain and the United Kingdom, Extant, Extinct or Dormant* and, in 1900–6, *A Complete Baronetage.* These multi-volume works contain biographical information on noble families including younger children and related commoners. Sir J. B. Paul published *The Scots Peerage* in 1904–14.

Newspapers originated in Civil War propaganda sheets of the 1640s. Titles are listed in *British Union-catalogue of Periodicals of the World ... in British Libraries*, the British Library's *Catalogue of the Newspaper Library* and *The Times* of London's *Tercentenary Handlist of English and Welsh Newspapers.* British Library catalogues, available on the Internet at <**http://www.bl.uk**>, provide keyword searching of over 50,000 titles. Public libraries hold files of provincial newspapers, either the original papers or on microfilm. The *London Gazette* from 1665 is the official source for government information, including army appointments, military decorations

and bankruptcies. Regional events may be noticed in *The Times*, accessed through Palmer's index from 1790, or popular prints such as *The London Daily Post & General Advertiser*, 1734–94, and *Gentleman's Magazine*, 1731–1883. Regional newspapers include *Worcestershire Post-man*, commencing 1690, and *Belfast News-Letter* of 1737, the earliest Irish title. Newspapers contain notices of birth, marriage and death; obituaries; notices of bankruptcy and sale of debtor's goods; reports on council meetings and court proceedings; celebrations of

The new town of Whitehaven attracted families from far afield in the late eighteenth century.

This sketch by A. D. Fordyce of houses at Polmuir, Aberdeenshire, was accompanied by biographical notes on the occupiers of each dwelling around 1830.

achievements in sport, the arts, industry and agriculture; and reports of disasters and dreadful murders. Whole pages of advertisements reveal a wealth of social background and perhaps pin down the date at which an ancestor set up in business.

Pictorial sources include photographs, paintings and drawings in library collections and municipal art galleries. Valued as fine art, portraits of ancestors may be found far from the family home, in national galleries and private collections, even overseas. Uncatalogued pictures are located through the bush telegraph in their home locality: family portraits in the rectory; pen-and-ink sketches on parlour walls. Artists of national renown specialised in scenes of provincial life, employing the locals as models, depicting people in their everyday clothes and activities. Printed views of places were produced as woodcuts, etchings, engravings and lithographs for books, broadsheets, newspapers, company letterheads and walls at home. From the twelfth century onwards, towns and villages were conventionally

A studio portrait from the glass negative archive of a professional photographer deposited for research in the public library.

drawn as though seen from the air showing both the layout of the town and the façades of the houses, though not necessarily to scale. The aerial view remained popular until the eighteenth century and was periodically revived thereafter. A prospect took its view from ground level. Between 1572 and 1618, G. Braun (editor) and F. Hogenberg (engraver) published *Civitates Orbis Terrarum*, views and prospects of 546 British and European towns. The *Theatrum Scotiae* of John Slezer in 1693 depicted major Scottish towns and their hinterlands of ridged fields and cottages. *Britannia Illustrata* of Johannes Kip (1708) and the collected *Antiquities and Venerable Remains* of S. and N. Buck may be available in the public library either as original prints or copies. Supplementing these well-known sources is a

Owners and occupiers of houses and building plots are named on Robert Ray's plan of the burgh of Elgin, Moray, 1838.

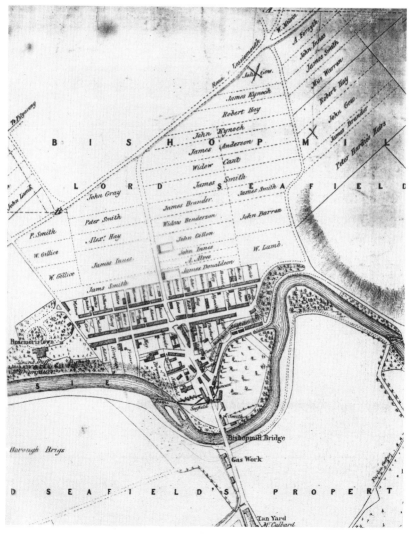

First edition 1:2500 (25-inch) Ordnance Survey, 1868.

welter of work by provincial printers illustrating the built environment and landscapes known to each generation of forebears.

Professional and amateur **photographers** alike created images of street scenes and public events. Ancestors stand among the crowds or peer from house windows to watch a ceremonial tree-planting or proclamation of a monarch. Photographic collections in the library may yield pictures of dwellings long-since demolished and, more rarely, interior images taken with magnesium flash. Picture postcards, notably the archives of James Valentine of Dundee, Francis Frith of Reigate and J. P. Gibson of Hexham, have provided crucial evidence for genealogists in search of a family house. Library collections include copy images obtained from national collections and individual photographic portraits from the archives of resident families and provincial photographic businesses. These may be captioned with the names of

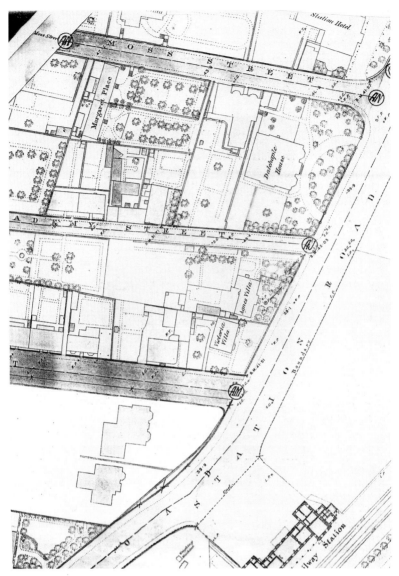

Surburban family homes and gardens on a 1:500 (10 foot) Ordnance Survey town plan, c.1870.

sitters and indexed in library databases.

A **plan** represents the landscape symbolically and schematically, as if viewed from above at a uniform scale. Printed plans at a useful scale appeared from the eighteenth century onwards, for example Rocque's Bristol (1742), Scalé's Waterford (1764) and Hochstetter's Norwich (1789). John Wood's atlas of forty-eight Scottish towns (1828) followed the fashion for including names of property owners. County maps at scales of 1 or 2 inches to a mile showing individual rural houses include the fourteen sheets of Joel Gascoyne's Cornwall (about 1700), emulated by William Williams's Denbigh and Flint (about 1720) and J. Noble and

J. Keenan's County Kildare (1752). The Ordnance Survey originated in military mapping of Scotland during the eighteenth century. Uprisings by supporters of the Stuart dynasty, especially in 1745–6, alerted the government to the need for accurate maps. From 1747 to 1755, William Roy prepared a 1:36,000 scale 'Great Map' of Scotland, recording peasant townships on the eve of clearance. Roy's map is now in the British Library but copies of relevant sections should be available in public libraries. In 1784, Roy moved south to fix a baseline at Hounslow for the first 1-inch (1:63,360) survey of England and Wales. Published 1-inch maps were reduced generally from 2-inch field surveys, with strategic areas and ultimately most of the country measured by field officers at much larger scales, up to 1:2500 (25.344 inches to one mile). These are now preserved at the British Library. Scottish and Irish 1-inch maps appeared from 1843 and 1855 respectively. Ordnance Survey 6-inch (1:10,560) mapping commenced in County Londonderry (published 1833). Mainland Britain was mapped at a 6-inch scale from the 1840s. 25-inch maps (1:2500 or 25.344 inches to 1 mile) commenced in County Durham in 1853, eventually covering all except unpopulated and uncultivated districts. At this scale the researcher sees an exact footprint for each dwelling showing fine details such as a bay window, front porch and privy in the garden. A general revision of the 6- and 25-inch maps was completed between 1891 and 1913, showing how the family home changed as generations passed. Published town plans at generous scales, variously 1:1056 (5 feet to 1 mile) and 1:500 (10.56 feet to 1 mile), commenced with Dublin and St Helens in the 1840s. Towns with populations exceeding 4000 were mapped nationwide by 1894. Guided by an old map, the genealogist retraces an ancestor's steps from home to school, workplace or chapel, following the route on foot and noting the buildings and landscapes that a forebear knew, and perhaps even meeting descendants of his neighbours and workmates. Unpublished Ordnance Survey archives for England, Wales and Scotland were largely lost in the bombing of Southampton in 1940. Irish records surviving in Dublin include manuscript plans, place-name books and other material of genealogical interest. An early intention to supplement Ordnance Survey maps with written *Memoirs* commenced in Ulster in 1830 but collapsed by 1840 with publication hardly begun. The *Memoirs*, now available in editions prepared by the Institute of Irish Studies at Queen's University of Belfast and the Royal Irish Academy, offer occasional references to individuals in connection with schools, houses, industries, churches, markets, fairs and public institutions:

> Tynan Abbey, the seat of Sir James M. Stronge, Bart, is situated about half a mile south west of the village of Tynan. The house, a remarkable handsome building, stands on an eminence 177 feet above the level of the sea. The demesne is extensive and well planted. Above a quarter of a mile east of the village of Tynan is the rectory, a plain neat building. The Reverend Mr Mauleverer is the present rector. About a mile and a quarter south of the village of Killylea is Fellow's Hall, the residence of J. T. Armstrong Esquire and nearly half a mile south of the same village is Darton House, the residence of M. Cross Esquire.
>
> A. Day and P. McWilliams (*Ordnance Survey Memoirs of Ireland, volume 1, County Armagh 1835-8*, 1990, page 127)

The public library is also first port of call for copies of maps in national archives. The published catalogue *Maps and Plans in the Public Record Office* covers in its first volume the British Isles from around 1410 until 1860. The following examples demonstrate the kind of material the genealogist discovers:

155. Kensington 1841
Plan of the several plots of ground for building on, now or lately part of the Royal Kitchen Gardens ... with names of tenants entered and the rents ...

Printed ephemera in the public library may include collections of popular poetry, broadsheets and bothy ballads, here offering a savage satire on the antics of dissenting ancestors and vulgar lampoons of casual labourers gathered for the harvest.

L.R.R.O.1/1002   MPE 874
841. Sutton Courtenay 1804
Two plans to Inclosure Award of 25 Sept. 1804 pursuant to 41 Geo III, c. 94.
Parchment. MS. Field boundaries, acreage, owners … Reference table gives old inclosures
K.B.122/789 *rot* 399)   MR 49 & 50
2834. Loddington and Thorpe Malsor [1798]
A freehold estate escheated to the Crown on the death of Mary Gardiner.
Parchment. MS., clrd. 4 chains to an inch. Adjacent owners. Reference table gives field names, quality and acreage …
(L.R.R.O.1/311)   MPI 251
2997. Rolleston [1598]
Lands in dispute. Ms., clrd. Occupiers, houses and churches in perspective …
(D.L.44/567)   MPC 241

The public library is the starting-point for archives held on microfilm, microfiche, CD-ROM, photocopy and printed edition. Parish registers on film and the International Genealogical Index (IGI) on fiche are among the family historian's principal interests in attending the library.

7
Discovering archives

Documentary sources are usually discovered just where all good archives should be, in their proper place at home: family papers in the attic; estate muniments with the land agent; official files on an administrator's desk. Researchers do not enjoy automatic right of access to documents in private hands, though tact, politeness and persistence eventually pay off in persuading careful custodians to open their archives.

Documentary collections may be located through the London office of the Historic Manuscripts Commission (HMC), appointed in 1869 to inspect and list archival collections. Registers of documents as well as transcribed texts compiled by HMC inspectors were included as appendices to various published reports. Catalogues of documents, known as calendars and arranged chronologically within each subject division, are a useful research tool. *Guides to Sources for British History* (HMC) include *Principal Family and Estate Collections*. Numerous documents have disappeared since their original cataloguing, for example one of Lancashire's most comprehensive archives, belonging to the Bootle-Wilbraham family of Lathom, was destroyed along with the family home in 1929. Others have merely moved house, perhaps to the secure storage of a library or university overseas, where British family papers are especially venerated. HMC maintains a register of manorial documents (MDR) established under the Law of Property Amendment Act of 1924. Also available at the HMC is the National Register of Archives (NRA), begun in 1945 'to record the location, content and availability of all archives and collections of historical manuscripts in England and Wales, other than records of central government, without limit of date'. Scotland and Northern Ireland operate registers on similar lines, based at the National Archives in Edinburgh and the Public Record Office of Northern Ireland in Belfast. The HMC website at <**http://www.hmc.gov.uk**> is a principal source for British archives. From the home page the researcher moves on to the MDR and NRA databases. The British Records Association (BRA) was founded in 1932 'to develop informed opinion on the necessity for preserving records of historical importance and … advise on the disposal of papers, deeds and documents of all kinds through its Records Preservation Section'. The BRA publishes the journal *Archives* and the series of pamphlets entitled *Archives and the User*.

Archives, strictly defined, are administrative records created for official purposes and retained in official custody. In popular usage the term archive describes almost any old document: paper or parchment; a roll, bound book or single leaf; handwritten (manuscript), typewritten or printed; even a photograph or audiotape. The word archives also denotes a place where old documents are stored. Archives may be the most rewarding source for the family historian. From a single document the careful genealogist teases out a variety of information that would surprise the original compiler. The thousands of documents available for each locality are the building blocks of family history. Archive sources have the authority of an eyewitness account because they were written by an ancestor's contemporaries, who were perhaps personally acquainted with the family. The researcher, though, appreciates that age is not a guarantee of accuracy. The sources may be tendentious, imprecise or downright dishonest. Few were written with future genealogists in mind. Various types of document are introduced in the Historical Association's *Short Guides to Records*, edited by L. M. Munby, revised and reissued 1994–7, and numerous pamphlets of the Federation of Family History Societies.

The county or borough record office, perhaps known as the archives or heritage

Genealogists at work: the searchroom of the county record office or heritage centre offers card indexes, calendars, microfilms, databases and, of course, archival documents.

centre, is a council service open to the general public. Addresses are in the latest editions of guides by Foster, Gibson, Helferty and the Historical Manuscripts Commission (see Further reading) and on the HMC website under **archon**. In England and Wales the county record office evolved from the court of quarter

An archive strongroom at the Moray District Record Office in the old tolbooth and prison of the burgh of Forres. Strict security arrangements mean that the researchers are seldom allowed a glimpse behind the scenes at the archives.

sessions presided over by justices of the peace who governed the shire from the sixteenth century until 1889. County archivists have added administrative records of bodies such as the town and county council, civil parish, highway authority, poor law union and school board. Non-official archives are deposited by lawyers, architects, industrialists, landowners and ordinary families to establish a wide-ranging genealogical resource. Services in Scotland were established chiefly from 1975 onwards. Archive searchrooms are open to genealogical researchers, though character references and advance booking may be required. A policy of closed access protects collections. Researchers browse lists, calendars and indexes to identify documents of interest, which are retrieved by staff. Offices usually insist that pencil, not pen, is used for note-taking to protect unique documents from ink smudges. The researcher may also be required to wear gloves, supplied by the office, when handling especially precious manuscripts. Documents cannot normally be borrowed, though photocopies may be purchased for home study.

Council archivists instinctively concentrate upon official archives. Governed by strict collection policies and cost-conscious councillors, archivists are cagey of soliciting or rescuing extensive collections of estate, business and family papers. The Keeper of the Records of Scotland summed up the position in seminal guidance for librarians issued in 1986: 'archival resources cannot possibly cope with the overwhelming bulk of paper ... produced ... The principle of selection is therefore firmly acknowledged ... in the long term interests both of historical research and of cost efficiency, an honest selection based on well-judged criteria must be attempted'. On this basis a manageable selection, perhaps a 5 per cent sample, is usually preserved. The bulk is destroyed. The ordinary family historian need not be so constrained. As chief user and beneficiary of archives the genealogist may assume the role of chief guardian of the heritage: campaigning for council funding, organising archival rescue, emergency conservation and storage, and at last, if need be, personally underwriting the cost.

Palaeography

Palaeography is the study of old handwriting. The genealogist becomes familiar with a range of styles in the course of reading archival documents and monumental inscriptions. Fluency comes through practice with help from primers and more formal instruction, for instance under the Cambridge University Continuing Education Series. Palaeography is crucial for dating and authenticating documents and for discovering, through affectations and eccentricities of hand, the authorship of anonymous manuscripts and perhaps character traits revealed to graphological analysis. Patience is the key to reading old documents. Each word is comprehensible if carefully considered letter by letter noting any special symbols that indicate abbreviation. Copying the form of each letter using traditional pen and ink helps to fix in the mind the shape of the characters, how they linked into words and developed through time. Genealogists hone their skills by studying illustrations with transcriptions in published books (see Further reading).

Writing was introduced to Britain by the Romans, whose letter forms were adopted and adapted by subsequent English, Welsh, Gaelic and Norse writers for devotional texts, memorial inscriptions, chronicles, sagas, annals, poetry and charters. A reformed script, with letter-forms resembling those adopted for modern print and typescript, was developed by scribes at the court of Charlemagne and adopted in England from around 960. This Carolingian hand was used for the writing of the Domesday Book and generally for legal and religious texts. From the thirteenth century onwards, inscriptions on memorial stones and formal legal, literary and religious texts were inscribed in an upright gothic book or text hand sometimes known as black letter. Scribes added various flourishes and linking strokes (ligatures) to permit rapidly executed or cursive writing for business and administration. From around 1370 features of business and text hands mated,

Examples of old handwriting taken from charters from Henry III to Henry VIII.

engendering a flowing joined-up, or currently written, mongrel script usually known as bastard hand. From this developed the separate stylish hands adopted by clerks in the several courts of government. These departmental set hands, or court hands, persisted until abolished by act of Parliament in 1731. In practice, though, varieties of court hand continued in use among lawyers for wills, deeds and legal writings until the nineteenth century. Secretary hand emerged during the sixteenth century. This current, sometimes slovenly, practical cursive script is the hand most familiar to genealogists researching parish registers, administrative archives, business and estate muniments. At this period too emerged humanistic or reformed Carolingian script. Introduced in Italy and spreading across Europe, this clear, upright lettering became the model for typefaces in printed books. The italic style cross-bred with secretary to produce the looped, joined-up round hand that remains in use today. Systems of abbreviation, developed to assist both reader and writer, are explained in palaeography primers and expansively described in A. Cappelli's *Dizionario* and C. T. Martin's *Record Interpreter*.

Languages

Genealogical sources appear in a variety of languages whose older forms present unfamiliar vocabulary and grammatical rules. Documentary languages can be self-taught with assistance from a published primer and dictionary (see Further reading). Professional tuition is usually available near at hand from the education authority or university extramural department. The English language originated among Germanic migrants who entered Britain in Roman times. Known as Anglo-Saxon, the language is found today in surnames derived from Old English place-names, nicknames and occupations. A more modern version emerged during the twelfth century as the spoken and written language of England, continuing dominant until about 1500 and a basis of provincial Scots dialect. The most comprehensive collection of English usage and vocabulary, including Scots words, is the multi-volume *Oxford English Dictionary* (OED). For genealogists the OED is an encyclopedic source for the shifting meanings of words including slang, obscenities, legalisms and technical jargon. The OED is available in affordable microprint and CD-ROM formats. Useful complements are J. Wright's *Dialect Dictionary* and E. Partridge's *Dictionary of Slang*.

Latin was used by the church, law, civil service, universities, manorial administration and businessmen throughout Britain and Ireland until officially abandoned in 1733. E. A. Gooder's *Latin for Local History* is 'a self-teaching manual and guide to the kind of Latin met with in historical records'. Norman French was introduced to England during the eleventh century. This was the language of the ruling class, spoken in court, castle and church, written in charters, legal records and acts of Parliament. French was also the language of romance, popular song and heraldry, contributing largely to English vocabulary, pronunciation and spelling. Native languages should present few difficulties to those family historians in Wales, Scotland and Ireland who are native speakers of Welsh and Gaelic. English speakers in pursuit of ancestors in Celtic regions may be challenged by documents and oral sources. Assistance is usually near at hand from bilingual natives, librarians and archivists.

Interpretation

Interpreting archival sources is a discipline termed diplomatic by scholars whose earliest efforts concentrated on Anglo-Saxon charters known as diplomas. This useful science enables the genealogist to authenticate and date a document by analysis of vocabulary, handwriting style, seals and signatures. Diplomatic study is relevant because a number of sources, for example early medieval charters, can be condemned as forgeries, written years after the persons mentioned were dead and buried. Diplomatic skills are called for when considering a legal document or even a simple family letter. Almost any statement can acquire an air of authority when written in faded ink on yellowed parchment and preserved in the archives. But truth is a shy creature inclined to camouflage itself within the web of words. For example, following the troubles of 1644–6 some 220 burgesses in the town of Elgin claimed for goods pillaged or burned by 'the common enemy', the royalist Marquis of Montrose. The claims, worth tens of millions in modern money, included quantities of gold, silver, arms, armour, bulls and riding horses. The genealogist must decide whether an ancestor, who regularly pleaded penury in tax assessments, was indeed the possessor of such wondrous wealth. Perhaps the claim really represented the style to which he aspired, rendered with all the careful attention to truth and detail usual in an insurance claim, especially enhanced by officials to exaggerate the common enemy's crime.

Downright forgeries may be rare, or perhaps too well contrived to be detectable, but documents may give incorrect fact through a copyist's error. Even genealogical records may tell lies, possibly unwittingly. A baptism once registered under one set of names can permanently conceal the true identity of a parent, because no further records survive. Though a healthy scepticism scrutinises most sources, in the end simple faith accepts or rejects. Law papers, most notoriously, cannot be expected to tell the truth, the whole truth and nothing but the truth concerning an ancestor. Judges, lawyers, witnesses, plaintiffs and defendants all grind personal axes. Legal processes may unravel this skein of conflicting interests, though more usually the genealogist finds that judgements in court add only another layer of dubiety and a stratum of law to bury the truth. The archivist's professional practice of sampling and weeding will inevitably weight the evidence. Restrictions on access to archives for terms of years are quite usual, perhaps denying the very existence of certain documents. The papers of Peter Anson (1889–1975), artist and historian of the fisher communities of eastern Scotland, were subject to severe restrictions. Innocuous documents relating to Anson's work in connection with the Scottish Fisheries Museum and the Apostleship of the Sea were released, allowing researchers to relish the portrait of a folksy, Catholic contemplative, happily integrated into the community of fishwives and seamen. The ultimate release of suppressed files will colour this impression with shades cast by Anson's contribution to power struggles among the clergy of the diocese of Aberdeen and the homosexual subculture of the Banffshire coast.

Dating

Methods of counting years and arranging calendars are of importance to genealogists seeking to interpret the dates given in documentary sources. The most familiar chronological convention is based upon the year of grace. The birth of Christ is reckoned as year 1. Years are then numbered backwards as BC (before Christ) and forwards as AD (*anno Domini*, 'in the year of the Lord'). Venerable Bede, writing around 700, was the earliest British historian to use the year of grace consistently. Regnal years of popes and monarchs were also employed. Thus an English writer might date a document 'in the tenth year of Henry III', which ran from 28th October 1225 until 27th October 1226. A Scottish writer would refer to the coronation of Henry III as happening during the second year of the Scottish king Alexander II, while Vatican sources dated the event to the first year of Pope Honorius III.

Dates within the year were expressed in the form 'Tuesday the twenty-second day of March'. Legal documents might even record the time of day. Alternatively, church festivals were preferred, for instance Christmas, fixed at 25th December, or Easter celebrated on the Sunday following the full moon on or after the vernal equinox, and occurring on any day between 22nd March and 25th April. Local festivals were uppermost in the minds of provincial scribes. Thus a Lichfield clerk might refer to *mille martyres*, the feast of the thousand martyrs of Lichfield. Writers

The memorial tablet of Nathaniel Collier at Jevington, Sussex, shows double dating for 1st March 1691 (Old Style), 1692 (New Style).

might date documents on the day before a festival (the eve or vigil) or after the holiday on the octave, which fell eight days later. Church lawyers gave the opening words of the gospel for the day, so that the twenty-second Sunday after Pentecost was known as *reddite que sunt Caesaris Caesari*, 'render unto Caesar that which is Caesar's' (Matthew 22:21). The year might be reckoned as beginning on various dates including 24th September, used by Bede in obedience to Roman convention, or the feast of Christ's conception, known as Lady Day, which fell on 25th March. During the sixteenth century, 1st January was adopted in Europe, with Scotland following suit in 1600. Progressive English writers recognised the continental practice, with double dates for documents written between 1st January and 24th March in the form '22 January 1592/3'.

Because the earth takes approximately 365.2422 days to circle the sun, human calendars based on whole numbers soon get out of step with the heavens. This difficulty was appreciated by the ancients, who periodically recalibrated their tables. In one of these reforms in 46 BC, Julius Caesar inaugurated a calendar incorporating leap years. Known subsequently as the Julian or Old Style, this remained in use during the Middle Ages, accumulating a discrepancy of ten days by the sixteenth century. A reformed, New Style, calendar was devised and indicted by Pope Gregory XIII on 24th February 1582. The Protestant British rejected this Gregorian calendar, though practical businessmen with European connections might use Old Style/New Style double dates in the form '31 May/11 June 1590'. Britain and Ireland were finally brought into step with Europe in 1752. The accumulated discrepancy, by then eleven days, was remedied by declaring the day following 2nd September as 14th September. As a result, the financial year shifted from Lady Day to 6th April. Traditionally minded folk celebrated Old Christmas in the first week of January.

8
Birth, marriage, death and adoption

During the nineteenth century, statistical registers under government control were introduced. District registrars were appointed to record and issue certificates of birth and death and to conduct secular marriage ceremonies at the registry office. This system commenced from 1st July 1837 in England and Wales; Scotland in 1855; Ireland in 1864 (Protestant marriages from 1845); the Isle of Man in 1849 (marriages) and 1878 (births and deaths); Northern Ireland in 1922; Jersey in 1842; and Guernsey in 1840 (births and deaths, marriages from 1841 except Church of England, which maintained its own registers until 1919). Registration was free but difficult to enforce. Despite penalties for non-compliance in respect of birth registration, introduced in 1875, many families continued to ignore the regulations, their unregistered babies storing up problems for future genealogists. Information was despatched by each district superintendent registrar to national registrars at general register offices in London, Edinburgh, Dublin and the various islands. Information was entered into registers, originally in manuscript. Each event was indexed by surname to facilitate searches. Indexes were completed quarterly on 31st March, 30th June, 30th September and 31st December for England and Wales and annually in Scotland. These registers of life events are sometimes referred to as vital registers, using a word derived from the Latin *vita*, meaning 'life'. There are official proposals to computerise indexes. The volunteer project FreeBMD digitising English and Welsh indexes for free on-line access has a search page at <**http://freebmd.rootsweb.org/cgi/search.pl**>.

The family historian obtains information by first personally searching the indexes

REGISTRATION
OF
BIRTHS, DEATHS, AND MARRIAGES.

NO PENALTY
AND
NO FEE
WHEN REGISTRATION TAKES PLACE
AS FOLLOWS:—
BIRTHS within 21 days.
DEATHS within 8 days.
MARRIAGES within 3 days.

W. P. DUNDAS,
Registrar-General.

Civil registration was free of charge and compulsory, though many still failed to register the births of their children.

V. R.

REGISTRATION

OF

BIRTHS, DEATHS, & MARRIAGES.

17ᵗ & 18ᵗ VICTORIÆ, CAP. 80.

CHANGE OF SYSTEM.

FROM and after the 1ST OF JANUARY 1855, all Registration in existing Registers of Births, Deaths, and Marriages becomes Illegal (except in the case of Births, Deaths, and Marriages occurring prior to 31st December 1854, which may be Recorded in the existing Registers until the 31st December 1855), and Public attention is earnestly called to the following Instructions relative to the Law as it will then be in force. Under the new system, all Births, Deaths, and Marriages, if intimated to the Registrar within the periods prescribed by the Act, will be Registered WITHOUT ANY FEE BEING CHARGED against the Informants.

BIRTHS.

SECTION XXVII.—On occasion of the birth of any Child, the Parents or Parent (or the Mother, in the case of an *Illegitimate Child*) must *within Twenty-One Days* thereafter, and under a PENALTY OF TWENTY SHILLINGS, in case of failure, attend Personally, and give information to the Registrar of the Parish or District within which the Birth occurred.

In case of the Death or inability of the Parents, the Person in charge of any Child born, the Occupier of the House or Tenement in which the Birth has taken place, and the Nurse present at the Birth, must attend and give information to the Registrar.

In the event of a failure to give the Notice above specified, the Parents, or other Persons above specified, and also any others having knowledge of the Particulars, shall, upon being required, Personally or in Writing, to do so, *within three Months* from the date of the birth, attend and give Information to the Registrar, under a PENALTY OF FORTY SHILLINGS.

SECTION XXIX.—Any Person who shall find exposed any New Born Child, or the Dead Body of any New Born Child, shall *forthwith* give notice of the fact to the Registrar of the Parish or District, or to the Inspector of the Poor, or to the District Constable, under a PENALTY OF FORTY SHILLINGS.

SECTION XXXI.—In all cases where *Three Months shall have expired* after the Birth of a Child, it is not lawful to Register such Births, except under the provisions of the 31st Section. The nature of these may be learned on application to the Registrar of the Parish or District.

DEATHS.

SECTION XXXVIII.—The nearest Relatives present at the Death of any Person, and the Occupier of the House or Tenement in which the Death took place, must personally give notice of the Death to the Registrar of the Parish or District, *within Eight Days* thereafter, under a PENALTY OF TWENTY SHILLINGS.

[*Turn over.*

of births, marriages and deaths. If the place of residence or registration is known, the appropriate superintendent registrar's office (popularly known as the registrar's), is probably the most inexpensive option. This offers the added bonus of a visit to the ancestor's home town to pursue oral and archival sources. In England and Wales, certain public libraries have purchased the microfiche index of civil certificates. The central office for English and Welsh births, marriages and deaths is the Family Records Centre, a branch of the Public Record Office, at 1 Myddelton Street, London EC1. Scottish searches are conducted at New Register House, Edinburgh, where computerised indexes assist the process.

Searches can be undertaken by officials for a fee. Indexes are examined in blocks of five years, usually two years before and after probable event date. For England and Wales applications for index searches with a view to obtaining certificates are accepted by post, telephone, fax and email. Cheque, credit or debit cards are all accepted at the General Register Office, PO Box 2, Southport PR8 2JD. For difficult searches it may be appropriate to employ a professional researcher, who will usually charge by the search or by the hour. Addresses may be obtained from *Family Tree Magazine, The Genealogists' Magazine* and family history societies. The website at <**http://www.origins.net**> contains information on parish registers, civil

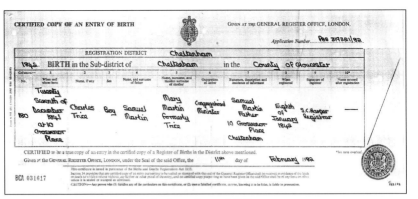

Certified copy (issued 1982) of a birth certificate of 1842.

certificates and census returns. Searching online, for a fee, is in certain instances possible, principally by surname, given name, parish and date. Official copies of the records can be ordered as paper documents directly for a fee.

In England and Wales, each birth index volume was arranged until 1911 under the headings:

Surname	Forename(s)	Superintendent Registrar's District	Volume	Page

From 1911, the mother's maiden name was included.

In marriage indexes, the surnames of the bride and groom were separately noted without cross-referencing until 1912:

Surname	Forename(s)	Supt. Reg. District	Volume	Page

If reference numbers, dates and names tally, the two entries for husband and wife will yield just one certificate. From 1912, the search was simplified by cross references:

Surname	Forename(s)	Surname of Spouse	Supt. Reg. District	Volume	Page

The death index was arranged under the headings:

Surname	Forename(s)	Supt. Reg. District	Volume	Page

From 1866, the age at death was included under a separate heading. Nameless foundlings follow *Z* in each index volume. In Scotland, the female deceased's maiden and previous surnames were indexed where reported.

The index reference allows an official to locate the information and provide a certificate for a fee. In Edinburgh the personal searcher's fee includes permission to make notes from the certificate. A birth certificate shows the child's name (if any), sex, date (sometimes time) and place of birth, father's name and occupation, mother's name, maiden or previous married surname, the informant's signature (or mark), description (for example aunt) and residence with date of registration. Scottish registration also recorded the date of the parents' marriage, if applicable.

A marriage certificate provides names, ages, occupations, residences, marital condition and signatures (or marks) of the couple, names and occupations of each father and whether deceased, date of marriage, whether by banns or licence, with signatures (or marks) of two witnesses and the name of the priest. Scottish documents indicate the name and maiden surname of each mother. Subsequent divorce may also be noted if reported. There may be up to four copies of a marriage record: with the Registrar General, the district registrar, at the church if a religious ceremony took place and in the family papers of the couple themselves. Researchers note that marriages might take place years after the birth of children. And children may have been born without any marriage ceremony taking place – to women who lived alone, with a succession of men or faithfully with one man as pillars of respectability within the community. Divorce in England before 1857 was achieved by private act of Parliament. Alternatively, the ecclesiastical Court of Arches might grant a legal separation or dissolution of the marriage on grounds of consanguinity, impotency or pre-contract. From 1858 jurisdiction was exercised by a new court for divorce and matrimonial causes, later the Family Division of the High Court of Justice. An act of Parliament of 1967 conferred jurisdiction in certain matrimonial proceedings on county courts. Divorce in Scotland fell under the jurisdiction of commissary courts from 1563 until 1830 and the Court of Session from 1830 until 1984, when sheriff courts began to share the burden. From 1984 the General Register Office for Scotland maintained a central register of divorces, adding also an appropriate note to marriage register entries. Papers relating to divorces are lodged with the appropriate court, but may be restricted for terms of years and weeded before release date. The grim course of divorce proceedings is usually traced in family papers and solicitors' archives.

A death certificate included the deceased's name, sex, age, marital status as relevant, occupation, date, place and cause of death, the signature (or mark), description and residence of the informant (perhaps a next-door neighbour, landlord, workhouse matron or relative) and whether the person was in attendance or merely present at the death. Information may not be wholly accurate, especially for an aged recluse. The reference number of a Scottish certificate will indicate if a fatal accident inquiry was required, leading perhaps to newspaper reports. Scottish regulations additionally asked for the deceased's usual address if different from the place of death, the time of death, marital status usually including names and maiden names of present or previous spouses, duration of final illness, names of medical attendant, name and occupation of the father, name and maiden name of the mother, and whether either was still living. In 1855, names and ages of offspring were

Certified copy (issued 1983) of a marriage certificate of 1854.

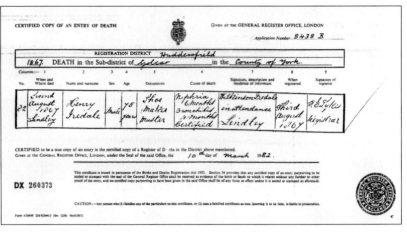

Certified copy (issued as a photocopy of the original in 1982) of a death certificate of 1867.

required, but this was an onerous task soon abandoned. If the circumstances of a death were unusual or suspicious, a coroner's court investigated. Collections of English coroners' inquests from the thirteenth century onwards are held at the Public Record Office and in some county archives. Confidentiality and weeding hamper investigation. The newspaper is an accessible alternative, especially for the more sensational or grizzly cases.

National registration of vital events allowed officialdom to make informed assumptions about ordinary people's lives. Nineteenth-century social scientists were intrigued and popular commentators scandalised by the registrar general's revelations. For example, an average of 24 per cent of children in the Scottish parishes of Kirkmichael and Marnoch over the period 1858–91 were illegitimate. In New Blyth, Aberdeenshire, for short periods the average soared to over 40 per cent according to W. Cramond's paper *Illegitimacy in Banffshire*, read to the British Association in 1892. Today, academic historians use vital registers to reconstitute families and compile data on the structure of populations, death rates, birth rates, age at marriage, longevity, illegitimacy, causes of death, occupations, social class, family mobility and family size. This research is useful to family historians in revealing whether ancestors conformed to general trends, and if not, why not.

The genealogist conducts detailed investigations on his own account, usually working backwards in time. The work begins with a set of known facts, such as a name, date and place. From these clues a birth, marriage or death certificate may be obtained. The names of father and mother on a birth certificate lead to their marriage certificate. This involves a degree of guesswork regarding the date of the wedding. While most folk married between the ages of sixteen and twenty-five, some deferred marriage, perhaps to realise an inheritance or develop a career. Second and third marriages of widows and widowers might take place even in old age. Taking the names, ages and dates on the marriage certificate as a new starting point, the search proceeds a further step to the births of bride and groom and so to *their* parents' marriage and births. Working thus, backwards, step by step, a pedigree can be traced to early Victorian times unless hampered by some irregularity, for instance when a father's name is unknown or undeclared, individuals change their names, a birth is not registered or the registrar enters details incorrectly. If the male line comes to a temporary halt, the female line invites special attention. When a mother brought up children alone her contribution to the family history was particularly potent.

79

Legal adoption has been possible in England and Wales since 1927, and from 1930 in Scotland. Many children were, before this and for various reasons, not brought up by their natural parents. Many an unmarried daughter handed over her inconvenient baby to be brought up as the youngest of her own mother's brood. The child may never have learned that mama was really grandma, and big sister its natural mother. Informal arrangements in these cases are traced through family papers, poor-law records and school registers rather than the registrar general's indexes. The introduction of counselling for adopted offspring tracing natural parents is a recent innovation. Genealogical research is facilitated by cross-indexing of birth and adoption certificates, the annotation of birth certificates and the maintenance of the adopted children register. These services do not, at present, extend to children conceived through the use of donated eggs and sperm. For adoptions from 1927 in England and Wales, short certificates may be obtained, showing date of birth, names of adoptive parents and date of adoption. Full adoption certificates are available to adoptees from the Office for National Statistics, Adoption Section, Trafalgar Road, Southport. Records of adoptions from 1930 under orders of Scottish courts are available to adopted offspring on reaching the age of seventeen from New Register House, Edinburgh.

If a thorough search of the usual registers fails to reveal relevant information then several separate series may be investigated. At the Family Records Centre in London the Registrar General holds:

registers of regimental and army chaplains, at home and abroad: births, marriages, deaths, some from 1761

army returns: births, marriages, deaths abroad from 1881

marine births and deaths of British nationals on British ships from 1837

registrations recorded by British consuls: births, marriages and deaths from 1849

war deaths: South Africa 1899–1902, officers and other ranks 1914–21 and 1939–48, navy officers and other ranks 1914–21 and 1939–48, air force 1939–48

Royal Air Force returns from 1920

stillbirths from 1927 (special request)

aircraft (British) births and deaths from 1947

Scottish registers include:

some births, marriages and deaths of Scots abroad from 1860

marine births and death from 1855

army returns of births, marriages and deaths from 1881

war deaths: 1899–1902, 1914–19, 1939–45

consular returns of Scots births and deaths from 1914, marriages from 1917

Scots marriages in certain foreign countries from 1947

aircraft (British) births and deaths from 1948

births and deaths of those of Scots origin in some Commonwealth countries from 1964

divorces from 1984

stillbirths from 1939 (special request)

9
Census

In 1753, a bill 'for taking an Account of the Population of Great Britain' was presented to Parliament – and rejected. A general suspicion that the census would be used by the government to tax the people more effectively was probably not ill founded. Some opponents feared that an enemy would benefit from knowing Britain's population and potential fighting strength. Others opposed this 'political arithmetic' on biblical grounds, quoting 2 Samuel 24:10:

> And David's heart smote him after that he had numbered the people.
> And David said unto the Lord, I have sinned greatly in that I have done:

Transient ancestors such as professional entertainers who escape notice in the census are readily traced through newspapers and their own publicity material, which leaves a paper trail across the country.

From 1793 the French war, dire prognostications of overpopulation and distress caused by poor harvests added to fears that a shortage of people might hamper economic growth and military capability. In 1801 the government, finding it 'expedient to take an account of the total Number of Persons within the Kingdom of Great Britain', instigated the first national enumeration. A census has been taken every ten years since 1801, except for the war year 1941, providing a snapshot of family life. From 1801 to 1831 the government was concerned with statistics, especially 'the progressive Increase or Diminution of the population', in order to facilitate economic planning. Once statistics had been extracted and published, individual household returns were destroyed. Only occasionally and by chance has documentation survived from the first four censuses.

From 1841 onwards the census was the responsibility of the Registrar General. On the night of 6th June 1841, each inhabited house was recorded with the name, age and occupation of every individual in residence, including visitors, servants and lodgers. A person's exact place of birth was not required. Returns were handwritten by heads of household on printed forms and then laboriously transcribed into books by census officials. Entries were arranged by census districts based on parish and town boundaries. It is these transcripts that researchers examine. Enumerators helped out by completing forms on behalf of illiterate households and adding information from personal knowledge to fill gaps in the information provided. This, and the transcription process, inevitably led to errors. Meanwhile, disaffected and mischievous individuals gave false information. Women lied about their ages. Men pretended to professions for which they were unqualified. Sweatshop owners, white slavers, travelling folk, brothel keepers, street walkers, burglars, owners of unlicensed lodging houses, shebeen (illegal distillery) managers, anarchists, adulterers, Fenians (Irish nationalists) and illegal aliens remained invisible, distorting the picture of the neighbourhood. In the register entry transcribed below, Richard Tomlinson occupied a four-roomed terraced house with his wife Elizabeth. The enumerator drew a single stroke under his household and then moved on to the six lodgers, finishing the list for this dwelling with a double stroke. The census did not enquire about the relationships among the occupants, though we might tentatively presume that the Tomlinsons were husband and wife.

1841: Sunday night 6th June, collected 7th June, Barnton, Cheshire

address	house inhabited or uninhabited	name	age to nearest five years	occupation	if born in same county, yes or no
Lydiart Lane	I	Richard Tomlinson	45	carpenter	yes
		Elizabeth "	35		"
		/			
		Mary Shiplin	60	widow	"
		Ellen Wilkinson	11		"
		John Palin	20	waterman	"
		Joseph "	15		"
		Samuel Bostock	15	rope maker's apprentice	"
		John Miller	30	pensioner annuitant	no
		//			

This difficulty was remedied in 1851 when relationships as well as parish of birth were recorded. The house surveyed below stood in a terrace of back-to-back cottages erected in 1810. The accommodation comprised one main room up and one down with a single fireplace, no running water and a shared outdoor privy.

1851: Sunday night 30th March, collected 31st March

Enumeration number and address	Name	Relationship to Head of Household	Married Unmarried	Age	Occupation	Birthplace
23 Bells Brow	John Haddock	Head	M	54	agricultural labourer	Little Leigh
	Elizabeth "	Wife	M	55	--	Barnton
	James "	Son	U	27	flat horse driver	"
	Ellen Ghorst	daughter	M	24	boatmans wife	"
	Elizabeth Millington	daughter	M	20	wife of labourer at Salt Works	"
	William Ghorst	Son-in-law	M	24	boatman	Middlewich
	Edan Millington	Son-in-law	M	21	labourer at Salt Works	Antrobus
	Elizabeth Ghorst	grand-daughter	U	5	scholar	Barnton
	Martha "	"	U	3	scholar	Middlewich
	James "	grandson	U	2		"
	Hannah "	grand-daughter	U	1 week		Barnton
	Rebecca Millington	visitor	U	17	dress-maker	Antrobus

This was a household in employment except for Elizabeth Haddock and her young grandchildren. James Haddock worked with the horses that pulled barges, known as

Researcher's record of a census search.

flats, on the River Weaver below Bells Brow. On the canal parallel to the river, boats carried salt, coal and pottery. Most of the Bells Brow community were involved in these industries or in servicing narrow boats at the inland port of Barnton within sight of their homes. Few residents had drifted far from their native parishes in central Cheshire.

Original household schedules from 1841 until 1901 were destroyed in 1904, though the enumerator's usually more legible transcripts are preserved for research at the Family Records Centre, 1 Myddelton Street, London EC1 (England and Wales) and New Register House, Edinburgh (Scotland). Census returns older than one hundred years have been microfilmed for consultation, for instance in public libraries, family history societies and (Mormon) family history centres of the relevant district. An expedition there brings the researcher to an ancestor's home town and the opportunity to visit the county archives and family home. In some counties volunteers have transcribed, typed, indexed or computerised the records. The computer project FreeCEN <**http://freecen.rootsweb.org**> is providing a database for English and Welsh censuses of 1841–91 to support searches under place, address and surname. A Mormon transcription project for the entire British 1881 census comprises full entries for each household and person, theoretically

The Mather family through three censuses.

Census of 1861 showing pupils at Margaret Bell's Winnington School for girls.

supplanting the original handwritten forms. This 1881 census, published on microfiche and CD-ROM, facilitates searches by region, county, address, surname, birth year or year range up to five. The CD-ROM is held in public libraries and may be purchased at the Church Distribution Centre (LDS), Birmingham. There are official plans to put all census returns on the Internet, beginning with 1901, involving the challenging task of transcribing and digitising the records. The researcher's starting point is the website at <**http://www.census.pro.gov.uk**>. The project's user guide *Census Online,* PRO and Qinetiq, 2001, explains how access to 1901 information is through a free search by address, person, vessel or institution. From here a pay-per-view facility opens transcription details and an image of the page in the original enumeration book. In Scotland a similar pilot for the 1901 census converted 1891 returns to digital images linked to computer index entries, available for a fee at Scots Origins, <**http://www.scotsorigins.com**>.

In conducting census research it is useful to devise a standard form on which may be entered the details of each relevant family at each successive enumeration. By this means, one family may be followed as it grows or shrinks, takes on new occupations and moves house or town. The example below refers to the same individual whose forename, surname and address all changed. But the town remained the same and the individual was traced by noting the coincidences of names, parentage and ages:

1851 Elizabeth Mather age 3 unmarried 9 Campbell Terrace
1861 Jane Mather age 13 unmarried 7 Wilson Street
1871 Elizabeth Bowden age 23 married 1 Midland Street
1881 Jane Bowden age 33 married 1 Midland Street

Family room (with tiny larder through the door) at the one-down, one-up Bells Brow cottage inhabited by thirteen people in 1851.

Keeping up with the movement of ancestors to new manufacturing villages is possible through censuses, particularly the 1881 return with national index.

The Irish situation is both less and more straightforward. The first census of Ireland was taken in 1813. Further enumerations were organised at intervals variously of five, eight and thirteen years. This need not trouble the genealogist, though, because it was government policy to destroy the detailed returns for 1861–91, while those of 1841–51 were lost in the civil war of 1922. Returns for 1901 and 1911 are publicly available.

10
Baptism, marriage and burial

Registration of church baptisms, marriages and burials in England and Wales commenced in 1538 under a mandate issued to clergy by Thomas Cromwell, chief minister of Henry VIII. Cromwell's order was a means of ensuring national compliance with the practices of the new church established following the king's breach with Rome in 1534. Parishioners meeting in the church vestry were obliged to provide secure storage for their registers in a 'sure coffer' with two locks. The instruction was taken to heart. At Penrith a parish chest of the 1660s secures the archives with three locks, six keys and four iron straps, each with hasp and padlock. Parliament in 1812 required a 'dry well painted iron chest, in some dry and secure place'. Safes dated 1813 still stand in vestries as object lessons in heritage awareness.

The maintenance of **parish registers** was, from the outset, a parochial responsibility. Fees were charged for inserting entries and supplying extracts from the registers. Registration was not compulsory but socially obligatory. Initially no regulations were issued concerning the format or content of parish registers. Records maintained on loose leaves or stitched quires, liable to be mislaid and misfiled, were occasionally criticised during episcopal visitations.

A **baptismal** register might record parentage, date of birth, places of residence and occupations. Early entries are brief: 'Ann Cooke bap 11 Aug 1586'. This was sufficient to register the acceptance of an individual into the Christian church by the pouring of holy water. We can probably infer that Ann was legitimate because registers were usually scrupulous in noting otherwise. Baptism is sometimes referred to as christening, though properly that term refers to one part of the

Above: *Monuments and memorials in the ancestors' native parish supplement written records and bring the researcher face to face with forebears.*

Right: *Medieval marriages were solemnised in church, but documentation seldom survives in ecclesiastical sources: this scene is carved on the font at Gresham, Norfolk.*

Iron safes for safe-keeping of parish registers were installed in church vestries following George Rose's Act of 1812. In most cases the records have been transferred to county archives. A few parish safes still contain the archives for which they were designed. This example is at Clifton, Cumbria.

ceremony, the giving of a personal name. Clerks might record two or three generations:

> Mary daughter of Randle Poole junior of Northwich, flatman, son of Richard and Lydia Poole of Barnton, and Kitty, daughter of John and Deborah Jones of Northwich, born 18 July, christened 17 August 1800 at Witton

Baptism usually took place about six weeks after birth. Certain sects such as Anabaptists and Baptists from the sixteenth century onwards required baptism in

Certificate dated 1817 of a baptism in 1771.

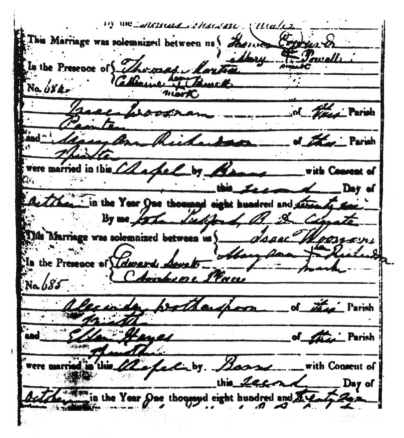

Marriage register, 1826.

adulthood when vows might be taken by the individual rather than by proxy through godparents. Printed standard forms for baptisms were introduced from 1st January 1813.

A **marriage** took place in church after a proclamation of banns read thrice to allow for objections.

> William Logie, Speymouth, and Jean Wiseman, Urquhart, were patrimonially Contracted and haveing Consigned pledges for their orderly proclamations were Married, 11 January 1740, at Urquhart

In the marriage register the nuptials of a landowner might be dignified with names of parents, grandparents, witnesses, titles and residences. It was probably felt a waste of the clerk's time, ink and paper to enter more than the baldest details of ordinary folk: 'John Sangster & Ellen Bowen 14 Oct 1592'. From this entry it is impossible to know whether the bride and groom were old or young, natives of the parish, previously married or accompanied by parents and witnesses. A marriage could be effected at short notice if the couple obtained a bishop's licence in writing. This was granted, according to church canons of 1604, only 'upon good caution and security taken'. The process first required a bond by two cautioners to guarantee that no pre-contract or consanguinity existed as an impediment. Also necessary was an affidavit or allegation as to the age of the couple, their marital condition and parental consent where appropriate. The bond and allegation were preserved in diocesan registry files and the process registered by the diocese. The licence of marriage itself was kept by the parish minister. The couple's copies of the documentation occasionally survive in the parish chest or among family archives.

From the seventeenth century onwards, a man and woman might marry privately without banns or licence in certain locations. These included the environs of certain prisons and chapels such as St James (Duke's Place), Holy Trinity in the Minories and St Benet at Paul's Wharf, all in London, and also several provincial locations, for instance Peak Forest, Derbyshire. In the eighteenth century there was an epidemic of **clandestine marriages**, the result of romantic elopements; the duping of gullible youths by Drury Lane 'actresses'; and the seduction of naïve heiresses by penniless adventurers. Officiating clergymen earned a comfortable living from the business. The genealogist who unearths a clandestine marriage will justifiably suspect that some forgotten family tragedy or scandal awaits discovery, perhaps as litigation in the commissary court, among the family papers or even in the newspapers. Registers of clandestine marriages are held at the Public Record Office and certain county archives. The 'great Mischiefs and Inconveniences' were remedied by Hardwicke's Marriage Act of 1753. The new law applied to all marriages except those of Jews and Quakers. Hardwicke's act required that banns 'be published in an audible manner in the Parish Church … upon three *Sundays* preceding the Solemnization of Marriage'. Marriages might be performed only in parish churches, following banns or licence. A new standard form of register was introduced with spaces for the signatures of the officiating minister, bride, groom and two witnesses. The law did not extend to Scotland, where a different theological attitude prevailed, regarding marriage as a human contract rather than a sacrament, and recognising until 1939 the legality of marriage by cohabitation and repute. One effect of Hardwicke's act was to reverse the flow of elopements. Couples now headed not to London but north to the Scottish border, where they declared themselves married before witnesses at the first opportunity, typically Lamberton tollbar or Gretna smithy.

Burial registers might be fulsome or frugal. A wealthy parishioner's passing could be an opportunity for eulogy and genealogy, the register entry recognising the pedigree, Christian virtue, political loyalty and parochial benevolence of the deceased. Poor folk expected short shrift: 'Eliz Smythe 28 July 1592'. Elizabeth might be an infant or a centenarian, married, widowed or single, good, bad or indifferent. As time went on, a little more detail was included:

Samuel Heathcote, Esquire, Buried, Feb. 16, 1784
Mary, wife of Wm Davies, Buried Jan. 26, 1784, aged 48

Vagrants, beggars and travellers dying as they passed through the parish might be registered simply as 'stranger unknown'. Printed standard forms for burials were introduced in 1813.

Medieval **churchyard** burial was normally a temporary expedient. After a few years the defleshed bones were disinterred and relocated to a charnel house freeing space for further burials. In these circumstances monuments were unnecessary. By the 1560s, leading parishioners demanded permanent graves and family plots with headstones or recumbent slabs recording at least the names and dates of the occupants. Humbler folk's grave markers were not always inscribed, even with initials, until the 1750s. A gloomy iconography of winged souls, skulls, bones, spades, coffins and passing bells persisted until the late eighteenth century. Genealogical information was usual by this date with occupations, relationships and residences carefully carved or, during a brief craze around 1810, cast in iron. In the

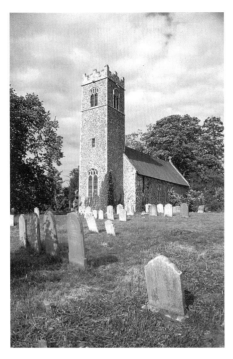

Ilketshall St John, Suffolk: inscriptions on gravestones in the churchyard may provide information to supplement parish register entries.

nineteenth century, death was celebrated even among poorer families with funerary sculpture depicting draped urns, broken columns and drooping angels.

Wealthy medieval folk might invest in a permanent resting place beneath the floor of the church marked by a slab inscribed with a floreated cross or an idealised portrait in brass. The prime site was in the centre of the chancel or before one of the several side altars, where the priest stood directly over the deceased to celebrate mass. Lords and ladies of the manor might commission life-sized effigies. A notable sculptural school in the west of Scotland depicted landowners as idealised warriors kitted out in a quilted surcoat (haqueton) over chain-mail with a conical helmet (basinet). Each stern warrior typically grasps the strap of his sword belt or the hilt of the weapon. Inscriptions were simple, genealogically informative and readily translated:

+ HIC IACET FINGONE MAC CARMAIC
ET FINLAID MAC FINGONE ET EOGAN
here lies Finguire, son of Cormac, and
Finlay, son of Finguire, and Ewan

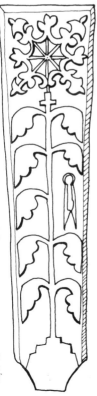

Grave slab of a wealthy wool merchant (his trade indicated by sheep shears) from Movilla Abbey, County Down: the merchant's name may be sought in family papers, title deeds, guild archives and records of pious donations to the church in which he was buried.

91

Grave slab of a Gaelic laird, depicted in a conventionally warlike manner, in the aristocratic burial ground of Iona.

Landowners and burgesses of the period 1520–1680 were portrayed with their sons and daughters prayerfully kneeling or staring complacently from neoclassical niches. Baroque details, comfortable couches and languid attitudes were affected by the gentry of the later seventeenth century.

Though a plot in the churchyard or a vault beneath the church may be traditionally associated with one family, the memorial stone usually records only the latest generations buried there. Occasionally a descendant has added an inscription naming distant forebears supposedly buried in the plot. Suicides and children not baptised might be denied burial in consecrated grounds. The quest for tidiness and low-cost ground maintenance has persuaded some church authorities to relocate gravestones or remove them entirely. Monumental inscriptions may be indexed and mapped in the public library, thus simplifying the search for a relevant grave where the full text can be photographed or copied. Weathered inscriptions require gentle cleaning with a soft brush and clear water. Lettering can sometimes appear more legible when viewed at night by means of a bright light shone obliquely across the surface of the stone, though nocturnal activities in a graveyard may attract the censorious attention of parishioners and the superstitious. Monumental inscriptions are a means of following migrating families. Robert and

Lettice Barnard and her children, realistically depicted on a memorial brass at Newnham Murren, Oxfordshire, 1593.

Susannah Smith of Gilling, Yorkshire, emigrated with their four sons and four daughters to Natal in the sailing ship *Haidee* in October 1860. Susannah died at their home Raisethorpe in 1877 aged seventy; Robert in 1881 aged seventy-six. Their stone in Pietermaritzburg tells the family story. Nearby lies William Stalker of Newhome, York Road, who died in 1900 aged seventy-seven and his wife Isabella, who died in 1913 aged seventy-one. His monument traces him to Forres in Moray.

In 1597, the Archbishop of Canterbury issued an order, known as a provincial constitution, whose terms covered the two ecclesiastical provinces of England and Wales. This obliged clergy to write registers on parchment rather than on paper and to copy any earlier records into the new volumes. Particular mention of the accession of Elizabeth I led many parishes to copy only registrations since 1558. Consequently, registers for the first twenty years of the system are not common. From 1597, clergy were required each year to transmit a copy of the registers to diocesan authorities. Known as bishop's transcripts, these documents sometimes provide more detail than parish registers, but also contain copying errors. The transcripts, preserved in diocesan archives, are usually now lodged in county archives. Registers were not always maintained during the Civil War and Commonwealth period, 1642–60.

From 1678, the word *affidavit* in a register indicates that the relatives of the deceased affirmed their compliance with the act of Parliament requiring burial in wool shrouds rather than the linen most folk preferred. This method of supporting the woollen industry was officially abandoned in 1814. Under an act of 1694, duties were levied on parochial registrations of 'Persons married, buried, christened or born', and also on bachelors and childless widowers. The duty proved difficult to administer even during the limited five-year term originally envisaged. Exchequer returns are lost but lists may be preserved in parish chests. Between 1783 and 1794 a second attempt was made by the government to raise money from register entries. The attempt was not a success. Paupers were exempted and so, while some people simply did not bother registering the births of their children, others accepted the stigma of pauperism to avoid the levy. Registers of some Anglican communities abroad were returned periodically to the Bishop of London and deposited in due course among the public records. Documents date from 1627, though most only from the 1820s onwards.

Following the introduction of civil registration from 1837 onwards, parish ministers continued to baptise, marry and bury. But a declining number of baptisms, particularly, were registered, while burials were often in municipal and commercial cemeteries or, from the early twentieth century, in crematorium gardens of remembrance rather than parish churchyards. Genealogists rely on church registers mainly to assess a family's religious affiliations. After 1837, marriages in church by licensed ministers were regarded as equivalent to civil registration, with register copies forwarded to the superintendent registrar.

Scotland's reformed church commenced registration from the 1560s. The records are popularly known as the Old Parish Registers or OPR. The survival and coverage of early registers is patchy, partly as a result of alternating between Presbyterian organisation based upon lay elders and episcopal control exercised by bishops. Records are notably thin for the Restoration era, 1660–88, because many were lost when unpopular episcopalian ministers, disparagingly known as 'King Charles's curates', were rabbled from their manses following the revolution of 1688. In Scotland, the established church centralised records in Edinburgh under the tutelage of the General Assembly, though parishes of independent temperament, notably in Moray, the Hebrides and Shetland, preferred their records to remain in the care of their own session clerks. The official repository is now the National Archives of Scotland.

In **Ireland**, registers of the established Protestant Church began after 1634.

Nonconformist baptismal register 1774–5.

Roman Catholic registers, if commenced at all, might be regarded as illegal, seditious and evidence of disaffection. Church registers deposited in the Public Record Office, Dublin, were destroyed in 1922. Church registers not in official custody at that date, including most Catholic registers, survived and may be found in parish or regional archives.

Registers of baptism, marriage and burial were maintained by sects dissenting from the national churches. Registers were potentially incriminating, so were kept hidden and ultimately lost. Registers were prised from sectarian custody following the introduction of civil registration. **Nonconformists** wishing their registers to be authenticated as legal evidence, say in respect of inheritance or poor relief, were required to deposit with the public records. For England and Wales some nine thousand registers were despatched, including indexed registers of Bunhill Fields nonconformist burial ground, London, 1713–1838, and registers of births maintained at Dr Williams's Library, London, 1793–1826. Unauthenticated registers deposited since 1837 include Bethnal Green Gibraltar burial ground, 1793–1826, and records of the British Lying-in Hospital, Holborn, for distressed poor married women, especially the wives of soldiers and sailors during the period 1749–1868. The Holborn archive details a child's baptism, sex and date of birth; mother's name, place of settlement, date of admission and discharge (or death). Spouses' names and occupations may be included together with medical notes, for example indicating a breech birth. Microfilms of nonconformist records are available at the Family Records Centre, London. Names are also indexed on the International Genealogical Index. Numerous dissenting sects and most Roman Catholic congregations retained their own records, which may survive among congregational archives, perhaps with a lawyer or among the family papers of church officials. Collections may be deposited in the county archives or central denominational repository.

During the nineteenth century, various scholars, record societies, the Society of Genealogists and the enthusiastic layman W. P. W. Phillimore made parish register data more accessible to genealogists, demographers and statisticians. Original registers were laboriously transcribed and printed. Records were indexed by Percival Boyd for the Society of Genealogists, including marriages during the period 1538–1837 and London burials, 1538–1853. More recently, microfilming has sidestepped the problems of transcription, avoiding error through miscopying or misprinting, but leaving researchers to decipher slovenly handwriting and faded ink exacerbated by murky photography. From 1966 onwards, registers and indexes were surveyed and listed in the series *National Index of Parish Registers*, edited by D. J. Steel for the Society of Genealogists. Separate volumes are concerned with nonconformist registers; Roman Catholics and Jews; English counties and regions; Scotland; and Wales. C. R. Humphery-Smith's *Phillimore Atlas and Index of Parish Registers* identifies, with maps, the location of English and Welsh registers.

Information from parish and other genealogical registers, together with pedigrees and histories deposited by family researchers, has been assembled by the Mormons into a database and published as a microfiche or CD-ROM index. This is known as the **International Genealogical Index (IGI)**. There is an emphasis on genealogically significant births, baptisms and marriages rather than deaths, and on the period from the commencement of church registers around 1540 to the start of civil certificates in the 1830s. Names have been collected worldwide. IGI does not index registers of organisations objecting on religious or legal grounds. There are numerous gaps in the coverage where registers are destroyed, illegible or not yet deposited in public archives. Wales is poorly represented before 1800, and even after that date the absence of rural nonconformist registers is noticeable. Most Irish established church and Catholic records are unavailable. There is a dearth of

International Genealogical Index (1981 edition) showing entries in Cumbria for the family name Blackburn.

The International Genealogical Index (IGI) is an invaluable source for following families across country, for instance those seeking a living after having been cleared from their land during centuries of agricultural reorganisation.

information from eastern Europe through loss or closure of records.

IGI contains millions of names arranged by country, county, then alphabetically under surnames or family names, subdivided according to given or first names. The various spellings of a surname may be drawn under one heading for ease of reference, but the careful researcher will independently seek all possible variants just in case. The index puts surnames in chronological order of event and shows the place or parish of occurrence or registration. IGI is a key to, rather than a substitute for, original registers. The detail of any entry must be sought in the original document preserved in public archives, retained by churches or alternatively held on microfilm by the public or university library. IGI offers separate indexes for the Isle of Man and the Channel Islands. In Wales and Monmouthshire, entries (mainly nonconformist) are alphabetised by surname and given name to take account of the use of the patronymic *ap*, 'son of'. Entries for a particular surname anywhere in Britain and Ireland, or narrowed down to a single parish at a certain date, can be researched with the IGI on CD-ROM. On the Internet the IGI is located through the Latter-Day Saints (LDS) church home page at <**http://www.familysearch.org**>, followed by the request *search for ancestors*. IGI is available for research at Mormon branch libraries and family history centres and in public libraries. For home study, appropriate sections can be purchased inexpensively provided the researcher has access to a microfiche reader.

11
Last will and testament

Last wills, testaments and inventories, generically known as probate records, unlock a door to an ancestor's home, revealing lifestyle, personal predilections and family relationships. An ordinary person before about 1910 did not normally write a will, particularly if relationships among siblings were cordial and possessions few. A wife did not require a will because her property became that of her husband, at least until the reforms of 1882 and 1893. However, the imprudence of failing to make a will might embroil potential heirs in litigation and infect families with rancorous resentments. An uncontested will needed no authentication by the probate authorities. Unproven wills may be preserved among family papers or with a lawyer. During the Middle Ages the disposition of an individual's worldly goods after death required a spoken death-bed utterance in the presence of witnesses. This is known as a nuncupative will. The practice was abolished by the Wills Act of 1837. A more secure means of disposition was a written document known as a testament, authenticated by the testator's seal or a signature witnessed by three reliable persons. A testator who wrote a holograph document in his own handwriting might dispense with witnesses in favour of an affirmation from several people. A testament disposed of goods and chattels, that is inanimate possessions and cattle, including clothes, farm stock, riding horses, hunting dogs, clothing, furniture, money, plate, household linen, buildings, rental income and the remaining term of leases. Land, including the ground upon which a house stood, could not be transferred by will, because the feudal owner required a public ceremony in front of witnesses.

To ensure a testator's wishes were followed, a testament was proved or authenticated by ecclesiastical courts, usually the archbishop, bishop or archdeacon and, in London, the Court of Hustings. When property was held in two or more archdeaconries, responsibility for proving the testament fell to the diocesan authority known as the consistory or commissary court. Property in two or more dioceses required the intervention of the archbishop. Wills and testaments proved at

A priest administers extreme unction while the family looks on; all perhaps hope for a deathbed bequest: the scene is carved on the late-medieval font at Gresham, Norfolk.

Following a death the lawyer read the will to the assembled family. This formal rite of passage might be dispensed with to save legal costs that eroded the value of the estate.

York are held by the Borthwick Institute, York, while those for Canterbury, commencing in 1384, are held by the Public Record Office but are available at the Family Records Centre, London. The Prerogative Court of the Archbishop of Canterbury exercised a general testamentary jurisdiction over England and Wales, proving wills of men of substance wherever resident, of people dying abroad or at sea or owning property in more than one archdiocese. The province of Canterbury covered Wales and England as far north as Staffordshire, Derbyshire and Lincolnshire, but not Nottinghamshire. Wills proved by diocesan courts and by districts historically exempt from the bishop's control known as peculiars are generally lodged in county archives. During the Commonweath, 1653–60, wills were proved in London under state jurisdiction. These collections are held at the Public Record Office.

In 1540, the English Statute of Wills permitted disposal of land under certain conditions. Males over fourteen years of age and females over twelve were allowed to make wills. A typical will begins with the name, residence and occupation of the testator. A clause of religious devotion precedes funeral arrangements, which, sensitively interpreted, may indicate an ancestor's religious affiliation and depth of faith. Real and personal property are then devised:

> unto my Wife Jane Skelton One full Moiety or half part of my Messuage Land and Tenement … Also All those my Four Meadows situate, lying, and being on the East Side of, and adjoining to Saint Bees Powe of the yearly rent of Two Shillings and Nine Pence Three farthings to the School of Saint Bees, and commonly called and known by the name of Walton Dykes, Also all those my Two fields or Closes, situate … in … Egremond … known by the name Brackenthwaite

(Cumbria Record Office, will of William Skelton of Lowkrigg, Cumberland, yeoman, proved 16th October 1741)

A will may offer glimpses of strained relationships and family scandals, as does that of Dr Alexander Gray, proved at Fort-William, Bengal, in 1807. Gray bequeathed a princely £20,000 'for the Establishment of an Hospital in the Town of Elgin … near a river … near the Pansport, formerly the property of my family, being an eligible spot for an Hospital'. He also left money to:

> the most abandoned and deliberately infamous Wife that ever distinguished the annals of turpitude, as proved by her letters and conduct to me … should she be reduced to distress, and become really penitent … [and] to a Sister, whose foolish marriage to a man who never had the prospect of supporting a family … has occasioned all my domestic misery … [and] to my Sister's Children, that they may not in their turn become the prey of unprincipled men …

The will of Francis Woosnam, a cooper, in Dethenith, Montgomeryshire, stands in stark contrast to the largesse of a wealthy professional man. Francis owned only a few shillings in 1731, but employed a writer to draw up a will that, with scrupulous fairness, divided his fortune evenly among five children, John, William, Euan, Cathrin and Betrish (presumably Beatrice). Each received 2s 6d. Francis's signature, a mark in the shape of a shaky inverted *W*, was witnessed by three acquaintances, Thomas Cleaton, Thomas Powell and David Ingram.

A will might be made out years before death. Some individuals periodically rewrote their wills and added clauses, known as codicils. Only the last will was

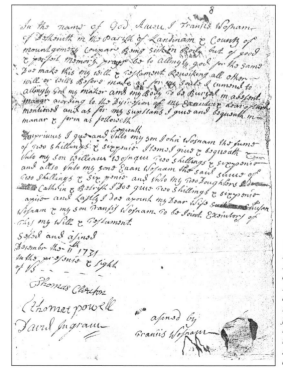

Will of Francis Woosnam, Dethenith, Montgomeryshire, cooper, dated 1731, proved 1732. Blemishes on the original document (picked up by the photocopier) result from over-strong ink bleeding through hand-made paper. Reading both sides of such documents can prove a real challenge.

deemed valid, though earlier versions among the family papers will reveal something of the testator's changing fortunes and family relationships. An authenticated will bears an official note of the date (perhaps years after death) and court of probate. One copy of the proved will was retained by the authorities; others were produced if required for family purposes. Normally the church court copied details of the will and supporting documents in a diocesan act book. The clerk also recorded the names of curators and tutors in cases of incompetency such as senility, idiocy, lunacy and minority. Where no will was found among personal papers after death, the church court could, on request, and for a fee, appoint administrators. Letters of administration specified names, dates, relationships and property valuations. Documentation was issued to the administrators and filed in court archives.

A will usually appointed executors, whose duty was to carry out (execute) the deceased's last wishes. An executor was obliged to keep proper accounts, claiming expenses out of the estate. Neighbours or colleagues of the deceased were appointed appraisers to compile an inventory of possessions. They usually toured the property room by room, incidentally leaving genealogists an intriguing record of the family home, listing all items of any value, say over 2d, including furniture, tools, clothing, farm animals, corn in barns, hay in ricks and debts. The inventory was despatched with any will for authentication. 'A true & perfect Inventorie of ye goods and cattell of Richard Skelton of Lowkrigge', dated 20th March 1656/7, lists the valuables of a comfortable husbandman:

List of the household goods belonging to James Calder sold by roup (auction) following his death in 1823.

In primis his Apparell	£2	00s	00d
Item Cattell younge & olde	£16	00s	00d
Item two old meares	£2	10s	00d
Item sheep younge & old	£6	10s	00d
Item Corne & hay	£5	00s	00d
Item Beddinge bedcloathes & yearne	£1	8s	00d
Item one little silver spoone		4s	00d
Item Brasse pewter & one Iron pott	£1	8s	00d
Item wood vessell		9s	00d
Item Chests & bedstockes		10s	00d
Item one Table, formes & stooles		8s	00d
Item grate, crookes, toungs & speet		6s	8d
Item one Ladder & Timber	£1	0s	00d
Item pullen		1s	9d

The Estate Duty office in London was responsible for collecting duty on certain legacies and residues as defined by act of Parliament in 1796. Appropriate wills and administrations were deposited for processing until 1894. Registers were compiled containing abstracts of wills. Original documents were returned for eventual filing in the relevant church probate registry. After 1858, wills were put into the principal probate registry. Estate Duty archives can fill gaps in diocesan records, for instance for wills of Devon, Somerset and Cornwall destroyed by the bombing of Exeter during the Second World War, and are researched through the Family Records Centre, London.

The Wills Act of 1837 permitted disposition of every kind of interest in real and personal property. It was necessary to put a will in writing, with the signatures of the testator or a representative and two witnesses. After 11th January 1858,

ADVERTISEMENT.

Public Roup

OF

CATTLE, HORSES, AND GREEN CROP,

AT ARDOCH OF DALLAS.

There will be Sold, by Public Roup, at Ardoch, on Wednesday, 6th November, 1839,

THE CATTLE and HORSES; TURNIP and PO-TATOE CROPS; FARMING UTENSILS, &c., belonging to the Heirs of John Findlay, deceased. There are NINE MILCH COWS, some of them near calving. From 40 to 50 head of YOUNG CATTLE. A Superior HIGHLAND BULL. Three WORK HORSES. One two-year-old COLT. And one one-year-old, do.; all in good condition, and to be sold without reserve.

The Roup to commence at 12 o'clock, noon, and credit will be given on approved bills.

A. CREYK, Auctioneer.

Ardoch, 29th October, 1839.

Printed at the Gazette Office, Forres.

Auction of farm stock to pay off debts following the death of John Findlay, 1839.

101

responsibility for proving and recording wills was transferred to a newly established Principal Probate Registry at Somerset House, London, and to district registries throughout England and Wales. Wills from 1858 are obtainable from district registries; the postal searches and copies department, Principal Probate Registry, York; or by personal visit only to the Principal Registry of the Family Division, London WC1.

In Scotland, secular commissary courts replaced medieval diocesan organisation from 1563, granting confirmation of testaments and exercising jurisdiction in districts corresponding to medieval bishoprics. Transcripts of wills submitted for registration are preserved in commissary books. In cases where an individual died intestate, that is without leaving a will, the commissary nominated an executor for a testament dative. Testaments were accompanied by inventories. The inventory of the possessions of the surgeon-poet A. D. Brands, compiled in 1869, describes a comfortable middle-class home:

Kitchen   11 Skellots & Pots £1 2s Toast Rack 6d Coffee Pot 1s American Clock 10s Dinner
   Set stone Ware £2 10s Facing and Italian Irons 2s
Pantry   8 Finger Glasses 2s 6d 3 Spirit Bottles 3s A few Custards 1s 6d 12 Ale Glasses 3s
   24 Dram Glasses 6s 5 Water Carafes 2s 6d 3 Hyacinth Glasses 1s 6d
Dining Room   Dumb Waiter 12s Sofa £2 5 Stuffed Chairs £1 Mahogany Book Case £7 10s
   723 Volumes Books £18 1s 6d
Silver Plate   Tea Pot $20^1/_2$ oz @ 5s £5 2s 6d 15 Dinner Spoons $31^1/_2$ oz @ 5s £7 17s 6d
Drawing Room   Whatnot and Ancient China Ornaments £2 15s Canterbury 10s Piano Forte
   £3 10s Rosewood inlaid with pearl small Secretaire £1 5s

Commissary records at the National Archives in Edinburgh are indexed down to 1823, when sheriffs were appointed commissaries. From 1876 onwards, annual printed calendars have been published listing confirmations and inventories granted in Scotland by county and name:

PAULET, Charles William, late of Staple Hill, Wellesbourne, County of Warwick, died 8 April 1897, at 12 Brunswick Terrace, Brighton, County of Sussex, testate. Certificate endorsed by Commissary Clerk of Edinburgh, 5 August, on Probate of the Will and two Codicils, granted at London, on 17 June 1897, to Bevil Granville, Mary Paulet, widow, the relict, and Ernest Knightley Little, the Executors. Value of Estate, £69,414 12s 2d.

Kirk sessions (pages 110–11) sometimes maintained testament books recording the wills of paupers obliged to bequeath their meagre possessions to reimburse the poor fund for dole received in life:

I Isabel Geddes in Park-Knockie of Ballintomb ... in order to reimburse the Poor Box ... hereby legate & bequeath to the said Kirk Session [of Knockando], all & Sundry Goods, Gear, Debts & Sums of Money as shall pertain or belong to me at the time of my Death, & nominate & appoint the Kirk Treasurer ... executor of this my Last Will & Testament

(Knockando Parish, 21st February 1778)

In Ireland, a principal registry in Dublin and district registries in the provinces were established in 1858. Earlier probate records deposited in Dublin were mostly destroyed in 1922. Wills from about 1900 onwards, copy wills from the 1660s onwards and genealogical abstracts prepared by Sir William Betham, Ulster King of Arms, from prerogative wills before 1799, are available for research.

12
The church

The Christian Church influenced the lives of everybody in Britain and Ireland from the cradle to the grave – and beyond. Archives of the two English and Welsh church provinces, governed by the **Archbishops** of Canterbury and York, are available at Lambeth Palace Library, London, and the Borthwick Institute of Historical Research, York, respectively. Archbishops exercised centralised administrative and judicial powers over belief, morality, appointments, taxation, church property, wills and testaments. Archbishops also administered the two faculty offices created in 1534 to assume the Pope's licensing powers and to refer to cases of plurality, when priests held several charges and incomes, and also to marriage licences and ordination of clergymen. Editions and indexes facilitate research.

Cathedrals were governed by a committee of clerics who began each meeting by reading a chapter of their rules or canons. Cathedral records are thus known as

The nativity of Jesus depicted as a homely scene of medieval childbirth: a midwife washes baby while mother recovers in a comfortable canopied bed; father is sent out of the way to the kitchen to boil water.

capitular, from the Latin *capitulum*, 'chapter', and are deposited in national or provincial research centres including county record offices. The chapter minuted decisions in act books, concerning appointment of staff, building programmes, liturgy and management of manorial estates and their resident populations. On 23rd July 1688, the dean and chapter of Durham convened for a disciplinary hearing. The background was King James VII and II's declaration of religious toleration that would particularly benefit Roman Catholics.

> Mr Henry Smith being called ... [the chapter] severely reproving him for being lately scandalously drunke; and for drinkeing undecent healths. He did thereupon confess, that some small time before that, he had been overtaken in drinke; and that he had drunke Confusion to ye first Obstructors of ye Reading of ye King's Declaration whereupon he was dismissed to a further consideration

Capitular records may remain with cathedral muniments if not held by an appropriate university or public archive. Irish records may be located through the Representative Church Body Library, Dublin.

Records of the **diocese and bishop** in England and Wales are in county and diocesan record offices, with certain collections in national archives and the Church of England Record Centre, London SE16. Protestant Irish records may be located through the Representative Church Body Library, Dublin; guidance on any Scottish sources may be sought through Scottish Catholic Archives, Edinburgh. The bishop licensed marriages, schoolmasters, midwives, surgeons, absentee clergy and dissenting meeting houses. He required territorial inventories known as glebe terriers under regulations (canons) of 1571 and 1604 listing parish property, tenants and benefactors. The bishop's courts heard cases involving moral lapses, matrimonial disputes, slander, property, inheritance and charities. The court of audience for sensitive cases involving the lapses and relapses of clergymen as well as matrimonial disputes was presided over by the bishop in person, or an auditor under his close supervision. The consistory court, chaired by a junior dignitary known as an official, decided mundane cases involving slander, money, property, and wills. Summary correction of offences such as sabbath breaking, perhaps arising out of a visitation of parishes, involved a decision by the 'mere office of the judge' and a fine, or public penance. Procedure by plenary jurisdiction involving opposing parties, written submissions and lawyers was recorded in act books.

Registers of a bishop's pronouncements survive from the eleventh century onwards. Among the oldest are those of Chichester, commencing 1075, and Llandaff, from 1140. Many are available in print. The *Register of Edmund Lacy, Bishop of Exeter, 1420–55*, edited by G. R. Dunstan for the Canterbury and York Society and Devon and Cornwall Record Society (Torquay, 1963–7) is an example:

> Bideford churchyard ... polluted by the burial of the body of *Maud, widow of John Hoper*, who had hanged herself, was not so polluted because she was insane
>
> (30th January 1420/1)

> *John Quynterell* of ... Honiton, excommunicate for ... driving away his wife and living in open adultery for several years with one Alice Erbers
>
> (26th November 1449)

> petition made by *John Bassett esquire* ... that Richard Penpons, Robert Byan and Anne his wife had procured the counterfeiting by Robert Huchyng of London, of his seal of arms, and so forged a deed
>
> (27th October 1451)

Charters concerning land, owners, occupiers and adjacent proprietors as well as law suits, pensions, ordinations, vicarages and charities were registered in chartularies. These are particularly informative in continuing for so many centuries, recording generation after generation of church tenants, perhaps the same family gradually climbing to fortune and fame. Correspondence, rentals, leases and account books reveal the church as landlord and its muscular dealings with tenants. These estate documents, which may begin at the Reformation, indicate that some families occupied the same property for generations. The church owned property in areas such as southern Wales and valleys of the Pennines where industrialisation from the late seventeenth century brought in population, enterprise and, of course, wealth. There was no keener guardian of lucrative commercial monopolies or developer of housing estates than the diocesan agency.

Periodically the bishop made a personal visit to parishes within the diocese. In advance of each visitation a questionnaire was despatched. Answers returned formed a basis for the prelate's inspection of the physical condition of property and the moral condition of parishioners. Following his visit, the bishop filed a report known as a *speculum* listing 'things found out'. Returns for the diocesan censuses of 1563 and 1603 occasionally resulted in dissenting individuals being named and shamed in church or JP courts. Bishop Henry Compton's religious census of 1676 included returns of individual parishioners in a few places such as Bispham, Broughton, Clayworth and Goodnestone-next-Wingham.

The **parish** in England and Wales was governed by a meeting of responsible male inhabitants assembled in the church vestry or robing room. Minutes and accounts of

Accounts kept by Thomas Edwards and John William, constables of East Harling, Sussex, 1604–5.

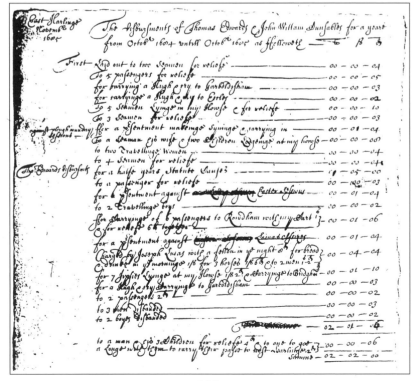

105

the vestrymen may survive from the fourteenth century onwards, lodged in the parish chest or at a nearby record office. Two vestrymen, acting as churchwardens, were responsible for altar cloths, manuscripts, relics, plates and similar treasures. Vestry records of building works identify ancestors as craftsmen or contractors. The vestry answered inquiries from central government, for instance concerning charities in 1816 and 1819–37; registered owners and occupiers as basis for the property tax known as a cess, assessment or rate, from 1601 in England and Wales; listed males of military age, householders, taxpayers and paupers. The vestry supervised parish schools and social welfare, making records of scholars, teachers, benefactors and recipients. Following an act of 1836, the vestry might submit corroborative property surveys to the poor-law commissioners, retaining drafts, maps and duplicate returns in the parish chest. Registers of church members, families and adherents were maintained.

Minutes and accounts of parochial officials such as the sexton, beadle, horse pinder (impounder) and hedge supervisor were known as town books. The constable was a key functionary, in touch with the whole community, liaising with the county lieutenancy and justiciary, compiling lists of adult males, for example for service in the militia, the part-time local defence forces of the Crown. The constable kept watch and ward and supervised the trained band and militia detachment. The supervisor of highways from 1555 required inhabitants to work a specified number of days on the public roads. He recorded those who fulfilled their obligations, those demurring and those wealthy enough to commute labour into a money payment.

From 1572 until 1834 (England and Wales), the parish administered **poor relief**. Paupers were maintained in their own homes with a dole of money, or offered bed, board and useful employment in the workhouse. The poor law drew little distinction between the feckless and the genuinely unemployed. The overseer's knowledge and judgement were crucial in determining the treatment a pauper might receive. Apprenticeship agreements, in a documentary format known as an indenture, show

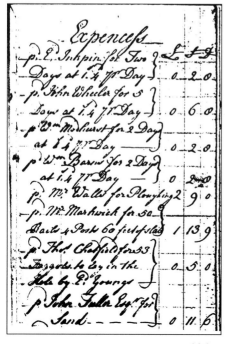

Payments to named individuals for work on the roads in 1768–9, from the accounts of the surveyor of the highways of Laughton, Sussex.

how individual pauper children were placed in employment, perhaps to learn a useful trade, perhaps as cheap hands for industrialists. Travellers described as Egyptians (gypsies), shipwrecked seamen and discharged soldiers making their way home are named as they passed through the parish, seeding the community with foreign genes and surnames, encouraged on their way with a dole or a flogging:

1793	Novr. 22	Carrying Home Edwd. Swetman & family to Brightling	£0 2s 0D
	Novr. 26	[By Cash] to Mr Philcox examining John Berry's wife	£0 1s 0D
	Decr. 16	To Hyland Thos. in need	£0 2s 0D
1794	Jan. 14	[Paid] Sus. Blunden 15 Weeks Allowance for her	
		Mother & Sister at 4s per Week	£3 0s 0D

(East Sussex Record Office, PAR 234/31/1/5, Burwash overseer's accounts, 1793–4)

From medieval times onwards, priests could claim one tenth, or a **tithe**, of the agricultural produce of the parish. In England and Wales, an act of 1836 permitted commutation of tithes paid in kind into a money payment. Southern and midland parishes had generally commuted tithes during the social and territorial reorganisation associated with enclosure of common fields. Under the new act surveyors were employed to map the parish, measuring each parcel of land, house and outbuilding. An accompanying document known as an apportionment recorded the names of owners and occupiers. Three copies of the tithe plan were prepared, now found in the parish chest and county, diocesan or public record office. Plot 200

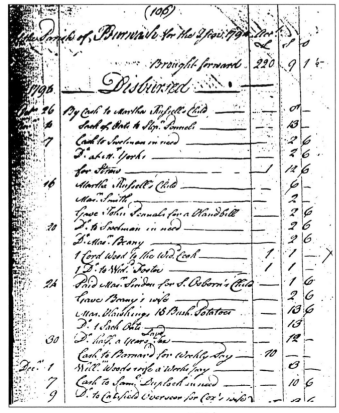

Accounts of money paid to named paupers of the parish of Burwash, Sussex, 1794.

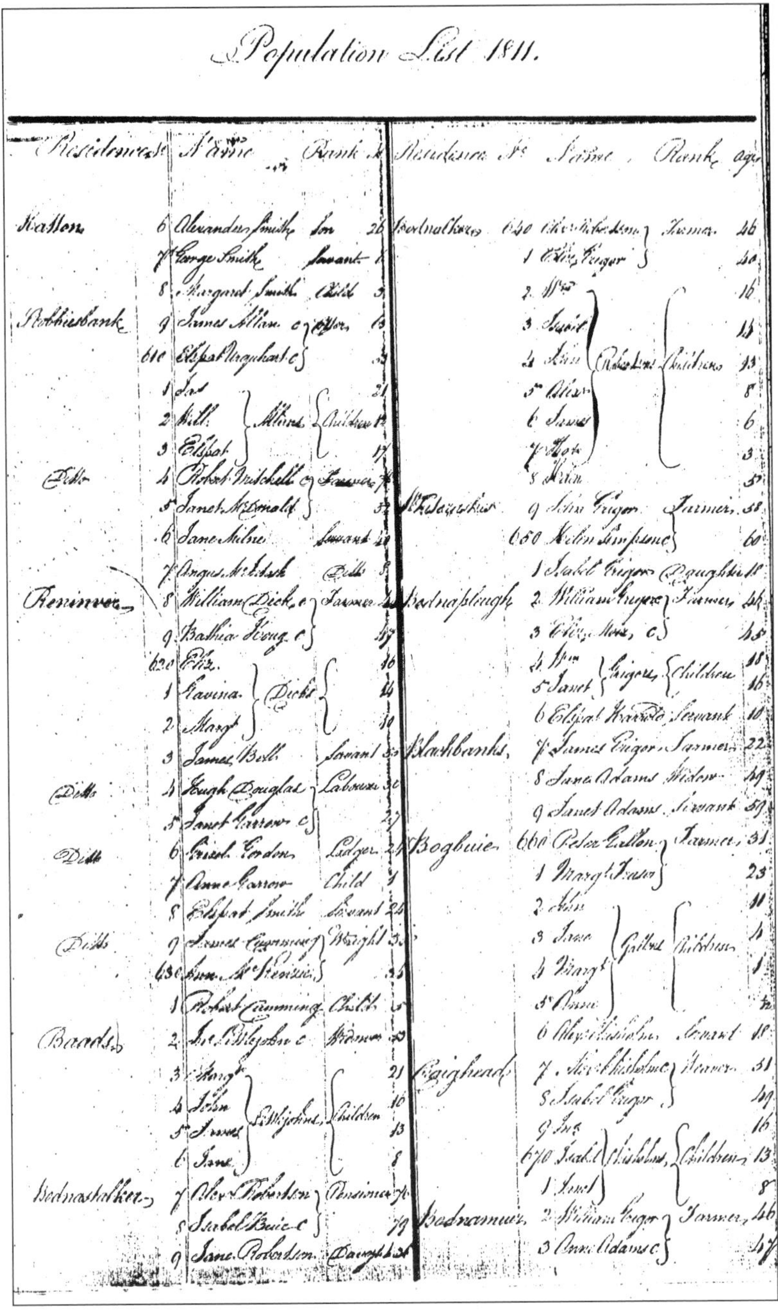

Population List 1811.

Residence &c.	No.	Name	Rank	Age
Kattan	6	Alexander Smith	Son	26
	7	George Smith	Servant	[illegible]
	8	Margaret Smith	Child	3
Robbiesbank	9	James Allan c	[illegible]	63
	610	Elspet Urquhart c		[illegible]
	1	Jas. (Allans)	Children	21
	2	Will. (Allans)	Children	12
	3	Elspet (Allans)	Children	17
Ditto	4	Robert Mitchell c	Farmer	[illegible]
	5	Janet McDonald c		57
	6	Jane Milne	Servant	40
	7	Angus McIntosh	Ditto	8
Reninver	8	William Dick c	Farmer	[illegible]
	9	Bathia Young c		47
	620	Eliz. (Dicks)		16
	1	Gavina (Dicks)		14
	2	Marg^t (Dicks)		10
	3	James Bell	Servant	[illegible]
Ditto	4	Hugh Douglas	Labourer	30
	5	Janet Farrow c		27
Ditto	6	Grizel Gordon	Lodger	[illegible]
	7	Anne Farrow	Child	4
	8	Elspet Smith	Servant	24
Ditto	9	James Cumming c	Wright	[illegible]
	630	Ann McKenzie c		35
	1	Robert Cumming	Child	5
Boards	2	Isa. Gilljohn c	Widow	[illegible]
	3	Marg^t (Gilljohns)	Children	21
	4	John (Gilljohns)	Children	16
	5	James (Gilljohns)	Children	13
	6	Jane (Gilljohns)	Children	8
Bednastalker	7	Alex^r Robertson	Pensioner	[illegible]
	8	Isabel Bruce c		79
	9	Jane Robertson	Daughter	[illegible]

Residence &c.	No.	Name	Rank	Age
Bednastalker	640	Alex^r Robertson	Farmer	46
	1	Eliz. Grigor		40
	2	W^m (Robertsons)	Children	16
	3	Isabel (Robertsons)	Children	15
	4	Ann (Robertsons)	Children	13
	5	Alex^r (Robertsons)	Children	8
	6	James (Robertsons)	Children	6
	7	Thos. (Robertsons)	Children	3
	8	Helen (Robertsons)	Children	5
[illegible]	9	John Grigor	Farmer	58
	650	Helen Simpson		60
	1	Isabel Grigor	Daughter	18
Bednasleugh	2	William Grigor	Farmer	46
	3	Eliz. Moir, c		45
	4	W^m (Grigors)	Children	18
	5	Janet (Grigors)	Children	16
	6	Elspet Harrold	Servant	10
Blackbanks	7	James Grigor	Farmer	22
	8	Jane Adams	Widow	49
	9	Janet Adams	Servant	[illegible]
Boghuie	660	Peter Gillon	Farmer	31
	1	Marg^t Fraser		23
	2	John (Gillons)	Children	11
	3	Jane (Gillons)	Children	4
	4	Marg^t (Gillons)	Children	1
	5	Anne (Gillons)	Children	½
	6	Alex^r Chisholm	Servant	18
Craighead	7	Alex^r Chisholm	Weaver	51
	8	Isabel Grigor		49
	9	Jas. (Chisholms)	Children	16
	670	Isabel (Chisholms)	Children	13
	1	Janet (Chisholms)	Children	8
Bednamuir	2	William Grigor	Farmer	46
	3	Anne Adams c		47

Returns for the national census of 1811 were ordered to be destroyed; this parish return, for Dallas, Moray, was preserved among kirk session archives.

on the tithe map of Barnton appears on the schedule approved by the commissioners in 1846 with the following information:

owner   William Clarke of the Ropery, manufacturer
occupiers Himself, John Goodier, Joseph Carter, George Capper, Joseph Eyres
property House, beershop, smithy, two cottages, cowhouse, garden and coal yard
acreage   0 acres 1 rood 30 perches

Irish tithe applotment books at the National Archives, Dublin, offer word pictures of property, owners and occupiers for 1825–7.

Census lists may be found in the parish chest and county archives. Inhabitants of Ealing, Middlesex, were listed by name in 1599, those of Stafford in 1622, populations of the baronies of Newcastle and Upper Cross, County Dublin, about 1652. Household heads were named in Knockando, Moray, in connection with the distribution of government grain as famine relief in 1782–3. The census of Littleover, Derbyshire, is probably associated with the national enumeration of 1811:

House Number	Heads	Families & Ages	Lodgers
17 Mickleover	Henry Watson, once Tithe Master & Farmer, now Labourer. Mary, his servant, now wife.	Amelia, 11 Dorothy, 9 Julia, 7 Ruth, 5 Jeremiah, 2	Thomas Cooper William Hodgkinson Robert Walhouse
			Apprentices
18 Mickleover	Humphrey Austin, Framework K[nitte]r Ann, Wife	Elizabeth, 2 Thomas, 1	John Peach Joseph Rowe
41 Littleover	John Tafft, Soldier, on half pay, having lost his sight in Egypt Rebeka, Wife. Harriett Hopkins, Boarder Maria Jennings, Do.	Esther Bythway, Neice 9	

Scottish records fall under the care of the National Archives in Edinburgh. The reformed church in Scotland, often familiarly termed the Kirk, was organised as a hierarchy of courts comprising General Assembly, synod, presbytery and kirk session, each creating minutes, accounts, correspondence and title deeds. The synod was concerned with an area similar to that of the predecessor diocese and with weighty matters referred upwards from parochial level through the presbytery. Synod minutes are occasionally enlivened, as when James Allan, minister of Rothes in Moray, was summoned to answer charges that he had imbibed the quietist doctrine of the Flemish mystic Antoinette Bourignon, a particular theological vogue at the time. Feelings ran high among Allan's supporters. Synod minutes recorded the riot that ensued:

> The Moderator observing a croud of people thronging into the Synod house uncalled, desired the Officer to shut the doors … and desired that those people that had thrust themselvs in should remove, & … come not in a disorderlie tumultuarie way … notwithstanding of which a great manie crouded in, & one of their number came to the Table & laid down a Paper & desired that it might be read
> (National Archives of Scotland, CH2/271/4, minutes, synod of Moray, 30th October 1705)

The presbytery's concern with churches, manses and schools resulted in periodic parochial visitations:

> There is also a Jacobite meeting-house in the town of Huntly, wherein Mr James Allan (depos'd by the Synod of Moray for error) serves, which is much frequented and encouraged
> (National Archives of Scotland, CH2/342/5, minutes, Strathbogie presbytery, 1736)

The kirk session, an influential parochial meeting consisting of the parish minister assisted by lay elders and deacons, supervised the moral, social and religious life of the community in co-operation with landowners, known as heritors, civil magistrates and the town council. The session supervised the parish school, where typically the session clerk served as schoolmaster. Church door collections for the use of the poor were disbursed to persons listed on a roll of paupers. Minutes also record exceptional payments to individuals in pressing need:

> given to Andrew Duncan a Blind man one Shilling eight pennies, and to another Beggar a half pennie
> To William Newlands a Lame Boy as a second moiety of his Apprentice fee £5
> To Margerat Murdoch in Newton being distressed with Severall running sores £1
> To Jannet Newland's children £2

The session was responsible for the parish mortcloth, a funeral pall to cover the coffin or shrouded corpse before burial. Accounts of fees for the hire of this item in some measure make up for the absence of burial registers and gravestones in some parishes.

Session records preserve sentences of outlawry and excommunication:

> William Grant syspect warlack ... Georg Sutherland and agnes Keith cohabiters in adultery ... alexr mekintosche for rept and murther ... normand Duncan for Beastialitie
> (Forres, 24th October 1650)

The session attempted to suppress superstition and witchcraft:

> Christian Paton in Drainie ... used Charming or Divination to find out things stollen; by putting in a Dish with water, peeces of paper whereon was written ye names of ye persons suspected for ye theft, & making her observations & drawing Conclusions from ye sinking of some of ye peeces
> (Drainie, 4th June 1705)

The session was particularly taxed with the control of fornication, not least because this led to illegitimate children who, morality apart, might require support from the poor fund. The chief contributors to the fund were, of course, the prominent parishioners who sat as session members. Investigations were thorough to the point of prurience, providing precise information regarding ancestors' activities and origins:

> Anne Falconar ... owned her being with child to Robert McPherson sometime servant to Mr Bailie ... Being asked when and where it was begot, answered in harvest last & also sometime after in the Castle Yard in the beginning of November
> (Forres, 4th May 1738)

Most families in Anglesey were nonconformist but were obliged to attend the parish church for burial, as here at Rhoscolyn.

Punishments generally took the form of a fine for men, paid into the poor fund, and a public shaming for women. Despite this, relapses and even trelapses are recorded.

Nonconformists were numerous and influential in certain parishes, for example Roman Catholics in Ireland and Methodists in Wales. Central archives of these churches may be available at national headquarters. Quaker archives (Society of

Quaker meeting houses were usually modest vernacular buildings. This example is at Monyash, Derbyshire.

111

Register of church members, 1843.

Friends) at Friends House, London, are eloquent in describing the 'sufferings' of members subject to prejudice and persecution. Some records are deposited in national archives:

> Because for Conscience Sake they Could not pay tithes ... The orphens of Robert Kirk & his wife, both deceased ... ye eldest not eight years of age had taken from them for tithe by William Tompson tithetaker ... 5 loads of hay 11 stooks of wheat & rye 30 three Stooks of oats and 8 Stooks of Barley all worth £1 5s -d
>
> (Public Record Office of Northern Ireland, T 1062/48, sufferings in Shankell, County Armagh, 1706)

University libraries are also suitable repositories. Methodist archives are centralised at the John Rylands University Library of Manchester. Records of individual congregations of Baptists, Huguenots, Episcopalians, Jews, Free Presbyterians, Unitarians, Sikhs, Moslems and scores of other sects include registers, minutes, accounts, membership lists and title deeds. Numerous churches, chapels, mosques, temples and synagogues have opted to deposit papers in county

Register of pew holders, 1826.

archives and libraries as a means of improving public access and awareness, particularly of the philanthropic and educational activities of nonconformity.

Medieval records of **religious houses** of monks, nuns, friars and the two military orders of Knights Templars and Hospitallers survive chiefly in the form of chartularies. Transcriptions of these volumes, published by record societies, are available in public libraries. Wealthy monasteries commanded extensive possessions. Beaulieu and God's House, Southampton, documented the people of estates scattered through Berkshire, Hampshire and Cornwall (Southampton Record Series, 1974, 1976); Missenden chartulary (Buckinghamshire Record Society, 1939–62) documented communities of peasants, craftsmen and merchants across the counties of Buckingham, Bedford, Huntingdon, Middlesex, Oxford, Suffolk and the city of London.

A few fortunate families have traced their ancestry back before the sixteenth century and therefore require records of the medieval church. Documentation within Britain and Ireland was usually acquired and preserved by the successor Protestant authorities. The church was centralised around the Bishop of Rome, the Pope, whose **Vatican** palace housed the administrative archives. A hierarchy of priests reached down to parish level where, for instance, an individual could be granted an indulgence for remission of punishment after death in return for a financial contribution to a hospital, or arraigned for heresy and moral incontinence. The public library can supply published editions, transcripts and indexes of papal archives, including registers, supplications, petitions, correspondence, licences, dispensations and bulls relevant to the diocese and parish. Reform of the papal secretariat from the twelfth century onwards resulted in systematic registration of documents, now accessed through dozens of index volumes summarising papal letters arranged alphabetically, diocese by diocese.

13
Justice of the peace

From the fourteenth century justices of the peace assembled in England and Wales for administrative sessions. From 1461 justices took over some responsibilities from county sheriffs to emerge as an important element in county government during the sixteenth century. The justices, often referred to as magistrates or JPs, met in petty or summary sessions, which might convene in any convenient location, such as the magistrate's own house or the village inn, and four times a year in formal courts of quarter sessions. Usually members of the gentry, justices qualified by social status rather than legal training. In the court of quarter sessions they were advised by a clerk of the peace, typically a lawyer, who minuted the proceedings, drew up schedules of business and was responsible for the court archives. JP records are usually in county and borough archives and the National Library of Wales. In Scotland, 'godlie wyse and vertuous gentilmen of good qualitie' were appointed justices from 1609 in imitation of the English system, though the courts did not achieve the same pre-eminence in county affairs. Records are now the responsibility of the National Archives in Edinburgh.

Court in session

Presentments gave the court information through a variety of legal documents. Cases involved highway robbery, theft, trespass, assault, riot, cattle stealing, witchcraft, rent arrears, debt, burglary, drunkenness, trading standards and profanity. As landowners, the magistrates were notably zealous in protecting property: enforcing laws against poaching, the cutting of estate timber, burning of heather moors, encroachment on manorial waste and vandalising hay ricks. On 18th December 1651, Caernarvonshire magistrates were offered information on oath by Lewis Moris of Aberdaron, yeoman, that 'one Evan John ap William of Aberdaron … hath for many yeares last past kept and still doeth keep one Blanch as his concubine … adulterously'. The grand jury in Caernarvonshire presented on oath that Richard Thomas Griffith, churchwarden of Llangwnadl, permitted in the presence of

> David ap Robert, weaver, Evan ap Richard, smith, Morgan ap Morgan, weaver, Thomas Griffith, weaver, David ap Griffith, smith, and Robert John ap Hugh publicke wakes to be kept, & buying & selling … of ale in the house of Richard ap Robert

This disgraceful assembly took place on Sunday 2nd October 1653. Furthermore, tobacco was openly purveyed and consumed – and on the sabbath too! The Knutsford sessions, Cheshire, on 6th October 1802 heard that William Almand aged 27, flatman from Barnton, did feloniously steal

> from a certain booth or tent, then situated or erected on the race ground, at Nether Knutsford … a barrel or cask, containing British brandy, the property of Jonathan Hooley of Kinderton

Almand, who had spent a miserable three months in Middlewich house of correction awaiting trial, was found not guilty.

Under Elizabeth I, bishops were commanded by the Privy Council to seek out 'disordered persons as refuse to com to church'. It was the duty of magistrates to enforce laws on religious uniformity and root out sectaries. In 1581, the Bishop of

Bangor reported to the justices that

> one Gaynor glyn ... wydowe ... sythen, the xviiith day of marche nowe last past ... hathe not repayred to her saied parisshe churche [of] Llandydno in the commote of Creythyn

Cases such as this might be prosecuted as an example to terrify other dissenters into conformity. In several counties in the 1650s it was presented that 'one George Fox hath beene lately in these parts and hath uttered seuerall blasphemies'. Presentment led to a formal accusation known as an indictment, for example in Bedfordshire in 1658: 'against William Athey of Harrold Butcher for that being Constable he spake these wordes, I care not a fart for any Justice of the peace in England'.

The justices heard evidence, questioned suspects and witnesses and sentenced the guilty. Imprisonment was expensive and not favoured when the law offered exemplary public punishments such as fines, flogging, mutilation, branding and banishment. Culprits were also exposed to ridicule in the wooden framework of the stocks or pillory; and in Scotland in the joggs – an iron collar fixed by a chain to the market cross:

> Thomas Mason hyrer in Forres ... pressed to enlist for a soldier ... turned me Crazie in the head ... ventured to go to the Castell Yard and carry away corn and straw ... to suport my horse. The Baillies ... appoint his hands to be tyed behind his back and a Label put on his Breast with these words in Capital Letters A NOTORIOUS THIEF and then to be brought from the Prison to the market Cross of Forres where he is to be put in the Joggs ... and thereafter to be drummed thro' the Town ... with a Sheaf of Corn & Straw upon his back, to which Burgh he is never to return
> (1773)

JPs as administrators

From the sixteenth century, an ever-widening net of administrative duties brought most families into the orbit of the magistrates. Individuals were documented as contractors and labourers repairing county highways, surveyors of parish roads, rate assessors, keepers of bridewells and gaols, attendants at lunatic asylums, and village constables. JPs took advice from men of skill in assessing claims for damage in commercial disputes. On 21st January 1785, Joseph Foster, master of a canal boat, loaded at Newton, Cheshire, 692 bushels of white salt for home consumption, paying the stupendous sum of £150 15s 6d in duty. Foster travelled along the Trent and Mersey Navigation until:

> Barnton Tunnel being an underground Passage the said Vessel being heavy laden ... Suddenly Sunk and went to the bottom ... being nine feet deep, wherby the said Salt being in Bulk, was intirely Lost ... through suction or wake of another Vessel passing just before and a high Wind abaft

The magistrates accepted this businessman's claim and permitted refund of duty.

Neighbourly disputes periodically erupted over encroachments in the fields and pasture of unenclosed landscapes. Here the records preserve the authentic voice of an ancestor in Tomcork, Moray, in 1750:

> John Grant ... Does keep great Numbers of Grasseing Cattle ... Upon the Common Liberty of the Town ... Likeways ... almost ever Day Upon My Ingrass and Corn ... And whenever I Challenge him ... he gives me the most provokeing Language ... Calling me a Damned Lyar and a Damned Develish Dog ... he plewed Some riggs of My Land ... in the Harvest time he Shears of my Corn

1812

Rafford

		und 30	ab 30
1	James Wilson Grieve at Burgie	un	"
2	William Robertson Farm Servant Burgie	un	"
3	Alexander Goodbrand Servant Burgie	un	"
4	David Muir Gardiner Burgie	un	"
5	John Spence Weaver Burgie	un	"
6	John Kynoch Labourer Mill of Burgie	"	ab
7	Robert Anderson Farmer Craighead	"	ab
8	William Mann Farmers Son Lawrenstown	un	"
9	James Simpson Servant Gaveny	un	"
10	George Ray Servant Altyre	un	"
11	Thomas Stronach Servant Altyre	un	"
12	Thomas Bowie Mason Lochnavando	"	ab
13	James Paul Mason there	"	ab
14	William Coul Labourer there	un	"
15	Hendry Dunbar Farmer Corstown	un	"
16	James Anderson Labourer Craigroy	"	ab
17	Alexander Macgillivray Farmers Son Phorp	un	"
18	George Hendry Farmer Remplet	"	ab
19	William Henry Servant Miltown	un	"
20	Robert Henry Servant Clunie	un	"
21	John Walker Labourer Baremure	un	"
22	John Nairn Servant Clunie	un	"
23	William Smith Student Forres	un	"
24	William Munro Servant Ley of Forres	un	"
25	George Mason Farmer Robins hog	"	ab

Individuals in the parish of Rafford, balloted as militiamen by the County Lieutenant of Elginshire, 1812.

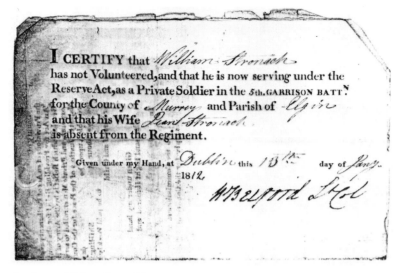

Certificate of William Stronach's service in the militia – unaccompanied by his wife Jean – 1812.

The justices resolved differences between master and servant:

> Bell Thomson ... three weeks absent from my service under pretence of illness ...
> On Monday I learnt that she had been very unwell ... and had in consequence been bled
> On Tuesday I heard she was worse
> On Wednesday she was speechless ...
> On Friday however ... She ... put on the thin and airy dress of a Bridegrooms maid ... to parade the Streets of Forres ... she attended the Ball in the Evening – danced – and remained there all night
>
> (Statement by Colonel Simon Fraser, 1836)

In this 1836 case, the justices supported the aggrieved Colonel, declaring Bell Thomson's 'wages for the current halfyear to be forfeited' and fining her £1 1s sterling 'to be applied for behoof of the poor'.

The militia was a primary responsibility of the county lieutenant, originally an appointee of the Tudor monarchy. Lieutenancy archives include lists of men eligible to serve in this territorial defence force. The actual work of mustering men fell to the justices. County justices chose by ballot or otherwise men required from enrolment lists compiled by parish constables. Militia units were, properly, home guard forces, but members could be required to serve for months at a time at high cost to affected families. Substitutes were therefore commonly paid, sought perhaps from far afield. Wives of militia men were considered for support from public funds when their menfolk were posted out of the county:

> I John Chisholm, a militia man serving in THE INVERNESS MILITIA do declare, That Elspet MacDonald [in Longbride, Elginshire] is my lawful wife, and has been so since the 10th day of December 1807. and that I have ... Two children ... Sophia aged 3⁴/₁₂, Hellen aged 2 years ... 11th day of January 1812.

During the Civil War period the administrative remit of the justices extended over the enlistment, pay and pensions of soldiers. Caernarfonshire JPs considered the petition of Richard Davies, late soldier under captains Smith and Barrowe. Davies claimed he was:

> at the first rebellious in Surrections in Ireland, under Sir Charles Coote ... dangerously wounded ... 3 Severall Bulletts in his bodie some whereof maye be felt, and hath 7en deepe & dangerous Cicatrices and cutts in Sundrye partes of his bodie, which have much debilitated his strength ... Som what hard of hearinge, & nowe verye impotent

Usually the court decision was written onto the petition before papers were filed. The absence of a note in the Davies case invites further research by descendants of this heroic (or accident-prone) warrior. Following the Restoration of the Stuart monarchy in 1660, magistrates' attention shifted to former royalist soldiers, for example, again in Caernarfonshire, with decisions regarding entitlement to pensions:

> Richard ap Robert Edmond an adged man of 63 years hath served in Scotland & other places under Sir John Owen hath a slender wound on the knee (not)
> John Williams of Bethkelert in Nasby fight hurt in the legge & in the thighe a great wound (not)

From 1662 onwards, JPs administered laws of settlement and removal concerning people likely to become a charge on the poor rate such as travellers, Egyptians (gypsies), unemployed men on tramp in search of work, pregnant strangers and unmarrried mothers. Session records may contain the petition by a parish for the removal of a pauper back to a place of birth or legal settlement followed by judicial examination to discover the parish and date of birth, details of marriage, age, occupation, children's names, spouse's name and parishes of previous residence. An order for removal might follow as in the case of Mary Flower, who appeared before justices at Richmond in 1815. Having no legal settlement there, no means of supporting herself and being 'with Child of a bastard Child', she was removed to Northallerton where her husband generously accepted the situation and baptised the child as his own son. According to session records in 1817, Mary Burgess walked the 25 miles (40 km) from Barnton, Cheshire, to Manchester, seeking the father of her unborn child. She failed and was required by the magistrates to return home. The authorities in Barnton sent their constable on expenses to appeal. His pleas were rejected. Mary's new child died at Christmas. She eventually got a man, perhaps *her* man, Francis Minchin, an artilleryman at Hulme barracks. Their first legitimate child, Dulcibella Caroline, was baptised at the parish church in 1821.

Magistrates might issue official passes and small sums of money to assist legitimate travellers to return home. Great Yarmouth justices were sympathetic to the plight of two shipwrecked sailors who appeared in the county in 1756. The men, survivors of the wreck of 'Tuscaney Galley, a merchant Ship of London', were given clothing, an instruction to travel to their home in North Wales within sixty days and a pass to ensure they were not prosecuted *en route* under vagrancy laws.

Licences and lists

JPs and their clerk of the peace licensed, supervised, assessed, registered, listed and taxed people. The clerk accepted for safekeeping personal testaments, wills, title deeds, marriage contracts and commercial agreements. Deeds of bargain and sale were enrolled from 1536. From 1552, the clerk recorded recognisances of good behaviour on behalf of licensed victuallers. From 1563, itinerant sellers of corn, fish and dairy produce, known as badgers, were licensed.

A LIST OF THE ELECTORS O...

SHEWING HOW THEY VOTED AT THE ...

The numbers mark the order in which the votes were given; and by being pl[...]
the Liberal Candidate, SIR ANDREW LEITH HAY, and who voted for MR 'T[...]
those who did not vote: the letter D. distinguishes those who, by having remo[...]

NAME AND DESIGNATION	LEITH HAY	DUFF
Rev. W. C. M'Laurin,		
John Sutherland, Coal-Merchant.		
Rev. P. Merson, Teacher.		
John M'Kinnie, Merchant,	1	
George Gatherer, Writer,	2	
Alex. Falconer, jun. Clothier,		
Dr A. Murchison, Residenter.		
James Mellis, Writer,		
Alexander Cooper, Writer,		
David M'Bean, Chemist.		
William Robb, Surgeon,		
John Mann, Baker,	3	
William Grant, Accountant,	4	
Robert Bain, Writer,		
Alex. Seivewright, Merchant,	5	
Alex. Forteath, Merchant,	6	
Alexander Stephen, Merchant.	7	
James Young, Brewer,	8	
James Alexander, Watchmaker,	9	
William Hardie, Baker,	10	
Peter Prown, Distiller,		
Alex. Gordon, Writer,	11	
William Gauldie, Merchant,		
John Forsyth, Merchant.		
Alexander Young, Brewer,		
Alex. M'Ewan, Cabinet-Maker,		
Lewis Anderson, Merchant,		
Admiral Duff, Residenter,	17	
William Chalmers, Residenter,	12	
James Murray, Merchant,		
George Mathieson, Skinner,		
James Culbard, Leather-Merchant,	13	
George Hay, Clothier,	14	
James Hay, Merchant.	15	
James Wilson, House-Carpenter,	16	
Alexander Grigor, Gardener,	17	
John M'Hattie, Blacksmith.		
William Robertson, Gardener,		
Alex. Sutherland, Residenter,		
John Shanks, Baker,	18	
William Innes, Residenter,		
Francis Gordon, Merchant,	19	
Joseph Cook, Shoemaker.	20	
William Arnott, Slater,		
James Dean, Farmer,	21	
Alex. Anderson, Gardener.		
George Sutherland, Gardener,		
Robert Roy, Sheriff-officer,		
John M' Hattie, Plasterer,		
William Anderson, Merchant,	22	
John Kynock, Tenementer,		
James Smith, jun. Miller,		
Robert Murdoch, Shoemaker,		
Alex. Sutherland, Nailer,	23	
John Smith, Blacksmith,		
James Donaldson, Merchant,	24	
Robert Hay, Cartwright,		
John Stuart, Wheelwright,	25	
James Simpson, Grocer,	26	
Robert Innes, Carpenter,	27	

NAME AND DESIGNATION	LEITH HAY	DUFF
Alex. Douglas, Farmer,	28	A[
Robert Stephen, Farmer,	29	A[
John Grant, Grocer,	30	J[
Alex. Culbard, Residenter,	31	W[
William Winchester, Cooper,	32	Ja[
A. C. Brander, Bookseller & Printer,	33	Jo[
William Russell, Residenter,	34	W[
John Taylor, Grocer,	35	R[
John Goldie, Squarewright,	36	ol[
John Murdoch, Carrier,	37	2[
James Cattanach, Cartwright,		34	L[
William Cattanach, Saddler,		35	V[
James Sinclair, Miller,		36	Lo[
John M'Naughtane, Residenter,		37	Vi[
William Lamb, Mason,		38	V[
Robert Munro, Vintiner.	38		..[
Alexr. Cruickshanks, Farmer.		39	N[
Peter Nicholson, Merchant.	39		iii[
James Cruickshanks, Merchant.		40	Al[
William Brown, Merchant.		41	Geo[
John Dunbar, Bookfinder.	40		Re[
Francis Taylor, Merchant.		42	Al[
Alexr. Brander, Banker.		43	Ja[
James Jenkins, Teacher.	41		Ja[
Geo. Bennett, Corn Merchant.	42		Ja[
Charles Thain, mason.		44	Jo[
Robt. Grigor, Skinner.	43		Ja[
W. Robertson, Farmer and miller,	44		Iol[
James Henry, merchant.	45		Ian[
Peter Thomson, merchant.		45	sa[
Alex. Clark, farmer,		46	Ja[
James Clark, Blacksmith		47	N'[
James Coull, Residenter,		48	Iol[
William Gordon, baker,	46		Ia[
Peter Smith, Dyer,		49	Ia[
James Gow, carrier,		50	Ab[
John Russel, Junr. merchant.	47		Ian[
Alexr Falconer, merchant,	48		Gr[
Wm. Skene, Manufacturer.	49		Al[
James Miln, blacksmith,		51	Jan[
Alexr Stephen, cabinet-maker.		52	Ar[
W. Gillan, Farmer,		53	Re[
W. Jack, nailer	50		Col[
Wm. Young, residenter,	51		'Col[
Hugh Gordon, residenter,		54	Alc[
Geo. Gordon, merchant,	52		Hu[
James Grant, Writer,	53		Jol[
W. Stephen, merchant	54		[Wr[
Donald Grant, mason,		55	Cap[
Alex Laing, sen. shoemaker.	55		Jol[
Alexr Phimister, Miller.	56		Jol[
Andrew Forsyth, builder.	57		Jol[
James Stephen, mason.	58		Jno[
John Leslie, merchant.	59		Jan[
Geo. M'Intosh, Shoemaker	60		Re[
Jas. Smith, Sen. miller		56	Jol[
Joseph Collie, merchant,		57	Al[
John Walker, Merchant,	61		Jan[
Allan Grant, road contractor.		58	W[

A. C. BRANER, P[...]

List of electors extracted from poll books of the burgh of Elgin showing how each cast his vote in the general election of 1841.

During the period 1662–89, a government tax of two shillings was imposed on household hearths. Village constables served as chimneymen submitting lists of those liable for enrolment at the sessions, with duplicate returns for the Exchequer. Returns for 1664 are notably complete. Until 1674, individuals were named, conveniently connecting ancestors with particular properties. From 1673, holders of public office registered oaths of loyalty to king and established church. Houses used as places of worship by dissenters were registered from 1689 until 1852. Land tax assessments for each parish were collected from 1692. The documentation recorded domestic, industrial and commercial properties with the names of owners and occupiers. Though not set out in any consistent form, parochial assessments remained stable, allowing researchers to follow a family's holdings from year to year, noting changes in the assessment that reflect acquisition or disposal of property. Returns for the period 1692–1780 are more likely to be found among estate muniments than in a session bundle. From 1696 until 1832, constables returned lists of men qualified for jury service showing name, abode, age and occupation. Window tax was collected from 1696 until 1851. Annual returns show the name and residence of the taxpayer with the number of windows in houses and business premises. Families affected by official road closures and diversions were recorded from 1697, including plans from 1773. Certificates of exemption from 'all Manner of Parish and Ward Offices', known as Tyburn tickets, were issued from 1699 as a reward for bringing a felon to justice.

Under an act of 1711, poll books recording men and their votes at parliamentary elections were deposited 'without any Imbezilment or Alteration', allowing genealogists to discover an ancestor's political leanings. In the Cheshire election of 1841, twenty-one electors were each entitled to two votes by virtue of owning property in Barnton, though several were not actually resident:

Name	Residence	How voted
John Plumb	Barnton	Whig (1)
Thomas Cross	Church Hulme	Whig (1)
Samual Cawley	Barnton	Conservative (2)
William Robinson	Church Minshull	Conservative (2)
Thomas Smith Entwistle	Rochdale	Conservative (2)
William Birkenhead	Northwich	Whig (1)

An act of 1715 compelled registration of papists with descriptions of their real property and, from 1717, also their wills and deeds.

From the eighteenth century, private acts of Parliament were passed for many parishes to divide medieval arable strips and common land into individual hedged and fenced fields. A large-scale plan was usually necessary to show appropriate property with names of owners and occupiers specified in an award. Documents were deposited with the clerk of the peace. About 7 million acres and thousands of families were affected, mainly in central and southern England. From 1780 to 1828, alehouse bonds issued by licensing magistrates were preserved. Registers of applications reveal a remarkable number of small family-run beershops, public houses and corner shops. In 1780, Parliament enacted that 'no Person shall vote for electing of … Knights of the Shire to serve in Parliament … which have not … been charged or assessed … by a Land Tax'. Annual assessments for each parish were until 1832 deposited with the clerk of the peace as evidence of electoral qualification. The rate in the pound was fixed and the tax made perpetual, enabling researchers to trace families through the records.

Date	owner	property	occupier	rate 4s in £
1750	William Ball	Leighs Brow	self	1s 5 $\frac{1}{3}$d
1760	Mary Ball	Leighs Brow	self	1s 8d
1773	Abraham Ball	Leighs Brow	self	1s 8d
1777	Abram Ball junior	Leighs Brow	self	1s 10d
1802	Abraham Ball	Leighs Brow	self	1s 10d
1812	Mary Ball	Leighs Brow	self	1s 10d
1818	Mary Ball	Leighs Brow	self	1s 10d

| 1820 | John Wilkinson | Leighs Brow | self | 1s 10d |
| 1831 | John Wilkinson | Leighs Brow | self | 1s 10d |

This data dovetails with information from other records. Church registers show that William Ball died in 1753, Mary in 1772, Abraham junior in 1805 and Widow Mary Ball in 1819. The census has John Wilkinson living with Ellen Wilkinson in 1841. In a tithe schedule of 1843, Ellen was a widow owning a cottage in Leighs Brow numbered 272 on the tithe map.

The clerk of the peace registered certificates issued to owners of sporting dogs and guns under acts of 1784 and 1785. Roman Catholic priests, schoolmasters and chapels were registered from 1791. Session records include deposited books of reference and plans showing property and dwellings in the vicinity of canals from 1792, subsequently also of railways, harbours, waterworks, gasworks and other public undertakings. Barges and bargees were registered from 1795 to 1871, establishing a prime source for a mobile community. Rules of friendly societies, masonic lodges and other suspect organisations were deposited from 1793, with membership lists added from 1799. The Forres St Lawrence lodge for 1817 included several dozen local residents as well as emigrés:

John Hoyes Esquire Grenada
Mr John Urquhart Merchant Gibraltar
Captain A.B. Campbell Native Bombay Infantry

Users of hair powder (clergy excepted) paid a duty of one guinea annually from 1795. Acts of 1795 and 1796 required returns of men liable for military service. From 1812, information regarding parochial charities and their property was deposited before making a return to government. In 1829, magistrates made returns of nonconformist and papist sectaries. Following electoral reform in 1832, registers of county voters were deposited, supplementing series of poll books, which continued until the introduction of the secret ballot in 1872.

cute the Offender to conviction; and I will give the Sum of **TWENTY POUNDS** to any Person who shall, within the same time, give me such Private Information as may lead to the discovery and punishment of the Offender.

Dated this 12th of December, 1838.

RICHARD MANDERS.

WE, the undersigned Gentlemen of the neighbourhood of Swords, being convinced that no trustworthy Person would be safe in the Service of his Employer, if Writers of such Letters, threatening Life and Property, were suffered to escape with impunity, do hereby offer a further Reward of the Sums attached to our several Names hereto affixed, to such Person as shall, within the period above mentioned, prosecute the Offender to conviction.

December 12th, 1838.

	£ s. d.		£ s. d.		£ s. d.
Charles Cobbe, *Newbridge,*	5 0 0	Patrick Bowden, *Oldtown,*	5 0 0	John Walsh, P.P., *Rowlestown,*	5 0 0
Talbot de Malahide, *Malahide Castle,*	10 0 0	James Brangan, *Swords,*	5 0 0	John M'Cann, *Swords,*	2 0 0
George Evans, M.P. *Portrane,*	10 0 0	Arthur Baker, *Balheary House,*	5 0 0	Elias T. Corbally, *Rathbeal House,*	5 0 0
Josh. Forster, *Swords House,*	5 0 0	Henry Baker, *Balheary House,*	5 0 0	Patrick Corbally, *Rathbeal House,*	5 0 0
Francis Howard, *Swords Glebe,*	5 0 0	Richard Smith, *Lissenhall,*	5 0 0	James Dodd, *Coultry,*	2 0 0
Andrew Crawford, *Auburn,*	5 0 0	Mungo Duckett, *Kilcreagh,*	5 0 0	W. L Badham, *Stormanstown,*	5 0 0
Thomas Crawford, do.,	-5 0 0	Peter Early, *Swords,*	1 0 0	Charles Frazer, *Hazelbrook,*	5 0 0
M. M. O'Grady, *Lamancha,*	5 0 0	Samuel Waters, do.,	2 0 0	Isaac Willan, *Carrickhill,*	5 0 0
N. Trumbull, *Beechwood,*	5 0 0	James Sandford, do.,	2 0 0	Austin Forde, *Forrest,*	3 0 0
Peter Aungier, *Lays,*	10 0 0	Joseph Segrave, do.,	1 0 0	James Monks, *Pickardstown,*	3 0 0
William Green, *Cottage,*	5 0 0	John Stamer, *Brazill,*	1 0 0	Michael Doyle,	3 0 0
John Arthure, *Seafield,*	5 0 0	Edward Cullen, *Rathbeal,*	1 0 0	J. Green,	1 0 0
Benedict Arthure, do.,	5 0 0	Patk. Lenehan, *Roganstown,*	5 0 0	Christopher Dodd, *Ballymun,*	2 0 0
James Carey, P. P., *Swords,*	3 0 0	Martin O'Reilly, *Lispopple,*	5 0 0	John Yourell,	2 0 0

A. THOM, PRINTER, ABBEY-STREET.

Farmers and businessmen supplemented the county police and magistracy with rewards of their own.

14
Town and county

Individuals as ratepayers, electors, merchants, tradesmen, paupers, debtors, criminals, councillors and public servants have been affected by the activities of town and county councils. Councils were responsible for the built environment, common lands, commodity prices, drains, education, elections, gas supply, highways, housing, lighting, markets, paving, police, poor relief, public health, sewerage, valuation, water supply and other social concerns, usually under some direction from central government. The military tribunal determined the fate of individuals seeking exemption from, or postponement of, service for family, economic or conscientious reasons during the world wars. Over the centuries, various authorities were created, including the borough, barony (Ireland), county commission of supply (Scotland from 1667), grand jury (Ireland), improvement commission, police commission (Scotland from 1833), poor law union (England and Wales from 1834, Ireland 1838), parochial board (Scotland 1845), board of health (England and Wales 1848), highway board (England and Wales 1862), urban and rural sanitary district (England and Wales 1872), county council (England and Wales 1888, Scotland 1889, Ireland 1898), parish council (Scotland 1894), urban and rural district and civil parish (England and Wales 1894). Access to these records in county and town archives has generally improved following local government reorganisations in 1974–5 and 1995–8.

Records may be fragmentary before the sixteenth century, though certain medieval boroughs have archives extending back to Norman times. The efficient organisation of towns and the privileges or liberties enjoyed by the inhabitants attracted immigrants from near and far. Burghs established in Scotland during the twelfth century were settled by Norman go-getters from Brittany, Flanders, England and Wales. This is usually the earliest period to which genealogies can reliably be traced.

Archives are voluminous from the sixteenth century onwards, stored in council muniment rooms or in the offices of officials. Documents not required for current administrative purposes are usually archived in the library or heritage service. Local government reorganisation, particularly in the 1970s and 1990s, has resulted in some relocation of collections. Documentation generated by organisations originally established as private enterprises may be held by councils, for instance grammar school records among education authority archives, almshouse muniments in social work files.

The merchant **guild** comprised the leading merchants and property owners who combined to protect their interests, regulate trade and maintain oligarchic control over borough governance and administration. The guild charter is sometimes regarded as the founding deed of a borough. Records may be sought in the offices of the guild's present-day successor or among town council archives. The papers may describe the prosecution of unfree traders whose activities threatened guild monopolies, the enforcement of trading standards and social welfare activities of the guild as burial club, friendly society and insurance company. Incorporations to promote the interests of craftsmen such as glovers, smiths, tanners, wrights and weavers appeared during the thirteenth century. Records include minutes, membership lists, records of apprenticeship, accounts of relief paid to indigent colleagues with quest and search books recording investigations into workmanship. Guild monopolies were eroded as new associations of masters and men emerged during the Industrial Revolution. Important among these were trade unions, which originated among working men's burial clubs and friendly societies. Records are located with branch officials, at union headquarters or among archives collected at Warwick University.

Town and county **council minutes** summarised transactions and decisions concerning operations such as water supply, public land, public health, houses, roads, education and poor relief. The performance of officials was investigated:

> Donald McCarter Constable of the 2d District, was found on the public Road in a State of beastly intoxication ... and was carried to the Police Station House in Elgin, – Dismiss him from the office of Constable
>
> (Elginshire commissioners of supply, 1840)

Individuals and families **petitioned** the authorities, usually in the hope of some practical or financial assistance:

> Isobell Gaull Daughter of the deceased James Gaull Sometime Wheelwright in Elgin, & now Spouse to Robert McAndrew late Glover in Elgin & one of the Out Chelsea pensioners, presently in ... the Island of Jersey ... humble application ... for ... a Small pittance ... towards Enabling me for Setting out for, & arriveing at the Said Island of Jersey
>
> (Elgin town council, 1756)

Group petitions included individual names, addresses, occupations, perhaps also signatures, allegedly genuine. In 1838, Elgin's prosperous citizens signed a paper seeking the suppression of a popular entertainment, offensive to their sensitivities:

> That James Cormie Dog trainer ... collected crowds of idle and disorderly persons to witness dog worrying, badger baiting and other cruel sports ... keeps quantities of the flesh of Old Horses and refuse from the Shambles for food to his dogs

Communal fears about public health from this era focused on overcrowded burial grounds, with corpses surfacing, tombs decaying and offensive exhalations of mephitic gas. Council and church authorities closed, developed or manicured sites, usually without recording monumental inscriptions or sorting ancestral bones.

Borough **courts** heard civil and criminal cases, but magistrates also copied into their court books bylaws, charters, rolls of freeholders, burgess acts, arbitrations and financial accounts. The court of Old Aberdeen wrote out the names of inhabitants on 11th May 1636:

Thomas Elmslie, wricht, and his dochter onlie

Thomas Robertsone, webster, his wyff, four bairns, Alexander Senzeour and William Ailes, servantes

Peter Barnet, his wyff and thrie uther strang women

James Innes, his wyff, his mother, ane bairne, Patrick Davidsone, Andro Bartlet, Williame Gordoune, Issobell Gibsone and Christiane Pattone, servants Elspet Gray, puddinwricht [maker of puddings], tuo bairnes, the one of them ane ydle sone in William Hayes land

A borough court book was a secure place to record private deeds, apprenticeship agreements and marriage contracts. At Winchester from 1303, council clerks accepted deeds for registration as a matter of course and perquisite. Registration applied in the newly drained and reclaimed lands of the Bedford Level in Lincolnshire from 1663. The three ridings of Yorkshire opened deeds registries between 1704 and 1735; Middlesex in 1708.

Disputes arose from the normal frictions of a crowded borough community as animals strayed across arable fields, boundary markers were interfered with, chimneys smoked, dunghills stank and neighbours cursed or cheated each other.

Courts protected consumers by enforcing weights, measures and product quality.

> John Moir & Alexr Hay & others Butchers in Cullen Did … buy a Lepper swyn or sow which they had the impudence to bring to the publick Markatt … As also … did sometyme aGoe buy … a Cow that Dyed of some ill desease And … salted the same … by which the lifes & health of people are In danger … The Balzies fyns … Fyftie merks And ordains them Remain in prisone for twentie four years.

Researchers may decide that this prison term handed down in 1725 was a clerical error, possibly for 'months' or even 'hours'.

Mercantile disputes were decided. Debtors were imprisoned and their goods auctioned off. Criminal cases including burglary, street robbery, assault, riot, arson and witchcraft were heard, creating voluminous records of ancestors in the roles of criminal, victim, witness, accomplice and court official. Punishments included fines, confiscation, banishment, flogging, branding, mutilation and hanging:

> Patrick Cantley … chapman … in Elgine … wes upon … the mercat even of Saint James Fair … at night challenged be George Gordon … and Hellen Ogilvie his spous for the stealling frae them of Tuo pair of pleads, tuo pair of Linnen sheits, Tuo coads and ane Chamber pott … and being Searched and Dankered … taken reid hand with the Fang … wes found guiltie … Ordained to be Immediatly taken to the pillar in the fish mercat … and ther his louge [ear] to be nailed to the Trone [public weighing machine] by the hand of the hangman … goods and gear to be escheat … worth nyne or ten thousand merks for the use of the common good
>
> (Elgin town council, 1698)

In this case the thief was no ordinary criminal. Patrick Cantley, though described as a chapman – a term usually applied to a pedlar carrying his wares in a pack on his back – possessed goods worth nine thousand merks. The merk was worth 13s 4d so the value confiscated in 1698 was £6000 Scots, approaching half a million pounds in modern money. Descendants naturally wonder why a millionaire merchant should need to steal clothes and chamberpots. Perhaps he was a large-scale receiver of stolen goods. Perhaps Elgin merchants conspired to ruin a competitor. In other cases a punishment was selected to fit the crime rather than the criminal, as in Cullen in 1722:

> Jean simpson … acknowledged the stealing of the plate … from Helen Ord … & the stockins out of John Ords shop And the Chamberpott … on new years day … take her out of prison & put her on the Cockstool … for ane hour … and Banished out of the town

Councils owned extensive tracts of land with associated buildings. **Property** was granted by charter or acquired through benefactor's gift and outright purchase. Title deeds to council property connect families with houses and land. A council's rent roll identifies tenants of land, fisheries, quarries and houses. This documentation also identifies tenants of council housing erected under acts of Parliament from 1919 onwards and agricultural workers enjoying subsidised dwellings from 1926.

A Rentrole of Carnarvon Town Lands for the yeare 1699

	£	s	d
Mr William Owen for a house without the Gates	00	08	00
John Jones for an Arch under the Bridg	00	01	00
Mr. Williams of Pentir for a Shop near the Pillory	00	05	06
Hugh ap William Davyd for a Garden	00	00	04

REGISTER of PERSONS Entitled to VOTE in the ELECTION of a MEMBER of PARLIAMENT for the COUNTY of ELGIN, 1909-1910.

Parish of Kinloss (Part of).—Part of County Council Division 'Kinloss.' No. 17. Ward No. 1.

No.	Christian Name and Surname of each Voter at full length.	Place of Abode.	Occupation.	Nature of Qualification.	Street, Lane, or other Place where the Subject is situate.
3306	Anderson, David	Kinloss	Surfaceman	Tenant and occupant of dwelling house	Kinloss
3307	Bruce, Charles Minto	Langeot	Farmer	Tenant and occupant of farm	Kinloss
3308	Brown, William Dalgarno	Langeot	Overseer	Inhabitant occupier of dwelling house	Kinloss
3309	Butler, Patrick	Milton of Grange	Farmer	Tenant and occupant of farm	Kinloss
3310	Cameron, Alexander	Kinloss Station	Retired crofter	Inhabitant occupier of dwelling house	Kinloss
3311	Cameron, Kenneth	California	Grieve	Inhabitant occupier of dwelling house	Kinloss
3312	Clark, Donald	Langeot	Grieve	Inhabitant occupier of dwelling house	Kinloss
3313	Clark, James	Seapark	Groom	Inhabitant occupier of dwelling house	Kinloss
3314	Coutts, David	Grangehall	Gardener	Inhabitant occupier of dwelling house	Kinloss
3315	Davidson, John	Newton of Struthers	Pensioner	Inhabitant occupier of dwelling house	Kinloss
3316	Davidson, John A.	Mill of Grange	Farmer	Tenant and occupant of farm	Kinloss
3317	Donaldson, Alexander at Grange	Whiteinch	Farm servant	Inhabitant occupier of dwelling house	Kinloss
3318	Douglas, Robert	Grangehall	Shepherd	Inhabitant occupier of dwelling house	Kinloss
3319	Duncan, John	Grangehall	Gamekeeper	Inhabitant occupier of dwelling house	Kinloss
3320	Forbes, Robert	Woodhead	Farmer	Inhabitant occupier of dwelling house	Kinloss
3321	Forsyth, George	Grangehall	Coachman	Inhabitant occupier of dwelling house	Kinloss
3322	Fyfe, George	Kinloss Station	Station agent	Inhabitant occupier of dwelling house	Kinloss
3323	Garrow, John	Findhorn	Residenter	Tenant and occupant of shootings and grazings	Links, Kinloss
3324	Grant, Alexander C.	East Grange	Ploughman	Inhabitant occupier of dwelling house	Kinloss
3325	Grant, John	Kinloss	Gamekeeper	Inhabitant occupier of dwelling house	Kinloss
3326	Grant, Peter		Farmer	Tenant and occupant of farm	Kinloss
3327	Kelly, James	Seapark	Farmer	Inhabitant occupier of dwelling house	Kinloss
3328		Dune Park	Gentleman	Proprietor and occupier of farm	Kinloss
3329	Matheson, Alexander	Easter Langeot	Farmer	Tenant and occupant of farm	Kinloss
3330	Milne, James	East Grange	Surfaceman	Inhabitant occupier of dwelling house	Kinloss
3331	Morrison, Adam	Kinloss	Carpenter	Inhabitant occupier of dwelling house	Kinloss
3332	Morrison, William	Kinloss	Cattleman	Inhabitant occupier of dwelling house	Kinloss
3333	Munro, Hugh	East Grange	Ploughman	Inhabitant occupier of dwelling house	Kinloss
3334	Munro, James	Broombank, Kinloss Bridge	Salmon fisher	Proprietor and occupier of dwelling house	Kinloss
3335	Murdoch, David	East Grange	Surfaceman	Inhabitant occupier of dwelling house	Kinloss
3336	M'Andie, John	Damhead	Salmon fisher	Tenant and occupant of dwelling house	Kinloss
3337	M'Arthur, Alexander	Kinloss	Grieve	Inhabitant occupier of dwelling house	Kinloss
3338	Maclean, Duncan	Kinloss	Shepherd	Inhabitant occupier of dwelling house	Kinloss
3339	M'Combie, William	Kinloss	Gardener	Inhabitant occupier of dwelling house	Kinloss
3340	M'Culloch, James	Kinloss	Ploughman	Inhabitant occupier of dwelling house	Kinloss
3341	M'Donald, William	Kinloss	Shepherd	Tenant and occupant of dwelling house	Kinloss
3342	MacEcheron, Rev. John	Kinloss	Minister	Proprietor and occupier of manse	Kinloss
3343	M'Iver, William	Grangehall	Watcher	Inhabitant occupier of dwelling house	Kinloss
3344	Mackay, Matthew	The Glebe	Sexton	Inhabitant occupier of dwelling house	Kinloss
3345	Mackenzie, Donald	Woodside	Grieve	Inhabitant occupier of dwelling house	Kinloss
3346	Mackenzie, John	East Grange	Ploughman	Inhabitant occupier of dwelling house	Kinloss
3347	Mackersack, John	Kinloss	Landed proprietor	Proprietor and occupier of lands of	Kinloss, Kinloss
3348	Mackersack, Robert Hardy	Newton of Struthers	Farmer	Proprietor and occupier of farm	Kinloss
3349	Mackintosh, James	Dunepark	Ploughman	Inhabitant occupier of dwelling house	Kinloss
3350	M'Leod, Donald	East Grange	Ploughman	Inhabitant occupier of dwelling house	Kinloss
3351	M'Millan, William	North and South Damhead	Ploughman	Inhabitant occupier of dwelling house	Kinloss
3352	M'Rae, Alexander	Hatton	Cattleman	Inhabitant occupier of dwelling house	Kinloss
3353	M'Rae, Thomas	North and South Damhead	Ploughman	Inhabitant occupier of dwelling house	Kinloss
3354	M'William, Charles	East Grange	Ploughman	Inhabitant occupier of dwelling house	Kinloss
3355	Nicol, George	East Grange	Grieve	Inhabitant occupier of dwelling house	Kinloss
3356	Paterson, James	Kinloss	Gentleman	Inhabitant occupier of dwelling house	Kinloss
3357	... James Grant	Grangehall		Proprietor of estate of	Grangehall, Kinloss
3358	Reid, James	East Grange	Ploughman	Inhabitant occupier of dwelling house	Kinloss
3359	Rhind, Alexander	North and South Damheads	Farmer	Tenant and occupant of farm	Kinloss
3360	Rhind, Alexander	Muirton	Farmer	Tenant and occupant of farm	Kinloss
3361	Robertson, George	Grangehall	Grieve	Inhabitant occupier of dwelling house	Kinloss
3362	Ross, Peter	Arduseline Cottage	Gatekeeper	Inhabitant occupier of dwelling house	Kinloss
3363	Ross, Hugh	Kinloss Station	Grieve	Inhabitant occupier of dwelling house	Kinloss
3364	Russell, William	Milton of Grange and Westwoods	Grieve	Inhabitant occupier of dwelling house	Kinloss
3365	Sellar, Colin Reid	Findhorn	Lessee of salmon fishings	Joint tenant and occupant of fishings	Findhorn
3366	Sellar, James	Findhorn	Lessee of salmon fishings	Joint tenant and occupant of fishings	Findhorn
3367	Sellar, John, sen.	Findhorn	Lessee of salmon fishings	Joint tenant and occupant of fishings	Findhorn
3368	Sellar, John, jun.	Findhorn	Lessee of salmon fishings	Joint tenant and occupant of fishings	Findhorn
3369	Sellar, John Cordiner	Findhorn	Lessee of salmon fishings	Joint tenant and occupant of fishings	Findhorn
3370	Sim, James	Kinloss	Ploughman	Inhabitant occupier of dwelling house	Kinloss
3371	Simpson, John	Muirton	Farm servant	Inhabitant occupier of dwelling house	Kinloss
3372	Simpson, Robert	Kinloss	Ploughman	Inhabitant occupier of dwelling house	Kinloss
3373	Simpson, William	Kinloss	Labourer	Inhabitant occupier of dwelling house	Kinloss
3374	Smith, Alexander, sen.	Kinloss	Late blacksmith	Tenant and occupant of dwelling house	Kinloss
3375	Smith, Alexander, jun.	Kinloss	Blacksmith	Inhabitant occupier of dwelling house	Kinloss
3376	Smith, William	Culterns	Farmer	Proprietor and occupier of farm and lands	Kinloss

Electoral roll marked by a Conservative party worker to indicate the political allegiance of each voter.

Building works in towns were officially regulated. In Scotland, the dean of the guild presided over a burgh court deciding neighbourhood disputes involving common gables, overhanging eaves, encroachments, nuisances and ultimately all building works. In industrial towns such as Glasgow, commissioners were appointed to regulate paving, sanitation, lighting and water supply. Archives relate to nuisances and to amenities requested or lacked by forebears from the 1830s onwards. Plans show houses inspected, erected or altered as well as commercial and industrial premises. Planning records supplement these architectural collections from 1944 onwards.

Registers of adult males qualified or chosen to serve in the militia were compiled by commissioners of supply, sheriffs, lords lieutenant, magistrates and other county or borough authorities from the sixteenth century. Councils registered highways, pharmacies, explosives, slum clearance, war comforts, caravan sites, dairies, shops and quarry employees under silicosis and asbestosis schemes. Councils also preserved election papers and electoral registers following the Reform Act of 1832. Clerks served as collectors of national assessed taxes on shops, windows, coats of arms, servants, horses, dogs and carriages. From 1904, vehicle registration files preserved detailed biographies of motor-cars, motorcycles (as much a part of some families as a child or spouse), as well as lorries, tractors and buses (essential to the family business), naming owners who are further documented in registers of drivers' licences and related correspondence. Registers recording the sale of plots

No.	Description of Subject		Proprietor, including Lessees of Lands and Heritages of more than Twenty-one, and of Minerals of more than Thirty-one Years.	Tenant and Occupier.
3176	House and Shop, 15,	Findhorn	John Mackay, senior, merchant, Findhorn	Rents under £4
3177	Do 134,	do	David Mackenzie, senior, thatcher	Said David Mackenzie
3178	Do 203,	do	Alexander Macphail, gamekeeper, Wester Moy, Forres	Rents under £4
3179	Do 193,	do	Widow Catherine Macphail, Findhorn	Said Widow Macphail
3180	Do 142,	do	Widow Alexander Main	do Widow Main
3181	Do 143,	do	James Main, tailor, Pierse Close, Forres	Rents under £4
3182	Do 174,	do	John Main (Nochall)	Said John Main
3183	Do 157,	do	John Main (Mauch)	do John Main
3184	Do 244,	do	William Main, sailor (Whirr)	do William Main
3185	Do 79,	do	Alexander Masson (Stous), fisherman	do Alexander Masson
3186	Do 118,	do	Alexander Masson (Beetle), do	do Alexander Masson
3187	Do 64,	do	Alexander Masson (Linkie), do	do Alexander Masson
3158	Do 202,	do	Barbara Allan or Masson, Stormontfield, Perthshire	Rents under £4
3189	Do 239,	do	George Masson (Cleverly), fisherman	Said George Masson
3190	Do 146,	do	George Masson (Tay), do	do George Masson
3191	Do 81,	do	David Masson (Sailor), do	Rents under £4
3192	Do 50,	do	James Masson (Cann), do	Said James Masson
3193	Do 101,	do	James Masson (Tiny), do	do James Masson
3194	Do 175,	do	James Masson (Pim), do	do James Masson
3195	Do 185,	do	Widow James Masson (Money)	do Widow Masson
3196	Do 33,	do	James Masson (Bowrie), fisherman	do James Masson
3197	Do 54,	do	Widow James Masson (Pittainer)	do Widow Masson
3198	Do 160,	do	Widow James Masson (Pica)	do Widow Masson
3199	Do 162,	do	John Masson (Jacky), fisherman	do John Masson
3200	Do 162,	do	Heirs of John Masson (Plout), fisherman	do Heirs
3201	Do 189,	do	John Masson (Cocky), seaman	Rents under £4
3202	Do 119,	do	Widow John Masson (Red Joan)	Said Widow Masson
3203	Do 113,	do	John Masson (Bower), fisherman	do John Masson
3204	Do 240,	do	Nicholas Masson (Duncan), fisherman	do Nicholas Masson
3205	Do 104,	do	Widow T. Masson, merchant, Findhorn	do Widow Masson
3206	Do 166,	do	William Masson (Carl)	do William Masson
3207	Do 158,	do	Representatives of William Masson, per John Masson (Plout)	Empty and not finished
3208	Do	do	James Matheson, carrier	Said James Matheson
3209	Do near Old Toll-house,	do	William Matheson, crofter	do William Matheson
3210	Do and Shop,	do	Robert Milne, Esq., London, per Messrs R. & R. Urquhart, Forres	Miss M'Hendrie
3211	Inn,	do	do	Captain James Storm
3212	House and Shop,	do	do	Mrs James D. Mackay
3213	Do	do	do	Mrs George Wood, innkeeper
3214	Do &c.,	do	do	Rents under £4

County property valuation recording officially the tee names of numerous individuals sharing the surname Masson, 1877.

and burials in the municipal cemetery may provide information not recorded on death certificates. Registers of adoptions maintained under the Children Act are a key source for tracing lost forebears, offering names and biographical details of children and natural or adoptive parents. Reasons for the adoption may be given, together with details of payments and occasional poignant pleas such as this from a Glasgow woman in 1920: 'Would kind lady adopt little girl 3 years bright & intelligent'. The burgh of Aberdeen registered apprenticeship indentures:

> Alexander Thomsoune, brother german to William Thomsoune, couper, [apprenticed to] the said William, 4 years and 1 year from Whitsunday 1648 Johne Fiddes sone to vmqll. [the late] Thomas Fiddes, induellar in Aberdene [apprenticed to] George Moresoune, tailyour, 7 years and 1 year from Lambes 1649 James Naughtie, laxfisher [salmon fisher], indwellar in Aberdene [apprenticed to] Andro Young, couper, 7 years and 1 year, from Whitsunday 1650

Financial records include cash books, ledgers, annual abstracts and digital records. These concern public buildings, services and servants including town clerk, treasurer, beadle, drummer, schoolmaster, scavenger and hangman. Voucher bundles comprising bills, invoices and receipts preserve the names of workmen engaged on council projects such as repairing the town gaol, maintaining the public clocks, erecting a house or school building. Also mentioned are the merchants who supplied materials such as a rope for the hangman, faggots to burn a witch, coal to warm the schoolhouse and drink to sustain the councillors. Account books and voucher bundles supply snippets of personal information that assemble eventually into biography: 'Give the bearer George Livie seaman in whythills two shillings sterling being ane object of Charety his wife having Brought furth three children at on Birth' (Cullen, 1726). The following example concerns engineering contractors, including a wright, receiving cash, food and probably drink too, while the work was in progress. We also glimpse the town treasurer, Thomas Hay, balancing the town's accounts in the upper room of his own home.

> 'The Compt of ye commond guid of the burgh of Elgin Maid In Thomas Hayis owerchalmer' Exoneratio
> Item of tua marks giffin to James Baxter wryght for bigging of ye bellhous … Item of twentie schillingis for tua dayis mait gevin to adam gordoun and his man ye tyme of ye vpputting of ye townis New Bell
>
> (10th January 1592/3)

Revenue was raised through a tax, calculated as a rate of so much in the pound on the value of property, and thus often referred to as rates. Property was listed with notional values and names of owners and occupiers in documents known as valuation, assessment, cess, extent or stent rolls. These may survive from the sixteenth century onwards. An act of 1744 opened rate books to public inspection, incidentally encouraging officials to make provision for their preservation. Scottish valuation was modernised in 1855. Irish valuation was undertaken by Sir Richard Griffith, commissioner of valuation from 1827 to 1868. Field, house and record of tenure books in the National Archives, Dublin, preserve Griffith's descriptions of family homes, for instance, Alexander Wilson's 'neat little cottage well furnished' with its small garden rented by the year for £5 'though worth seven guineas' in the townland of Corporation, Killybegs, County Donegal, in 1839. Valuations are used to trace, year by year, the houses and other properties a family owned or occupied.

Council **correspondence,** surviving in neat indexed letter books, single-subject files and intriguing bundles tied with string, ranges over the gamut of public interest, noting individual and family involvement in abattoirs, building, education, evacuation, farming, fishing, housing, military tribunals, nursing, poor relief, schools, slums, squatting and venereal disease. An ancestor's letters to government are more likely to be preserved if out of the ordinary: a refusal to accept evacuees; a complaint about an obscene book in the public library; a description of slum property improved by an absentee landlord; a compliment on the efficiency of officials. Council departments (education, housing, social work, finance, legal) held files for terms of years before making a selection for permanent preservation.

Reports on people and places were compiled by officials, as here by Sergeant James Douglas of the new police force of Elgin in 1840:

> James Douglas. & Donal Cameron Both Common Vagrents travling in the Countrey with littel Excus … I took them, Into Custatey Last Night for feighting in ther Lodgings and Loked them up … brought them Before Balies Wilson and Walker
>
> (Elgin town council, 1840)

Reports by the borough surveyor, roads surveyor and county librarian prove genealogically valuable as they refer to individuals, their homes and connections with the council as consumers or suppliers of services. Overcrowded, insanitary or dilapidated housing was of particular concern. Owners and occupiers were visited and recommendations made in respect of compulsory purchase, demolition, rehousing or renovation.

Nineteenth-century social reform revolutionised secular provision for support of the old, infirm, disabled, unemployed, feckless and idle **poor**. Minute books record decisions reached at meetings of the board. The inspector's pocket book records visits to paupers' homes:

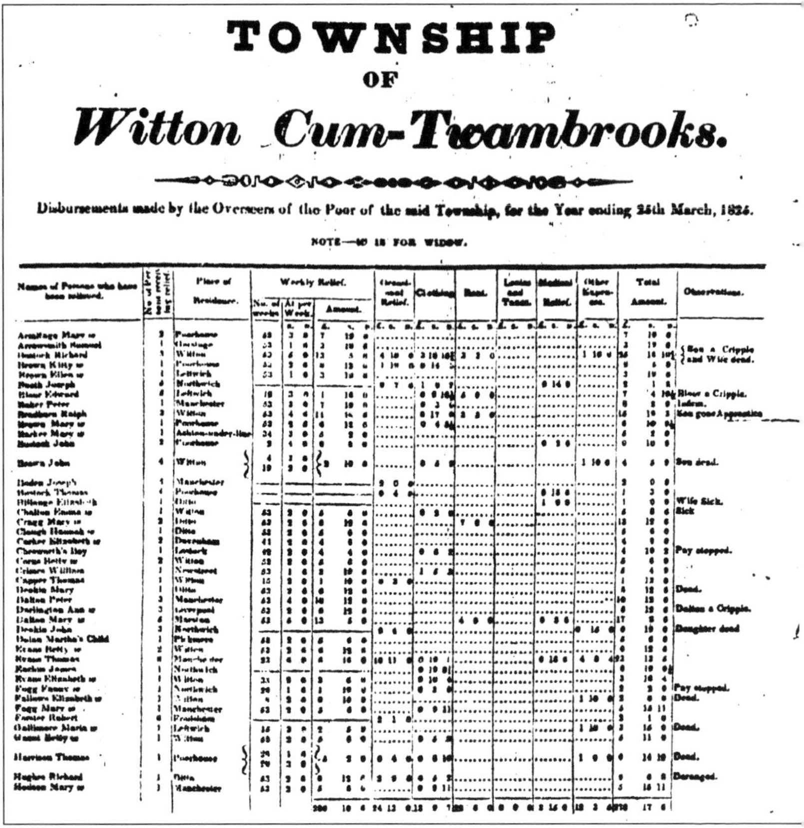

TOWNSHIP

OF

Witton Cum-Twambrooks.

Disbursements made by the Overseers of the Poor of the said Township, for the Year ending 25th March, 1825.

NOTE.—w IS FOR WIDOW.

Names of Persons who have been relieved.	No. of Persons receiving relief.	Place of Residence.	Weekly Relief. No. of weeks	At per Week.	Amount.	Occasional Relief.	Clothing.	Rent.	Leases and Taxes.	Medical Relief.	Other Expenses.	Total Amount.	Observations.

Payments to the poor in a Cheshire parish, 1824–5.

> Margaret Giels or Gatherer … Ramsburn, Rothiemay Age 43 years … 1870 This Pauper has … been burdened with the support of her son Adam who has two of his fingers amputated in consequence of an injury by Machinery. Her son George is dead, and she gets no assistance from either of her other sons who are most notorious Poachers. Isabella has had 2 illegitimate children. All the daughters dress gaudily, but give little help to their Mother … 1881 Re-admitted, and allowed 2/6 a week … 1892 Been very Poorly. ordered dr. to get some Beef & Cordial … 1893 allowance increased 6d per week … 1896 Died

Formal registers of poor are trenchantly informative. These examples are from Keith in Banffshire:

> Jane Symon or Smith: Son John a useless fellow, and just got married to a woman about as useless, and stupid as himself … Daughter … [has] about a dozen Bairns … and but a Small Croft

> Alexander Johnston: has acquired an inveterate taste for Paragoric or some other horrid opium stuff which … leaves a smell in the Parochial Board office for hours after he has left

Rates also supported the poor receiving indoor relief, that is inside the workhouse. Records normally offer biographical information on each inmate and details of diet, illnesses, childbirth and death. An example from the punishment book of the Elginshire union's poor house in 1899 shows how breaches of workhouse rules were dealt with:

> Elspeth Gow 30: Using obscene language. Ill treating her child. Bringing in whisky and refusing to work when the bottle was taken from her. Also with threatening to stab a servant. Punishment: porridge milk stopped for two days

From 1909 onwards, old age pensions committees were established to administer payments to people aged seventy or above. Surviving documentation includes minutes, letter books, registers and accounts. Claimants born before civil registration might experience some difficulty in proving their ages:

> Mrs. Ann Falconer, 10, Milne's Wynd, no evidence of age was produced … the Claim could not properly be allowed, but a note was produced – which the Claimant had handed to Bailie Stewart – shewing that the Claimant was … over seventy years of age and allowed her 5/- per week
>
> (Forres pensions tribunal, 1912)

In Ireland, memories of the 'Big Wind', a gale that ravaged the northern and western counties on 6th January 1839, were accepted as evidence that an individual was over 70.

Boys and girls were bound **apprentice** by the council for a term of years to learn a trade such as printer, shoemaker, smith or mechanic. A formal agreement was written out twice on a single page. The copies were then separated with an indented cut and retained by the master and the parent of the child. A third copy might be

'The Riding of the Marches on 1st October 1840' by Charles Cranmer (1780–1841). The painting, gifted to the burgh of Forres in Moray, offers careful portraits of the town councillors, officials and townsfolk involved in this ceremonial perambulation of boundaries. In reality, though, few owned horses as magnificent as the prancing thoroughbreds upon which they were mounted by the artist.

lodged for security with the authorities, especially in the case of pauper children. Many of these unfortunates, regarded as a burden on poor rates, if not disposed of as farm labourers or domestic servants, might be apprenticed to master sweeps, farmers or mill owners as cheap labour, with little hope of learning a useful trade. Apprenticeship indentures contain details of the child, the master and financial arrangements.

Parish **schools** were established from the seventeenth century. The activities of public boards of education under an act of Parliament of 1870 (1872 for Scotland) are recorded in minutes, accounts, reports and correspondence. Each school maintained its own registers of admissions and withdrawals. These show in standard format a pupil's name, age, parentage, date of admission, previous schools and date of leaving. The reason for leaving may also be given in short form: 'Dead ... gone to Canada ... took work'. There are confidential files on individual pupils and log books documenting significant events. The head teacher of Drainie School commented in 1883 on a pupil who later became prime minister: 'J (Ramsay) Macdonald has passed well, but should attend to History'. On the whole, though, log books are more revealing of staff than pupils:

9 Feb 1899   Miss Woosnam has been away from school, since Thursday last
                 ... through sickness
13   Miss Woosnam is still unable to attend school
20   Miss Woosnam is still away
27   Miss Woosnam returned to school to-day.
(St Luke's Church of England public elementary national schools, Mersey Park, Old Chester Road, Lower Tranmere)

Miss Woosnam married on 30th April 1899.

School board archives may also include minutes of governors' meetings, applications for financial assistance, punishment registers, testimonials for teachers, correspondence with parents and records of fees.

Town and county government finances depended upon the prosperity of small businessmen, their staff, suppliers and customers.

15
Property and business

Estate muniments are documents concerning the administration of landed property. A landowner might be defined as the possessor of at least 1 acre (0.41 ha), a standard employed in the parliamentary command paper recording the name and address of every owner of 1 acre and upwards in Britain, 1872–3, known as the New Domesday (1874: C.899, 1097). Extensive estates are administered by the state, the Crown, the Church, aristocracy, gentry, the National Trust, industrialists, charities, universities and financial institutions. Documentation may remain in the possession of the present, or sometimes a previous, owner of the estate: stored in an opulent muniment room or in an agent's dusty attic, at the aristocrat's mansion, estate office, lawyer's archives or public record office. Obviously the smallest properties created and preserved little in the way of archives. The National Register of Archives may know the present location of collections. Estate muniments connect people with places, guiding the genealogist to landscapes an ancestor knew, owned and cultivated; to fields ploughed by him or her and hedgerows planted; to houses inhabited and factories worked in.

A **manor**, or barony in Scotland and Ireland, was an estate held in fee (feu), conditional, that is, on performance of some military, religious or financial service for a superior who in turn owed fealty to his lord, and so on upwards through the hierarchy to the monarch. Feudal land law insisted that every piece of ground belonged to someone. No individual could be a lord without holding land in fee. The practice of intermediate or mesne lordship (subinfeudation) sends the genealogist to study the archives of the particular manor as well as of the superior lords. A manor might consist of a compact estate with a single village or scattered holdings in several counties. The lord or his agent resided in a manor house. The home farm (demesne) could be a discrete block of fields or a series of scattered strips and enclosures intermingled with tenant holdings. Wealthy landowners moved from manor to manor to consume the contents of barn and cask, leaving complex genealogical trails for family historians to follow.

The manor was a principal administrative unit in England and Wales until the seventeenth century (in Scotland until the eighteenth), though customary and copyhold tenures were not legally abolished until 1925. The lord or lady of the manor governed through a manorial court where petty functionaries such as

Manor court roll of Alciston, Sussex, 1288.

hayward, aletaster, reeve (administrator) and beadle (court officer) were appointed. Disputes were decided and community life regulated by the lord's steward, who preserved a record of proceedings on parchment rolls:

> Katherine daughter of John Kentyng also known as Candelman formerly wife to John Corte of Stalham, widow, is a serf of the lady of the manor by blood … who owes the lady for permission to reside outwith the manor, 6 pennies
> (Norfolk Record Office, Ms 6020, 16 B 5, Antingham, 17th September 1438)

The peasant relinquished land only to the manor court. A successor or purchaser gained entry on payment of a fine, as recorded in the manor court roll, in documents known as surrenders and admittances. These were written out and used as title deeds to land known as copyhold, held by copy of the court roll. Considerable acreage reverted to the manor following the Black Death of the 1340s:

> Those tenements remain in the hands of the lord … tenements which belonged to Simon Meleward that is to say, one messuage and half a wista of land in Blachyngton … because no one fulfilled the duty of attending the manor court following the tenants' deaths
> (East Sussex Record Office, SAS G18/6b, Alciston, 13th June 1349)

On the death of a manorial tenant, the lord was compensated for allowing an heir to inherit. This might be paid in kind, as a prime beast or item of furnishing, or in cash. The payment was known as a heriot, literally 'trappings to support an armed force', underlining the military basis of feudal landholding and society. The manor court maintained the peace, punishing offenders with flogging, stocking, mutilation, fines, ducking, branding and hanging. The lord sat as coroner to hear evidence in cases of unnatural death:

> It happened through mischance … that a certain William Miles went to a certain place called the Lynkes next to the hospital of St James of Sefford. He there dug in a certain hole and, in digging, was suddenly crushed by earth falling upon him so that he died.
> (East Sussex Record Office, SAS G18/3, Alciston, 11th November 1288)

A landowner permitted a tenant to occupy a portion of an estate under conditions specified in a **lease** (tack in Scotland). Leases were granted for a term of years or during the lifetimes of specified individuals. Oral agreements, permitted under Scots law until 1449 and English until 1677, in practice remained common for much longer. This and the illiteracy of peasants eased the landowner's task when peremptory eviction was called for. The operative words in an English lease were 'demise, grant and to farm let'. A *habendum* clause defined the term of the lease, a *reddendum* rents and services, and a *consideration* the one-off payment due on inception. The 99-year lease was popular as a means of effecting improvements to property at the expense of the lessee. The lessor's descendants eventually recovered the property, together with any buildings erected. In Lyme Regis, Dorset, a merchant named Solomon Andrew granted in 1680 a 99-year lease to William Trew, who, as a hellyer or tiler, was in the building trade and probably also what we might today call a property developer. The lease incidentally noticed neighbours, in this case John Okenshott, also redeveloping property, and one Francis Swetland. The lease belongs to the muniments of the Baker-Wilbrahams of Odd Rode. Leases granted for the lives of specified individuals usually referred to two or three generations of the same family. On 7th September 1704, Richard Arderne of Harden granted a lease to Peter Woodward of Alvanley, Cheshire, husbandman, for the lives of Woodward, his wife and the infant son of Thomas Woodward of Manley, yeoman.

Small Farm
TO BE LET,
IN THE IMMEDIATE NEIGHBOURHOOD OF FORRES.

THE FARM OF CLOVENSIDE, as for many years occupied by Mr Alexander Lillie, the late Proprietor, measuring nine Acres imperial, or thereby, is now to be Let, with immediate entry. There is a comfortable Dwelling House, and suitable Offices.

The Conditions will be seen, and all necessary information obtained, on application to R. & A. Urquhart, Writers, with whom written Offers may be lodged till the 14th October next.

Forres, 21st September, 1849.

Printed at the Gazette Office, Forres.

A small family farm to let, 1849.

Annual rents and services comprised two shillings per annum and one fat hen at Christmas. Leases might be employed as security for money loans. Here the demise specified a long term of 500 years or more, cancelled on repayment of principal and interest. A mortgage may evidence family penury, or alternatively an era of estate expansion with money raised to finance agricultural or industrial development. Mortgage documents relating to a family home may include descriptions and plans of internal fixtures and fittings.

Financial accounts with names of contractors may be preserved from the fourteenth century onwards for expenditure on estate buildings. Personal and household accounts are a prime source for references to tradesmen and craftsmen whose own papers are lost. A rental lists tenants and their holdings:

A Rentroll of the late estate of Sir William Williams of Vaynol ... 1696
William Morris ap William Thomas & William ap Humphrey for Eu: Mawr presents 6s rents £28
Richard ap Humphrey for Stinking Poole presents – rents 10s
William Thomas ap William Lewis for Kefn: y: Lann presents 6s 6d rents £8 18s 4d
(Caernarfonshire Record Office)

A **survey** was a word-picture of a property, particularly popular from about 1540 to 1780. An ancestor's home may be described:

One litle house adioyning the Churcheyard ... newly reedified consisteth ... a hall, a kitchen & a buttery roome upon the first storye & three lodginge roomes over them

upon the seconde storye & seller vaulted under the buttery
(Hatfield House Library, General 41/7, 1606)

A survey named the occupiers of lands in the open fields:

One close of pasture called Hobb Ridinges abutting north on the lands of John
Richardson, south on Barnton townfeild 5 Acres 2 Roods 10 perches One parcell of
arrable called Dichland in the Common field abutting northeast on Oxhay, being the
land of Mr. John Venables, John Varnon on the east side, Judge Warberton on the west
side 0 Acre 2 roods 32 perches
(Swynehead chartulary, demesnes in Barnton, Cheshire, 1620)

Estate **correspondence** related to land management. Family letters may be
mingled with business correspondence about crop yields, market prices, rent arrears
and suppliers of goods:

Acquaint Dykesides widow ... that she will pay up the last leessie [penny] of the
present Rent with the arrears ... which if she faills ... I'll not take it in good pairt but
that I'll effect it ane other way not so agreeable to her
(Stoneyforenoon estate, Moray, 22nd March 1729)

A defect in the title to Drumduan Estate, Moray, in 1846 resulted in genealogical
investigation, preserved in a letter from estate lawyer Thomas Davidson to the laird:

First – that Major Fraser of Castle Leather near Inverness was the common ancestor
of Col Fraser Drumduan and of you
Second – That Castle Leathers had besides several daughters. two sons. the eldest of
whom Robert ... came to reside at Kinnudie, and afterwards at Inshoch Castle ... the
eldest son of Robert was Captain James Fraser of Kincorth, and that you are now the
eldest son in life of Captain James ...
Third – That the second son of Castle Leathers was Captain James Fraser sometime
of Mavisbank ... who had four sons the youngest of whom was Col Simon Fraser of
Drumduan ... it would appear that Drumduan's father was the brother of your
Grandfather but which of them was the elder ... has not been ascertained

Occasionally an estate worker's journal has survived. Richard Yarnold in the
kitchen garden at Knowsley recorded temperatures three times daily:

1820 April 14	Different sorts of seeds sown Viz Irish Golden beet. best red beet. Altringham carrot ... Florance Coss Lettuce, black spanish Lettuce ... London Leek Salsafy & Scorzonera 47:56:50 Very fine
June 14	The first peas gather'd the first mellon cut and the first grapes gather'd for the parlour. Mellon seed sown for the 5th crop 51:61:59 Fair
June 30	Ice got for the first time this season out of the new Ice house 54:60:59 Stormy

This document shows the family enjoyed vegetables such as salsify (oyster plant)
and scorzonera (viper's grass) which today might seem unusual and exotic. Recipe
books among family papers indicate how food was prepared and served.

Estate **maps** from the eighteenth century onwards delineate houses, fields, rentals
and names of proprietors, tenants and occupiers. Communities may be represented
on the eve of clearance and enclosure. When an estate was sold, perhaps as a result
of bankruptcy or failure of heirs, plans and wordy descriptions emphasised property
values, noting also the names of sitting tenants.

Title deeds to properties owned or occupied by ancestors may be sought with the present owners or their agents. Deeds are lengthy documents, but the genealogical gist is usually readily extracted: names of buyer and seller, their residences and occupations. A preamble in the form of a *whereas* clause recited previous owners and occupiers, while witnesses were possibly relatives by blood or marriage. A deed of 29th October 1530, relating to property adjacent to Trinity College, Edinburgh, refers to family relationships in the era before parish registers. The parties concerned in the transaction were all of one family, comprising William Achinson, son and heir of the late George Achinson and heir apparent to his mother Margaret Broune, who was presumably George's widow though this was not stated. In accepting the property, William promised his mother he would receive Thomas Achinson, his brother, from her and sustain him in meat, drink, clothes and other necessaries as was becoming, during the space of five years for the singular love and certain other favours often done by her to him. Charters were the usual means of conveyance from the eleventh century onwards, offering an uncomplicated fee simple and referring to sellers, buyers, witnessses and neighbouring landholders:

> one acre of land with appurtenances in Eskyr ploughgate in a field called Mayneskyr
> which acre lies in breadth between John Lang's land on the east extending in length

Plan of the coffee estate of Mousagalla, Ceylon, 1864; genealogists might trace descent from the owners, the managers or the coolies.

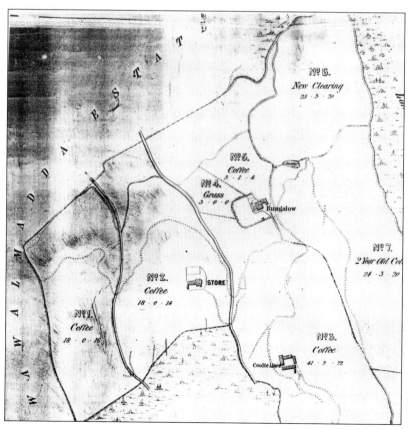

Mr. Palin. Tunnel Top.

Originals examined at Fletcher's.

Abstract of Indenture. 1881. between (i) John Eaton, of Cotton,
in the County of Chester, farmer, and Thomas Eaton of Sproston,
farmer. (ii) John Wood of Crewe, joiner. (iii) Mary Lea of Eaton
near Congleton, widdow, and Ann Wood of Holmes Chapel, spinster.
(iv) Algernon Fletcher of Northwich, gent. (v) said John Eaton,
Thomas Eaton, Samuel Eaton of Holmes Chapel, famer, Thomas
Bolshaw of Holmes Chapel, butcher, and Elizabeth, his wife.

Reciting. Thomas Cross, late of Holmes Chapel, farmer, being at
time of death seised of hereditaments and estate
of inheritance in fee simple in possession free from incumbs by
his will dated 2/2/1846.......bequethed all his real and personal
estate to his son John Cross and Thomas Eaton upon trust as to
one third part for his dau. Catherine, wife of said Thos Eaton
......and trust for his dau. Elizbeth Tomlinson, wife of Phillip
Wood.....remaining third upon trust for his son Thos Cross called
the Younger for his life, and afterwards to his wife.

And Reciting...said Thos Cross died 22/1/1847 leaving John Cross,
Thos Cross, Catherine, wife of Thos Eaton the Elder, and Eliz.
Tomlinson, his only children surviving......will proved at Chester
July 1847.

And Reciting....said Eliz. Tomlinson died 9/5/1848 leaving said
Phillip Wood, her husband and ⋈ John Wood, her son and heir at
law surviving.

And Reciting the said Thos Cross the Younger died without issue
in 1868 in New Zealand.

And reciting by indent 19/1/1871 John Wood did release and convey
all that part share entitled as heir of Eliz.Tomlinson Wood to
Thos Eaton in trust.

And Reciting.....Thos Eaton the Elder had dated 2/1/1871
devised all estate vested in him as trustee or mortgagee unto
said John Eaton and Thos Eaton. Thos Eaton the elder died 28/11/1871.
Will proved at Chester.

And Reciting...Phillip Wood died 6/10/1871.

And Reciting ...John Eaton and Thos Eaton were seised of the
moiety of hereditaments in Barnton and the moiety held as follows:
¼ vested in John Eaton in his own right, ¼ vested in Thos Eaton
in his own right, ¼ vested in Samuel Eaton, ¼ vested in Elizabeth,
wife of Thos Bolshaw.

And Reciting......sum of £245 agreed upon as value of moiety of
said hereditaments and agreed between parties 2,3,and 5 that
£245 be paid to John Wood, Mary Lea and Ann Wood (sisters of
John Wood) in equal shares by John, Thoa Eaton party thrto Saml1
Eaton and Eliz.Bolshaw as purchase money of said moiety.

All that moiety or ½ part share or other that part share of interest
vested in the said John Eaton and Thos Eaton party thrto by virtue
of the provns of the said recited indent of 19/1/1871 or expressed
and intended to be ofand in All those 3 mesauages situate near
Tunnel Top in Barnton now in resp occupation of Wm Allen, John
Jackson, John Siddall as tenants....all that field situate in
Barnton contg 3a 1r 36p stat.meas, now occupied by Wm Hayes as
tenant and all other estates if any in Barnton devised by will of
Thos Cross deed.

Below: *Title deeds to the family home include various types of document and copious
evidence for the genealogist. The large parchment beginning with the words 'Know all Men'
is the probate copy of a will preserved as evidence of title.*

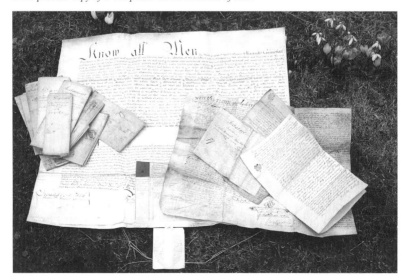

Advertising the family business, 1841.

from the said Thomas Alford's land on the south as far as John Peickeston's land at the north

(National Library of Ireland, Sarsfield Vesey Mss, D3330, deed 2, 10th April 1439)

Later deeds include the bargain and sale (one document) from 1536 to 1841 and the lease and release (two documents) from 1614 to 1841. Final concords and recoveries arose from court cases contrived to establish a title. Accumulated deeds were bundled up and catalogued in the useful document known as an abstract of title.

A **marriage settlement** protected the interests of individuals. An estate might be settled jointly on husband and wife, the wife retaining possession of the jointure even in widowhood, and as dowager exerting an influence for several generations.

137

FORRES & ELGIN CARRIER.

ROBERT MASSON begs to inform the Merchants, Tradesmen, and public generally of **FORRES** and **ELGIN**, that he has arranged with JOHN JAMES, long Carrier between the above mentioned towns, to fill his place in that capacity; and trusts that, by unremitting care and attention to Goods and Orders committed to his trust, and Uniform Low Charges, to merit a share of public favour.

Goods and Parcels to be taken in at his own house, CAROLINE STREET, Forres; and at Mr R. Gill's, Harrow Inn, DALMENY PLACE, Elgin.

Forres, 28th May, 1850.

PRINTED AT THE GAZETTE OFFICE, FORRES.

A family transport business, 1850.

An entail, restricting succession to an estate, perhaps by excluding specified individuals or preventing division of the property, may be symptomatic of significant relationships among family members. An entail might be broken by collusive action known as a common recovery from the fifteenth century onwards or by act of Parliament from 1512.

Business records

Records have usually been considered necessary for running a factory, shop, hotel, bank or market stall. Archives include minutes of meetings of shareholders and directors, financial ledgers, cash books, vouchers, correspondence, employee files, wages books, plans, title deeds, catalogues and product samples. Ancestors are noticed as owners, shareholders, employees, suppliers and customers. Business records may be held on company premises, or lodged with a lawyer, library or archive. The chemical giant ICI, in occupying Winnington Hall estate and school, acquired useful genealogical items such as Florrie White's commonplace book and a window pane scratched 'Mary Summers My Last Term Thank God'. Nearly 30,000 collections have been recorded by the National Register of Archives and there is access to information at <**http://www.hmc.gov.uk/business/busarchives.htm**>.

Names of **lawyers** who served as company secretaries and the present addresses of partnerships may be traced through law and commercial directories. Managers are protective about confidentiality, even after a century or more, but perseverance may be rewarded with access to an Aladdin's cave of family muniments, business archives and genealogical treasures. An example is provided by the provincial law firm of Davidson & Leask of Forres. There were 892 volumes of letter books and 293 of legal drafts relating to over one million documents in family boxes and bundles, including records of Thomas Davidson, a banker with connections in the Baltic; a leading hydropathic hotel; water, gas, railway, and shipping companies; toll

Metal deed boxes in a lawyer's strongroom contain family muniments comprising legal documents and all kinds of precious or sentimental collectanea.

A family butcher sets up in business, 1852.

NEW FLESHER.

GILLIES M'EDWARD,

RESPECTFULLY intimates to the Inhabitants of FORRES and surrounding country, that he has commenced business as a FLESHER in that Shop formerly occupied by Mr M'GRIGOR, east of Mr CHARLES MACDONALD'S Baker, where the

VERY BEST HILL MUTTON MAY BE HAD AT FOURPENCE-HALFPENNY PER LB.

G. M. earnestly solicits a trial, and as he has determined to slaughter only superior animals, and sell on the smallest profits, the public may rely upon being well and cheaply served, if encouragement be given.

HIGH STREET,
Forres, 10th September 1852.

PRINTED AT THE GAZETTE OFFICE, FORRES.

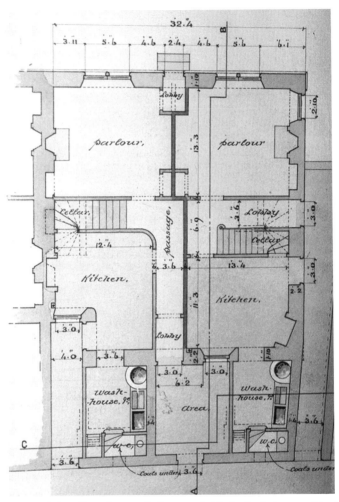

An architectural plan allows the genealogist to see inside the family home and to visualise dwellings now inaccessible, drastically altered or demolished.

bridge and turnpike road records; commercial nurseries, farms and salmon fisheries; property developers and house builders; a boot manufactory, a bobbin mill and a working men's union known as the Society of Wrights from 1789.

Fire insurance was a thriving business, operated from London, Bristol, Edinburgh and Glasgow by the 1720s. Each property insured was marked by a lead badge, known as a firemark, bearing a company logo and policy number. Registers preserved by fire companies identified clients and properties. Companies continuing in business may hold and make available to researchers information dating back three centuries. Many series are deposited in county archives. Guildhall Library, London, has indexed and made accessible on microfiche the archives of over eighty firms, including the Hand-in-Hand, established 1696, Royal Exchange of 1720 and Sun Fire from 1710 which specialised in provincial business, notably in East Anglia.

The **architectural** profession in its modern form emerged during the eighteenth century as master masons and house carpenters benefited from a building boom in an era of commercial prosperity. Architectural practices were founded as partnerships of two or three principals, whose successors may still be at work in the firm's original offices. Past and present architectural practices may be traced through professional directories, and it is usually possible to negotiate access and study plans of an ancestor's house, shop, farm or factory together with files of specifications and correspondence. Architects' papers may be deposited subject to rigorous weeding in libraries, county archives, the three Royal Commissions on Historical Monuments and the British Architectural Library of the Royal Institute of British Architects, 21 Portman Square, London W1.

Estate agents and auctioneers accumulated documentation in connection with the sale of family homes, businesses, stock-in-trade, furnishing and personal effects. Descriptions and valuations of property with plans and photographs indicate an ancestor's lifestyle.

Turnpike trusts, established by act of Parliament to build, repair and maintain roads and bridges, financed operations through tolls farmed out to contractors. An ancestor who served the trust will be generously documented in minutes and accounts. A keeper's cottage may still stand at the roadside. From the bay window the officer watched for traffic, collecting the toll before turning open a gate across the road.

The aged, sick, lunatic and orphans were cared for by private **charities**. Registers of inmates document an ancestor's diet, life and death, as here from the governor's book of General Anderson's Institution, Elgin:

> Mrs Donaldson died here this afternoon between 4 & 5 o'clock. She sunk under the gradual decay of nature ... Her death was sudden – she had just partaken very heartily

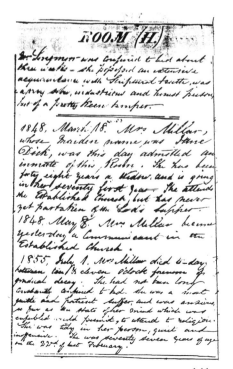

Mrs Longmoor and her 'keen temper' died in Room H at Anderson's Institution, Elgin, to be succeeded by the 'inoffensive' Mrs Millar, formerly Jane Dick. 1848.

of some soup … a few minutes afterwards, she was lying in the bed quite dead … In her youth she had addicted herself to guilty pleasures, and was a great sinner

(26th April 1853)

Education was organised through institutions for the most part independent of government. Universities, colleges, inns of court and public schools were, in many cases, founded to provide schooling free for promising poor boys and for a fee to those with money. Grammar schools catered for the sons of merchants, gentlemen and professional men. Orphans and poor boys might attend charity schools such as Christ's Hospital, founded in London in 1552. Schools for the lower classes proliferated during the nineteenth century, especially under the encouragement of the Society for Promoting Christian Knowledge, founded 1698, and the Anglican National Society of 1811. Registers of admissions, matriculations, scholars and graduates are normally preserved and may be edited for publication. Records in school and college libraries or lodged with lawyers and county archivists relate to the achievements and misdeeds of scholars and teachers.

the Committee of Management … are decidedly of the opinion that a *Female Teacher*

A pharmacist's prescription book gives a clue to an ancestor's ailments, 1852.

will not be able to maintain a sufficient degree of authority over boys ... to keep up that discipline which forms so distinguishing and essential a feature of the Lancasterian system ... therefore Resolve ... to place a *middle aged man* as Teacher ... *Mrs. Don's services, as Teacher, will be dispensed with*

(Elgin Education Society, 3rd February 1824)

A subsequent minute showed that the middle-aged man who replaced the unfortunate Mrs Don was, however, observed several times about town 'in a state of inebriety' and dismissed before he could begin work and infect the boys with his moral weakness.

Educational establishments registered the names, ages and parentage of scholars, with perhaps a telling character assessment. One word sufficed in Anderson's Institution, where boys and girls were variously categorised as 'trifling ... dull & dogged ... good scholar ... lazy ... sly'. One of the better scholars, James Thompson, twice absconded in 1854 after being flogged by the governor, Reverend John Eddie, a man 'of an exceptionally sensitive temperament'. Thompson's sufferings eventually emerged in a letter dated 1870:

> Nearly all the boys that were in the Institution in my time were stripped ... we could not well see the performance, except when the victim, creeping under the lash, moved too near ... the School door ... If we did not see we heard well, and more than that we have seen the marks of the strap black and blue on the skin of the victim ... Mr John Stalker, watchmaker, High Street, Dingwall on the 24th of October last:– 'I was stripped five, if not six times. It is a little severe but very wholesome'.

Medical records concerning individuals made by dispensaries, pharmacists, physicians and surgeons may be available from health board or county archives, possibly also from successors of the original practitioners. The adoption of particular archival rules and financial controls have affected the preservation of records. An ancestor's ailments can be inferred from a pharmacist's prescription, though medicines were generally multi-purpose and tending to alleviate symptoms rather than cure underlying causes. Nursing, medical intervention and subsequent procedures were closely costed in the past to ensure proper remuneration for doctors and others in attendance. The daily progress of an illness was narrated in medical casebooks, which occasionally survive in a doctor's family papers, usually discovered after clearance of a bank vault or lawyer's safe. An accumulation from around 1800 was found by Bristol and West Building Society staff in the wine cellars of an old building acquired for offices.

16
Parliament

Parliaments in England, Ireland and Scotland met irregularly during the Middle Ages, the members establishing various *ad hoc* arrangements for preserving records. From 1621, clerks of the English House of Lords maintained an archive of journals, petitions, bills and related documents at Westminster. Here records remained, suffering depredations from damp, vermin, neglectful keepers, weeding and, finally, the great fire that swept though the Palace of Westminster in 1834. Archives of the Lords and Commons eventually found a home in the House of Lords Record Office in the Victoria Tower at Westminster. The Scottish Parliament until the union of 1707 comprised the three estates of prelates, barons and burgesses, whose records are the responsibility of the National Archives in Edinburgh. Records of Irish Parliaments before the union of 1801 remain in the library of Dáil Éireann, the National Archives or the National Library, Dublin.

The activity most usually associated with Parliament is making laws (statutes) of the realm. These acts are dated by the year of the monarch's reign. **Public acts** concerning poor relief, hours of work, public health, military conscription and similar matters rarely mentioned individuals, but their impact on families could be enormous. An example is the Irish statute 25 Henry VI chapter IV of 1447, which bears the self-explanatory title 'An Act that he, that will be taken for an Englishman, shall not use a Beard upon his upper lip alone, the Offender shall be taken as an Irish Enemy'. Chapter III of 1465 required all Irishmen living in or near the anglicised territory around Dublin, known as the English Pale, to wear English clothes rather than native kilts and to trim their beards after the English fashion by 'shaving of his beard above the mouth'. The law further required that Gaelic surnames be

Record of Parliament held at Perth in 1369, listing members attending.

abandoned in favour of

> an English surname of one town, as Sutton, Chester, Trim, Skryne, Corke, Kinsale:
> or colour as white, blacke, browne: or arte or science, as smith or carpenter: or office,
> as cooke, butler, and that he and his issue shall use this name

Irishmen beyond the pale were deemed barbarous beyond redemption and so not worth the trouble of legislation. A subsequent act of 1495, 10 Henry VII chapter XX, sought to anglicise or emasculate family mottoes, replacing martial examples derived from war cries such as *Cromabo* and *Butlerabo* with loyal invocations of *St George* and *King Harry of England*. Though the Gaels of Scotland originally arrived from Ulster, their return as Protestant landowners during the sixteenth century was resented by the native Irish. The Catholic monarchs Philip and Mary thus in 1556 gave assent to an act of Parliament forbidding recruitment of Scots mercenaries and also marriage with 'eny Scottisshe man, woman, or mayden'. Scottish merchants and mariners were, however, to continue their traffic across the Irish Sea.

Public acts occasionally refer specifically to individuals, families and their estates. The Irish act of 25 Henry VIII chapter II restrained the landowner Nicholas Husse, Baron Galtrime, from enjoying the profits of the parsonage of Galtrime. This church, dedicated to the Blessed Virgin Mary, had been donated to the priory of Newton beside Trim during Edward IV's reign. Husse naturally thought his own family's historic claims were paramount. The government of Henry VIII asserted the integrity of church lands, perhaps envisaging confiscation for the Crown in the not too distant future. In 1661, the Scottish Parliament took under consideration the case of Helen Gibesone and Christian Blaikie, who 'confest the abhominable cryme of witchcraft in entering into paction with the divell', and commissioned a number of responsible persons to 'put them to the tryell'. Parliament then turned to happier matters, granting a handsome reward of 'one hundreth pund sterling' to John Gordoun and Alexander Strachan for the arrest of a bandit named William Roy Menzie, thus freeing the Brechin district 'of the robries and outrages committed be the said William'. Also in 1661, Parliament addressed the case of an Orcadian laird:

> vpon the sexteinth of October last, that the said David [Sinclair] his father wes
> removed by death James Moodie of Melsetter in Wause in Orkney accompanied with
> nyn or ten complices to himselff came to the saids lands & house of Rysay, and most
> vnchristianly & inhumanlie fell vpon the supplicant (he being bot ane minor) in ane
> hostile and most violent maner … intrometted with the dueties of the saids lands of
> Rysay & haill cornes & cropt … As also most barbarously entered the petitioners
> duelling place … and thrust him out at doores, and beat him to the great effusion of
> his blood, and did cast out all the plenishing out of his house … .

Public acts (superseded or current) of the Westminster legislature are located through chronological and alphabetical indexes, while texts can be read in *Statutes of the Realm*, also known as *Statutes at Large*. Original rolls of medieval Irish Parliaments were destroyed in 1922, though there is a printed selection of acts for 1310–1800. Published by the Record Commissioners, *The Acts of the Parliaments of Scotland* (APS) include charters and writs from 1124 referring to families and individuals.

Of direct concern to family historians are *private* or *local and personal* acts, which arose from petitions by town councils, corporations and individuals concerning such matters as the enclosure of common land, tithes, estates, charities, transport undertakings, public works, divorce and naturalisation. From 1571, the titles of private acts were included in volumes of sessional papers as well as in series of statutes of the realm. There are various chronological and analytical indexes to

Statutes of the realm.

THE

STATUTES
AT L·A·R·G·E,
PASSED IN THE

PARLIAMENTS
HELD IN

I R E L A N D:
FROM

The Third Year of EDWARD the Second, A. D. 1310,

TO THE

Twenty fixth Year of GEORGE the Third, A. D. 1786 inclufive.

WITH

MARGINAL NOTES, and a Complete INDEX to the Whole.

PUBLISHED BY AUTHORITY.

IN THIRTEEN VOLUMES.

acts from 1797 onwards. Texts of private acts were included in sessional papers, occasionally from the sixteenth century, more consistently from 1796. Some acts not published in the local and personal series were collected in special sessional volumes entitled *Private Acts*. Individual volumes are also available from 1798, though all acts were included only from 1876. Private acts of a strictly personal nature, for example concerning divorce, change of name and naturalisation, might never be printed, though the manuscript text may be consulted at Westminster. Copies of private acts, printed and manuscript, with background papers can also be sought in relevant estate archives and family papers, lodged with provincial lawyers and archive offices. From 1792, organisations proposing public works such as docks, waterworks, railways, bridges, tramways, canals and turnpike roads were obliged to deposit with Parliament drawings, plans and explanatory books of reference. Documentation refers to promoters, opponents, contractors, architects, surveyors, agents and engineers. Landowners and tenants of property affected by or adjacent to the proposed development are particularly noticed, their lands described and valued; their houses depicted on plans that predate or usefully supplement the Ordnance Survey.

Journals of the English House of Lords from 1510 onwards and Commons from 1547 indicate how closely Parliament might be involved in the affairs of families, for instance when rural landscapes were enclosed and villages deserted. Printed and indexed journals are held by public libraries. The following extract from a journal of the Irish House of Lords, now in Trinity College, Dublin, concerns contractors

Right: *Index of private acts of parliament concerning naturalisation, divorce and enclosure, 1801.*

(*Private*) 41° GEO. III.

94. An Act for dividing, allotting, laying in Severalty, and inclosing the Open and Common Fields, Common Meadows, Common Pastures, Commonable Lands, and Waste Grounds, within the Parish of *Sutton Courtney*, and the Hamlet of *Sutton Wick*, in the same Parish, in the County of *Berks*.

95. An Act for naturalizing *Cornelius Paas*.

96. An Act for naturalizing *John Daniel Baum*.

97. An Act for naturalizing *Elizabeth Winsla*.

98. An Act for dividing, allotting, and laying in Severalty, certain Common and Open Fields, Common Meadows, Commonable Lands, Commons, and Waste Grounds, lying within the Parishes of *Barkway* and *Reed*, and the Hamlets thereto belonging, in the County of *Hertford*, and for extinguishing all Rights of Common, Sheepwalk, and Shackage, in, over, and upon the Lands and Grounds within the said Parishes and Hamlets.

99. An Act for dividing, allotting, and inclosing the Open Fields and Common or Car, within the Township of *Molscroft*, in the Parish of *Saint John* of *Beverley*, in the East Riding of the County of *York*; and for making a Compensation in lieu of the Tithes thereof, and of certain ancient inclosed Lands in the same Township.

100. An Act for dividing and inclosing the Common and Open Fields, Meadows, Pastures, Commonable Lands, and Waste Grounds within the Parishes of *Lavenden* and *Brayfield*, otherwise *Cold Brayfield*, in the County of *Buckingham*.

101. An Act for dividing, allotting, and laying in Severalty, the Open and Common Lands and Grounds within the Parishes of *Down Ampney*, in the County of *Glocester*, and *Latton* and *Eisey*, in the County of *Wilts*.

102. An Act to dissolve the Marriage of *Jane Campbell* with *Edward Addison* her now Husband, on Account of his incestuous Adultery with the Sister of the said *Jane Campbell*, and to enable the said *Jane Campbell* to marry again, and for other Purposes therein mentioned.

103. An Act for naturalizing *David Court*.

104. An Act for naturalizing *John William Pfeil*.

105. An Act for naturalizing *William Harre*.

106. An Act for naturalizing *Henry Suthmier*.

107. An Act for naturalizing *John Haring*.

Below: *The sensitive genealogist is able imaginatively to visualise episodes in the lives of ancestors: here the present generation takes a seat at the fireside of Alexander Auldpotts in 1809 – a household under threat of eviction as agricultural change results in the clearance of peasant communities.*

employed by the Archbishop of Armagh who:

> about May 1661 had agreed with Mr Woodward & Mr Jacob Rowse for sowing Cutting & carrying downe of 100 Tunn of good Timber from the woods of Shellelagh to the towne of Wexford And ... paid ... £20 for a tunn of Iron which the said Rowse did Undertake to send to Drogheda ... the said parties respectively have failed in performance ... whereof his Grace hath been frustrated of his Intention in building

A first approach to the journals is made through printed calendars:

> FELTHAM'S Petition, complaining that his Wife hath been taken away, was referred to the Chief Justice of the King's Bench ... Petition discussed ... 18th June 1663

> [Bill] For Sale of the Estate of one Savery, the Commons having made Amendments to the Bill, whereby a particular Fact was alledged ... 18th April 1733

> [Petition] Of John Wilson of South Molton Street, Wine Merchant, and William Williams of Bond Street, Hatter, Creditors of Thomas Reynolds, Esq., a Lunatic ... 18th February 1819

> [Ireland:]

> A Return of the Names of all Persons committed under the Insurrection Act ... specifying the Nature of the Offence ... 29th March 1824

> Returns of the Total Number and Names of all Magistrates, Constables and Sub-Constables ... and distinguishing those who profess the Roman Catholic Religion ... 10th May 1824

Parliamentary **sessional papers** accumulated in their thousands. The archive includes the protestation return of 1642, comprising certificates collected in English parishes of males subscribing the oath of protestation, swearing to 'maintaine & defend ... the true Reformed Protestant Religion expressed in the doctrine of the Church of England ... the power & Priueledges of Parliament. The Lawfull Rights, & Liberties of the subject'. Sessional papers have been printed since 1660. Bound collections from 1801 onwards are held in eleven major libraries. Larger public and university libraries offer microform editions as well as 1112 volumes of reprints published by the Irish University Press, Shannon, and accessed through breviates (detailed catalogues) arranged by L. Hansard and P. and G. Ford. When Parliament investigated matters such as poor law, trade, factory hours and public health, evidence was taken as a dramatic dialogue, preserving the authentic voices of people in the past. When investigating the overcrowding of urban graveyards in 1842, a select committee took the advice of an expert in the field, a professional gravedigger:

> I dug a grave on a Sunday evening ... on Monday morning I finished my work, and I was trying the length of the grave to see if it was long enough ... and while I was in there the ground gave way and a body turned right over, and the two arms came and clasped me round the neck; she had gloves on and stockings and white flannel inside, and what we call a shift, but no head ... it was a very stout body, and the force that she came with knocked my head against a body underneath, and I was very much frightened ... It had never been in a coffin; it is supposed that they took the head off for sale

Neil Mackinnon, a cottar at Ferrinvicquire, aged fifty-eight, was questioned by the

POST MERIDIĒ sederūt Dñi antedci

In þe actioun and cauſ pſewit be mariouñ glen þe ſpous of vmquhil robert ſchaw aganis robert of Danzelſtouñ for the wrangwis vexatiouñ and diſtrubling of þe ſai. mariouñ ī þe landſ of balgarane 't takin 't w'halding fra hir of twa horſ out of þe ſaid landſ Baith þe ſaidſ ptiis beand pſonaly pñt þ richt reſſoñs 't allegatioñs hard 't vndſtad The lordſ audito'ſ decrettſ and deliſis that for ocht þ' þai haf zit ſene or that Is pducit or ſchewin before þaī that þe ſaid Robert has done na wrang ī þe Intrometting w' þe ſaid lādſ 't taking and withalding of þe ſaid twa horſ out of þe ſaid landſ

Minutes of a committee of the Scottish Parliament adjudicating the case of Marion Glen, widow of Robert Schaw, 1489.

Royal Commission (Highlands and Islands), 1892:

5830. Do you pay rent? – No.
5831. How much land have you? – Not the breadth of my foot.
5832. Have you any stock? – I have one cow.
5833. Where does it feed? – On the hill.
5834. Whose hill? – On the crofters' hill.
5835. And do you pay anything for that? – Yes.
5836. What do you pay? – A very small sum; it is the price of the grass, 6s.

Herman John Falk, a Cheshire salt owner, answered questions concerning his immigrant employees, adding a chapter to the family histories of their descendants:

In the year 1868 there was a great strike in the salt district ... My father ... imported a large number of Germans ... at lower wages ... 1871 ... the Germans became very independent and conspired with the Englishmen for a rise of wages ... There were no English employed after 1877, because Hungarians were introduced ... They are most obedient and docile ... In this country ... they chiefly wear sack clothing ... Their beds are made of sacking filled with straw ... I do not think they have ever worn a nightshirt at any time

The Falk family is further documented in a local and personal act, 26 George II chapter 6, which declared in 1753 that '*Jacob Valk* son of Nicholas Valk by Ann his wife born at Westsanen in North Holland ... having ... given Testimony of his loyalty ... is hereby from henceforth Naturalised'.

17
National libraries

National libraries in London, Dublin, Edinburgh and Aberystwyth preserve the published literary heritage of the nation. Unpublished manuscript holdings of genealogical interest include private, estate and business muniments, the archival collections of antiquarians, and official papers from national and provincial sources.

The **British Library** originated under an act of Parliament of 1753 entitled:

> An Act for the Purchase of the *Museum*, or Collection of Sir *Hans Sloane*, and of the *Harleian* Collection of Manuscripts; and for providing one General Repository for the better Reception and more convenient Use of the said collections; and of the Cottonian Library, and of the Additions thereto.

A national lottery raised £300,000 for the establishment of a museum, library and archives. The institution opened at Montagu House, London, in 1759. The British Library, breaking free of the Museum, opened new premises at St Pancras in 1998. The department of manuscripts is open to readers undertaking research that cannot be pursued elsewhere. Printed catalogues that may be available locally in the public library as well as unpublished catalogues held at the British Library itself are specified in M. A. E. Nickson *Index of Manuscripts in the British Library* (1984). This was compiled from indexes to catalogues of the Additional and Egerton manuscripts acquired 1783–1945, various 'special collections', accumulations of charters and rolls, and the foundation collections of Cotton, Harley and Sloane.

The Cottonian collection was accumulated by the antiquary Sir Robert Cotton (1570–1631). His private library was shelved in fourteen cupboards, topped with classical busts, which provided the classification system whereby the collection is still accessed. In 1700, an act of Parliament confirmed the Cotton family's wish that the library be 'kept in the house at Westminster called Cotton House ... for public use and advantage'. Transferred to Ashburnham House nearby, the library was damaged by fire in 1731. The surviving manuscripts were later removed to the new British Museum, where the keeper of manuscripts, J. Planta, commenced a catalogue in 1793, published by the Record Commissioners in 1802. The following examples give a taste of the catalogue:

> *Faustina*, E.II
> 1. Miscellaneous pedigrees, and various genealogical notes, concerning many noble families in England: with an alphabetical index, fol. 6. but not referring accurately to the collectanea.
> 2. An alphabetical index of the names of the gentlemen of Kent, in the time of K. Hen. VII.
> 3. An alphabetical list of arms granted since Anno 10 Eliz.
> *Titus*, C.X.
> 5. Rent roll of the manors of Acton trussell, and Bednal, belonging to John E. of Oxford.
> 10. Three law papers; 1. a fine and recovery, concerning various estates; 2. and 3. relating to estates of the earl of Essex.
> 17. Genealogies of several Irish families, and some papers on the state of Ireland.

A Record Commission catalogue of the collection of Robert Harley (1661–1724) followed between 1808 and 1812. The Harleian manuscripts are notable for heraldic visitations:

List of genealogies in the Harleian manuscripts.

—(CHAP. III. *Genealogies.*)—continued.

SECT. II.—*Welsh Genealogies.*—continued.

	Vol.	Pag.	Cod.	Art.
Collections, &c. (*cont.*) -	III.	243	·5058	1
- - -	ib.	332	6153	1
Cradock-Vraith-vras Defcent	II.	36	1412	42
Glyndowre (Alicæ) Stemma -	I.	446	807	84
Gruffith ap Cynan, Defcent -	ib.	646	1279	3
Gryffyth (Fam.) Pedigree -	II.	474	2094	7
- - -	III.	332	6153	1
Gwyn (Fam.) Defcent -	II.	561	2218	23
Gwyne (Fam.) Pedigree -	ib.	80	1500	19
Gwyn vara Dyvoa Defcent -	ib.	36	1412	42
Ideo (Lord of Luvel) Pedigree	ib.	80	1500	20
Jeftyn ap Gurgh -	ib.	36	1412	42
Lewis (Fam.) Pedigree -	ib.	474	2094	3
—— (Fam.) Defcent -	ib.	561	2218	23
Llewellyn (Prince of Wales) Defcent -	I.	38	139	81
- -	II.	561	2218	1
Lloyd (Fam.) Pedigrees -	ib.	474	2094	4—6
Middleton (Fam.) Pedigree -	ib.	475	2094	41
Mofton, or Moftyn (Fam.) Pedigrees -	ib.	397	2012	15
- -	ib.	475	2094	43, 45
Owen (Fam.) Pedigree -	III.	332	6153	1
Powis (Lords of) Pedigrees, &c. of -	I.	42	139	282
Price (Fam.) Pedigree -	III.	332	6153	1
Pugh (Fam.) Pedigree -	ib.	332	ib.	1
Rees ap Tudor, Defcent -	II.	36	1412	42
Tanat (Fam.) Pedigree -	III.	332	6153	1
Thomas (Fam.) Pedigree -	ib.	123	4181	16
—— (Hugh) Genealogical Hiftory of Wales -	ib.	418	6823	1
- - -	ib.	421	6831	1
- - -	ib.	444	6870	1
Trevor (Fam.) Pedigrees -	II.	475	2094	10, 44
- -	III.	123	4181	20
Williams (Fam.) Pedigree -	II.	475	2094	12, 13
Wynne (Fam.) Pedigrees -	ib.	474	ib.	9, 11

1174.

An Heraldic Book in Fol. consisting of loose Papers, Pedigrees, &c. all bound up together. They contain,

1. A Descent of Longe.
2. Descent of Butler of Sharebrock; with rude Tricks of the Arms of divers Families.
3. Descent of Harvey alias Smarte of Thurley in Com. Bedford.
4. Descent of Cobb of Sharne.
5. Rude Tricks of the Arms of Bury, & of some other families.
6. Pedigree of Colman, to A.D. 1610.

In 1757, George II donated the royal library, including spoils from monastic archives with books and manuscripts accumulated by English sovereigns since Edward IV. The royal library brought the privilege of compulsory copyright deposit of all books published in Britain and Ireland. The royal library was the first of the 'special collections', followed by Lansdowne (1807), Hargrave (1813), Burney (1815), King's (1823), Arundel (1831), Stowe (1883), Ashley (1937), Yates Thompson (1941). *A Catalogue of the Lansdowne Manuscripts in the British Museum* appeared in 1819:

Num. 88

75. A draught of the Will and Testament of Mr Michael Hicks, which seems to be the first he made, and that in haste, dated Aug. 24, 1603.
86. Mr Joseph Earthe, in affliction for the loss of his child, thanks Mr Hicks for his friendly consolation, &c. 1603.

98. A copy of an order in Exchequer, signed by Mr. Henry Fanshawe, concerning a copyhold at Orsett in Essex, Feb. 13, 1603.
99. The voluntary disposition and confession of a woman servant in Mr Hicks's family, pregnant by a fellow servant, Jan. 4, 1602.
100. Peter Makinson, Mr. Hicks's Butler, his complaint that a fellow servant has by slanders prevented his marriage with a woman servant of the family, 1603.
101. Peter Makinson's bond for 40*l.*, given to the Overseers of Low Layton, for maintenance of a child with which the young woman servant in Mr. Hicks's family was pregnant, and who had sworn it to him, Jan. 7, 1603.

The two series known as Additional and Egerton manuscripts comprise miscellaneous gifts, purchases and bequests from 1756 onwards. Saxon, Norman and later charters and rolls that have strayed from the public records form separate and genealogically valuable series. There are also estate muniments, administrative records, drawings, paintings and heraldic documents.

The **National Library of Scotland** originated in the collections of the Faculty of Advocates founded in 1682. The library was established by act of Parliament in 1925 and housed in premises on George IV Bridge, Edinburgh, with money from Sir Alexander Grant of the biscuit makers Macvitie & Price. The library is now a principal research centre with family and estate papers, newspapers, business records, charters, rentals, plans, photographs, antiquarian papers and Ordnance Survey maps.

The **National Library of Wales** in Aberystwyth was founded in 1907. The library holds diocesan, capitular, parish and nonconformist church records. Estate, family, business and institutional records are extensive, perhaps filling gaps in collections available in public libraries and archives. Typewritten, printed and computerised finding aids are available, with copies also held by certain public libraries. The catalogue to the Coleman Deeds (1921), compiled by F. Green, offers an example of a carefully contrived finding aid, perhaps making travel to Aberystwyth to consult the original document unnecessary:

> a lease from Phillipp Hoby of the Abbey of Neath ... to Gwenllyan Jenkin, widow, and John Jenkin, both of the parcel of Koed ffrank ... of a messuage and lands called *Tyre Myrick Hopkin* and *Tyre Gwillim Howell*, in the said parcel of Koed ffrank ... Rent: £6 and 2 pullets at Christmas, 2 days' work with oxen and to keep two horses to carry coal from the pits ... and a heriot of the best beast on the death of any tenant (29th October 1672)

The **National Library of Ireland** originated in the manuscript and book collections of the Royal Dublin Society, which became during the eighteenth century a metropolitan centre for the study of Irish civilisation and history. The library expanded its own archives under a policy of acquiring 'everything relating to Ireland or to Irishmen that comes on the market' and is now a major research centre for family and estate muniments, maps, drawings, photographs, ecclesiastical archives and architectural plans.

The **Royal Irish Academy**, Dublin, was founded in 1785 for promoting the study of science, polite literature and antiquities by collecting manuscripts and other historical sources. The academy's published *Proceedings* from 1836 onwards are required reading for family historians and genealogists interested in the Irish sphere of influence, which embraced also the Celtic west of mainland Britain. The library holds the collections of Sir William Betham, herald and Celticist; Edward O'Reilly of Cavan, lexicographer and jurist; John O'Daly and Hodges & Smith, Dublin book dealers; and the Ashburnham muniments from Stowe, Buckinghamshire. Chronicles, genealogies, surveys, chartularies and other medieval texts have generally been published, usually with English introduction and translation.

The genealogist's nearest **university** may collect archives relating to its own graduates and also estate, business and family papers from across a broad hinterland. Universities have developed archives originating in the research interests of academic staff. Warwick is a recognised centre for trade union archives. Manchester (John Rylands) holds valuable collections of ecclesiastical and estate muniments. Durham holds capitular archives and Glasgow actively collects Scottish business records. Leicester is proud of its department of English local history, with holdings of manuscripts, research materials and correspondence accumulated from throughout England and collectanea of the doyens of local history W. G. Hoskins and H. P. R. Finberg.

Trinity College, Dublin, has unrivalled sources for the history of Ireland and Scotland including the historical confection of the *Yellow Book of Lecan*. Manuscripts of the Celtic scholar Edward Lhwyd (1660–1709) include the twelfth-century *Book of Leinster* from Terryglass, County Tipperary, mingling saga, genealogy, legendary invasions and lists of provincial chieftains, and designed, it seems, specifically to tantalise the genealogist with aspirations to royal blood. Trinity also preserves Archbishop Ussher's manuscripts, secured for Ireland by Oliver Cromwell and including collections of hagiography, documents strayed from the Cottonian collection and annals from Margam Abbey, Glamorgan, covering the period 1066–1232.

The Department of Irish Folklore at University College, Dublin, inherited the mantle of the Irish Folklore Commission of 1935, a prime source of oral history and rural reminiscence in verse and prose. The folklore archives cover a range of interest, including linguistics, onomastics (names), houses, religion, agriculture and domestic economy.

Edinburgh University's School of Scottish Studies is a national centre for the study of oral history and rural life with notable photographic and film collections such as those of the anthropologist Werner Kissling (1896–1988) illustrating the occupations and folk customs of rural families and fisher households. There is also a tale archive and material relevant to the study of surnames and regional dialect. Also in Edinburgh, at the National Museums of Scotland, is the archive of the Scottish Ethnographic Institute, offering photographs, sound recordings and other sources for family history, rural tradition and popular culture. Associated with this is the European Ethnological Research Centre, sponsor of the series *Sources in Local History*, whose published titles include editions of Scottish diaries and memoirs.

The colleges of Oxford and Cambridge are major landowners, maintaining extensive collections of manorial and estate muniments relating to their territorial possessions. The Bodleian Library of Oxford holds collections of deeds, manorial rolls and the papers of historians, academics and antiquaries drawn from various regions of Britain. The Bodleian holds the collections of the seventeenth-century hereditary Irish *sennachie*, or traditional wise man, An Dubhaltach MacFirbhisigh, and the Anglo-Irish scholar Sir James Ware. Cambridge University Library holds ecclesiastical records from Ely, estate muniments especially from East Anglia, enclosure documents for Cambridgeshire parishes, records of people involved in fen drainage and promiscuous title deeds, travel journals, manorial rolls, terriers, private correspondence, pictorial sources and household accounts, including research materials from distant localities such as Newtown, County Down.

18
National archives: fiscal

Public records are the official memory of national government. Public records are deposited in the Public Record Office (PRO) at Kew; the National Archives of Scotland (NAS, formerly known as the Scottish Record Office), Edinburgh; the Public Record Office of Northern Ireland (PRONI), Belfast; the National Archives (An Chartlann Naisiunta), Dublin; and the National Library of Wales, Aberystwyth. There are also repositories in the Channel Islands and the Isle of Man. Offices publish comprehensive guides to collections as well as concise introductions to genealogical research, such as the PRO's handy series of over one hundred family fact sheets concerning militia musters, probate records, enclosure awards, taxation, death duty, immigrants, emigrants, apprenticeship and tithes. The PRO's family history magazine *Ancestors* and the *Pocket Guides to Family History* are useful purchases. Detailed finding aids (catalogues) of the PRO are made available by the List and Index Society. Each national archive has set up a website offering some catalogues and guides, allowing genealogists to plan research campaigns in advance

Medieval Exchequer officials count money and record payments on parchment rolls while Crown debtors languish in prison below.

of a visit to the capital. The PRO is at <**http://catalogue.pro.gov.uk/**>. Microfilms and photocopies of documents may be ordered by post for home study.

Research among the public records normally follows investigation of documents and sources in the regions where ancestors lived and worked. Many public records are in some form also available regionally, in printed editions, published calendars, on microfilm and via the Internet. Editions are listed in two volumes entitled *Texts and Calendars*, edited by E. L. C. Mullins, and in *Texts and Calendars since 1982*, accessed through the Historical Manuscripts Commission website. It may be necessary to consult original documents only occasionally to clarify an unclear reading from a microfilm or an ambiguously abbreviated calendar entry. Particular-instance files are not available outside the public record offices and so for the fine detail of an ancestor's dealings with government a visit to the public records is essential. Public records are, on the whole, arranged and classified according to depositing departments. Thus at the PRO, Admiralty archives bear the reference code ADM, Exchequer E, Chancery C and Home Office HO. There are catalogues to most series, particularly those most often sought such as hearth taxes and wills.

Richard Tonebrige's property in Waltone, Surrey, from the Domesday survey of 1086.

The Court of **Exchequer**, the financial arm of government, originated in England during the twelfth century, its name arising from the departmental abacus, a chequered cloth upon which clerks moved various counters including hobnails and horseshoes to aid arithmetic. The earliest public record is the Domesday Book of 1086. This comprises a survey of revenue and lordship ordered by William I. Fortunate genealogists have traced pedigrees back to the barons, knights and merchants who arrived with the Conqueror and whose landholdings are recorded in Domesday, perhaps displacing a native Saxon. The survey covered England, except London and northern counties. The book has been edited and indexed in county volumes by J. Morris for Phillimore of Chichester.

Exchequer archives down to 1832 are a source for families dwelling and working in royal manors, forests, palaces, military works and mining communities who might pay dues to or receive money from sheriffs responsible for administering the ancient demesne (domain/property) of the monarch. Financial accounts, writs, returns, extents and inquisitions were prepared to accompany the principal Exchequer records. Sheriffs appeared annually before Exchequer to submit accounts relating to Crown rents, profits of justice, forfeitures, feudal incidents (income), fines for encroachment on Crown land, trespasses in forests, fee farms from boroughs and treasure trove. Payments were written up on broad parchment rolls, known as pipe rolls (E 372), which may be studied in editions published by the Pipe Roll Society. A second record of transactions was made by cutting notches on wooden tally sticks. A tally stick served as a receipt for the sheriff that could be authenticated, even by an illiterate official, by comparing notches with a duplicate retained in Exchequer archives. When these obsolete records were burned in 1834, the resulting conflagration destroyed most of the Palace of Westminster and

VILLENAGII EJUSDEꟄ MANER'.

Alañs P'pos' Alañs ad Portam Joñes ad Portā WiꟄꟄs ad Portam Robs Barun WiꟄꟄs ſit RaꟄ Joñes Man RaꟄs le Long WalteꟄs de Schepe Amples' filia P'ꞏpos' RiꟄs ad Portam Alañs ad le Forche Joñes le Bole PetꟄs ad le Brok WiꟄꟄs Joſep Alicia Campiun Allex' de Barliwey Henr' de Barliwey Tecle ad le Broc Joñes ſit Walter' WiꟄꟄs Gerard Joñes de Barliwey WiꟄꟄs Duraunt RiꟄs in le Mer Alañs ad le Gocer WalꟄs ſit Betricie RaꟄs Clarice RiꟄs ad PetꟋn Matilda Scot quor' quilibet eoꞁ ten' x acꞏꞃ ꞇre cuſtumabit & valent opa & ꞓſuetudines ſingulꞁ eoꞁ p ann' ad voluntatē dñi ix s. ij d. & faciet p ann' vijˣˣ xij opa & tres ꝑcarias & vj gallin' xx ova.

COTEREL'.

Henr' Taylur ten' unū croftū q' contin' tres roꟄ Ꞔre p xiiij d꞊ p ann'.

Cecillia le Lung ten' j cotag' q' ꝯtin' di' roꟄ p xx d. & ij gallin'.

EdwarꟄs Oter ten' unū cotag' p xvj d. ij gallin'.

RiꟄs ad Portā ten' j cotag' p xij d. ij gallin'.

Angnes Agath ten' j cotag' p xiiij d. ij capon' & ij gallin'.

Thom' Mercꞏtor ten' ij cotag'.

Reginald Textor ten' ij cotag'.

Hug' Bercator Wariñs Toy Bele Scampeyn Robs Triturator Bartholom' de Pilketon' quor' quilibet cotag' ſolvit dño p ann' xiiij d. ij gallin' ꝑciū ij d.

Et oñes dant ſcutagiū dño ſuo.

EborarꟄs de Orewelle ten' j hydam q' ꝯtin' vjˣˣ acꞏꞃ Ꞔre & pꞏti geldabit dño Regi & ten' p ſocagiū de dño Henr' de Bokeſwore & iꟄm Henric⁹ de RicarꟄ de Frivile & iꟄm RicarꟄs de dño Reg' et debet unā ſectam ad comitatū CANT' & hundreꟄ de WETHERLE & dat de aux' Vic' xij d. de vis' iij s. & ſolvit dño ſuo p ann' p Ꞔco tenem' xxxvj s.

LIBERE

Robꞇs de Perey ſuꞋ' fuit ad reſpondū dño ꝶ de phͦo quo waͤo clam' here libam warennā in oñibꞁ dñicis ꝑris ſuis in BULEꞇON', SUꞇꞇON', ELKLE, WARROꞂ' & KERNEꞇHBY & here ꞏ̄icatū & fer' in ELKLE & emend afſiſe ꞓvis' fracꞇe de oñibꞁ tenenꞇ' ſuis in vi� ꝑdcis ſine lic' & vot &c.

Et Robꞇs ven' Et dic' qꟄ ipͤe clam' libam warennā in BULEꞇON' & SUꞇꞇON' p cartam dñi J. ꝶ avi dñi ꝶ ſic dat' anno rᵉ ſui quintodecio quam pſert & que teſtat' qꟄ ꝑdcis J. ꝶ conceſſit Robto de Percy avo ꝑdci Robti de Percy nūc cujus hes ipͤe eſt libam warennā in ꝑris ſuis de BULEꞇON', SUꞇꞇON &c. Clam' eciam here libam warennam in oñibꞁ dñicis ꝑris ſuis de ILꟄEKLEY, WARROL & KERMEꞇꞇBY p cartam dñi H. ꝶ ꝑris dñi ꝶ ſic dat' anno rᵉ ſui tᵉceſimo qꞏnto quam pſert & que teſtat' qꟄ ꝑdcis dñs H. ꝶ conceſſit Petᵉ de Percy patᵉ ꝑdci Robti de Percy cujus hes ipͤe eſt libam warennā in ꝑdcis viꟄ Clam' eciam here unū ꞏ̄icatū ſinglis ſeptim' p diͤm M'cur' apud maꟄ̄iū ſuū de ILLEKLEY Et feriam ſinglis annis dur' p ocꞇo dies videꞇ in vigil in die & in cᵉꟄino Sꞇi Luce Ewangle & p quinꞁ dies feqͤntes &c. Et dic' qꟄ ipͤe & oñes antec' ſui a ꝶpe dat' ꝑdcaꞁ cartaꞁ ſemp continue uſi ſunt ꝑdcis libtat' & hoc patᵉ eſt ꝶificare &c.

Et Roꞇꞃs de Hegh'm qui ſequit' p dño ꝶ pet' qꟄ inquir' p dño ꝶ quatᵉr ipͤe & antec' ſui uſi ſint &c. Ido inquiratᵉ &c. Rot. 22. d.

List of servile tenants on the manor of Orwell, Cambridgeshire, as shown on the Hundred Rolls; dues for their crofts and cottages are paid in pennies and poultry.

innumerable state archives. In Scotland, royal revenues were sometimes transferred to burghs for a fixed annual payment.

The Crown was vigilant that feudal rights should not be eroded. When Edward I returned from crusade in 1274 he ordered commissioners to enquire into Crown rights throughout the kingdom. Evidence was collected in each borough and in the ancient county divisions known as hundreds. Information collected for the years 1275–6 has been published with indexes in the *Hundred Rolls* (Record Commission, 1812–18). Royal justices, when despatched on circuit around the provinces, were authorised under the Statute of Gloucester of 1278 to enquire further into Crown rights and were empowered to demand that lieges prove *par quel garant* ('by what warrant') privileges were enjoyed. Investigations of franchises are published in *Placita de Quo Warranto* (Record Commission, 1818). For example, Ralph Basset of Weldon was summoned to Northampton on Monday next after the feast of All Saints 1329. Ralph claimed a large raft of rights including view of frankpledge (village peace-keeping), waif (right to abandoned property), gallows, punishment cart, courts, manorial jurisdiction, suit for recovery of stolen goods, collection of tribute and the right to amerce thieves in the manors of Pighteslee and Weldon. The Crown's attorney,

Property and privileges of Robert of Percy as investigated by 'Quo Warranto' proceedings in the reign of Edward I.

Richard Aldeburgh, knowing that only frankpledge and waif had previously been claimed, set a date 'when he shall hear judgement in the presence of the Lord King'.

Exchequer officials enjoyed wide patronage over privileges and honours. Departmental fine rolls recorded payments by individuals for Crown grants of wardship to handle the property of wealthy minors, letters of denization concerning residence and naturalisation, pardons for trespass or law breaking and the enjoyment of lucrative public offices. A principal source of royal revenue arose from feudal incidents, that is taking profits from the estates of tenants in chief as far as feudal principles permitted. Henry VII exploited to the full his rights to administer the estates of wards and minors following the death of a tenant in chief. Henry VIII went a stage further, establishing a special court to collect depositions, surveys, decrees, pedigrees and inquisitions. Estate muniments despatched as evidence were retained by the court, remaining in the public records after the court was abolished in 1660.

A second source of revenue arose from duties on foreign trade. **Customs duties** were levied on imports at London and provincial ports from 1275 onwards, commencing when Edward I targeted wool, fells, skins and hides. Collectors' accounts (E 122) name vessels, their masters and owners, dates of sailing and arrival and ports of origin with details of cargoes carried. Scottish duties were also levied from the thirteenth century. Here, to simplify procedures, trade in staples including wool, hides and fish, and in luxuries such as wine and wax, was limited to royal burghs. English administrative reforms of 1550–72 designated legal quays for foreign trade where port books daily recorded details of imports, exports, ships, cargoes, masters and merchants. London port books for 1696–1795 were destroyed by official weeders. In 1671 a Board of Customs was established for England and Wales, embracing Scotland from 1723 and Ireland from 1823. Bounties on whale and herring fishing (about 1750–1825) required customs certificates for each voyage concerning the ship, catch and crewmen. Board minutes are supported by correspondence with collectors in the outports, establishment records and reports on specific ports and problems from the 1830s. Individuals are particularly noticed, as here in 1813: 'The Conduct of Henry Comper, a Boatman in absenting himself without leave … from Drunkenness' and 'James Sammes … a Competent Tidewaiter [appointed] … in consequence of the insanity of Mr. Richard Chiverton Coastwaiter at Ryde'. Excisemen collected duty on some goods such as whisky during manufacture or before sale.

Taxation records include lists of individuals. Even the humblest villager may be mentioned, albeit as 'not liable' through poverty. This, though, may not be the whole story and the researcher should consider the possibility of untruthfulness in an ancestor's tax returns. English medieval taxation archives begin during the twelfth century. Records, grouped together as E 179, include scutage (related to feudal military service), tallage (concerning towns and royal demesnes), hidage and carucage (both due on ordinary lands). During the thirteenth century, payments known as subsidies were demanded as one-tenth or one-fifteenth of the value of movable goods belonging to clerics and laymen, as here in 1225, translated from the original Latin:

> Nicholas Peterson owns one cow worth 4 shillings, and one heifer worth 18 pennies, and one horse worth 3 shillings and one small measure of barley worth 3 pennies, and one bushel of wheat and barley worth 7 pennies
> The sum total of one-fifteenth of the above is 7 pennies and one halfpenny

Subsidies for 1295–1332 are relatively complete. After 1334 the levy became, in effect, a land tax requiring a fixed sum from each parish or borough. Periodic reassessment from 1489 to tax income and movables proved unsuccessful, though lists of 1524–5 and 1543 are considered reliable for genealogical purposes. Poll taxes put a price on the head (poll) of individual inhabitants. That of 1377, at one groat or 4d a head, caused disquiet. Three groats in 1380 conspired with social, economic and political factors in the generation following the Black Death to spark off the Peasants' Revolt. After Charles II's restoration in 1660, Parliament revived the subsidy as a source of revenue. The tax was not successful, though records for a few counties survive (reference E 179) in London with duplicates in county archives. Records of seven poll taxes during the period 1660–97 may be found in county archives and estate muniments rather than in London. In Scotland, the poll taxes of 1693–9 graduated payments according to social and financial status, also roughly estimating each person's wealth: 'James Cowper, taylor, Issobell Gellan, his wife, and John Cowper, his sone: valuatione is 1s 8d, stock extends not to 500 merks'.

A fourth medieval source of income was revenue from **Crown estates**. This property was kept separate from the ancient demesne of Domesday and administered by the royal household rather than Exchequer. The royal bedchamber was a preferred treasury in which the monarch could exercise close personal control over the administration of funds, hence the term chamber finance. Families living or working in town and country areas held even temporarily by the monarch are documented in financial accounts, rentals, leases, extents, surveys and grants. Tudor monarchs were notably possessive of income that could be siphoned away from sheriffs. In 1512 a department of general surveyors of the king's lands was

'Valor Ecclesiasticus' showing tenants with Welsh patronymics holding church lands in the diocese of Bangor, 1535.

formalised. Then, during Henry VIII's assault on the church, his officials in 1532 succeeded in collecting annates outside Exchequer's control. These 'first fruits' or profits from a benefice for the first year after the death or resignation of the incumbent brought in a good income directly to the Crown. The king also took one-tenth of the value of each benefice as a one-off payment. Commissioners valued parishes in *Valor Ecclesiasticus* (E 344) of 1535, published in six volumes by the Record Commission. Records of the institution of individual incumbents with related documents for 1544–1912 (E331) are among the most genealogically productive.

After 1536, Henry VIII seized monastic religious property. A Court of Augmentations of the revenues of the Crown was established, sufficiently powerful to absorb the wealth of English and Welsh guilds, chantries and colleges in 1545. Tens of thousands of monks, nuns, friars, chantry priests, lay brothers, foresters, miners and labourers, not to mention all the ordinary peasant tenants of church-owned estates, were affected by this transfer of ownership. Families were closely documented during their involvement as managers of the estates or when retained to work the enterprises. Genealogists consider the unsettling effect of the social, economic, political and liturgical changes of this era on individual ancestors as a significant chapter in the family history. Individuals with wealth or guile enough to curry favour with Crown officials obtained estates by grant from the 1530s onwards. Not a few families date their rise to gentility from the property revolution of the Tudor period. The continuing process of carving estates from Crown lands is documented in surveys, valuations and conveyances enrolled among the public records. Copies of these documents are often at the top (or bottom) of the deed bundle.

The surveying, valuation and disposal of the properties of 'Charles Stewart, late king of England' after 1649 benefited numerous supporters of Parliament, not all of whom lost everything following the restoration in 1660. After Charles II's restoration royal finance was in a parlous state, partly through the loss of feudal incidents and the impoverishment of Crown estates. Parliament granted new taxes in each English and Welsh county, based on an assessment of the value of physical features such as houses. The window tax of 1696–1851 is researched chiefly from documents held regionally, rather than in the public records. Hearth tax records of 1662–74 are lists from each parish of householders paying two shillings per fireplace. The lists include women, who are usually poorly documented elsewhere. From the number of hearths assessed the researcher may infer the social standing of the household. Poor families were listed but not liable. Four to seven hearths implies the substantial dwelling of a merchant, landowner or prosperous industrialist, which may still stand in the locality. The most complete parish lists date from 25th March 1664. In Scotland, Parliament granted a hearth tax in 1690, with some returns surviving from 1691–5. William III met the cost of his European wars by disposing of Crown estates, in bulk, to favoured or wealthy subjects.

Apprenticeship indentures were taxed from 1710 to 1811. The master paid 6d stamp duty for every £1 he received for agreeing to train the young person. The rate was enhanced to a shilling for every pound over £50. Tax registers were arranged under London City or Country, according to where the duty was paid. Payment was due at the end of the apprenticeship term. Registers show the name, address and trade of the master with the name of apprentice and date of indenture. Parents' details were required from 1752. Indexes of names have been compiled to assist researchers. Masters were excused payment for apprentices taken at the common charge of a township, parish or charity. Reference to such pauper apprenticeships may be followed up in relevant parochial or charitable records in county archives. The apprenticeship indentures themselves were private agreements and may be sought in family or business archives.

Taxation records in Scotland included a window tax of 1748–98, inhabited houses

Cheshire householders paying hearth tax in 1664, preserved in an early photocopy.

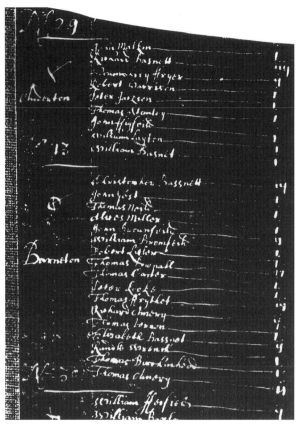

1778–98, male servants 1778–98, commutation 1784–98, shops over £5 annual rental 1785–9, female servants 1785–92, owners of carts, carriages, horses, farm horses, dogs, clocks and watches up to 1798. The detail varies, for example servants may be named, though their masters as taxpayers are always identified. Bachelors were charged double rates. In Britain, a duty was payable on legacies from 1796, extended in scope in 1853 in England and Wales to embrace succession to personal, leasehold and real estate. Registers of bequests, 1796–1894, provided the deceased's name, date of will and probate, executors' names and addresses, and duty paid. The archive is readily accessed through List and Index Society number 177. Scottish taxes on legacies and succession generated series of registers, accounts, inventories and indexes covering the period 1796–1907. The records offer additional information, including date of death, relationships among legatees and lawyers' names. Until 1868, heritable feudal property, chiefly land, perhaps with buildings thereon, could not be transferred by will, and so information from tax records is somewhat limited during the early years.

From 1798 separate tax assessments were consolidated, though this did not ensure the consistent retention of returns. The *schedule E* required names of butlers, coachmen, cooks, gardeners and gamekeepers in each household. Families paid a tax on each named male steward, bailiff, clerk, bookkeeper, apprentice, shopman, warehouseman, porter and cellarman. Proprietors of coffee-houses, taverns, inns, ale-houses, lodging-houses and hotels were taxed on each named waiter. A postmaster, innkeeper or coachmaker paid on each groom, postillion or coachman. There was a tax on drivers and guards of public stagecoaches or carriages. In *schedule D* families were charged for the luxury of carriages and riding horses while male servants were specifically named on *schedule C*. Records of the innovatory tax on incomes, collected 1799–1816 (E 181–2), provide the names of individuals arranged by parishes. Abatements were given according to the number of children, allowing researchers to infer family size from the level of tax. There are also various parochial tax ledgers in the public records, for London from 1857 and the provinces from 1864.

Throughout Britain and Ireland, the Finance Act of 1909–10 initiated a national survey of land ownership specifying every separate holding, though title deeds remain the chief source for genealogists.

Tontines and annuity schemes were an effective and popular means of raising money for the government. Eleven schemes were floated from 1693 to 1789, including the notable Irish tontines of 1773–7. These schemes were lotteries based on the life expectancy of nominees. An original participant was guaranteed an annual income based upon an investment, but dependent on the survival of a nominated individual. Of course a nominated child might die before an elderly relative and so the tontine was a gamble. When a payment ceased, the income was paid into a central fund for survivors. Thus, over the years, fewer and fewer people received larger and larger payments. The state, of course, took a cut at every stage. Some 15,000 individuals participated in tontine schemes. Registers with indexes show names, residences, marriages, deaths and wills of those involved.

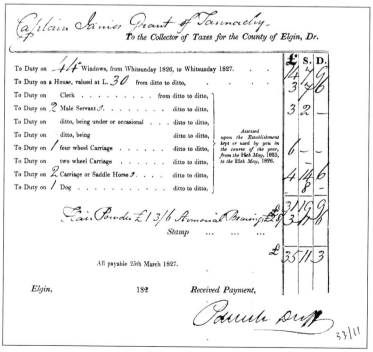

Tax return of Captain James Grant of Tannachy for windows, house, servants, carriage, horses and dog.

19
National archives: secretarial

Chancery was the nation's civil service in England, Ireland and Scotland. The head of the department, the Chancellor, was entrusted with the Great Seal of the kingdom, which authenticated documents issued by central government. The Chancellor's clerks made copies of royal charters granting lands and privileges, before despatch to individuals, boroughs and religious houses. These copies survive on the English charter rolls from 1199 until 1516 (C 53). The original documents are, of course, in the hands of the recipients or their successors. Charter rolls have been edited and published. Grants may be reiterated with copies preserved in confirmation rolls (C 56) and the series of *cartae antiquae* (C 52). Patent rolls from 1201 contain copies of documents issued patent (open) for all to see. Letters patent usually begin with the words 'to all to whom these presents shall come' and include grants of land, licences or pardons for the alienation of property, presentations to benefices, denization and honours (C 66). Letters close were issued folded, closed and sealed with the wax of the Great Seal, to be opened and read only by the addressee. These documents, concerning such matters as subsidies, family settlements and pardons, are consulted on some twenty thousand close rolls (C 54), some of which have been published. From the fourteenth century, individuals

The Court of Chancery around 1455; the table is strewn with documents to be authenticated with the Great Seal.

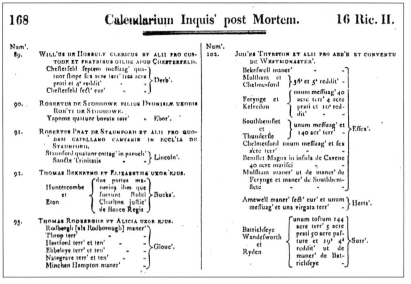

Calendar of inquisitions 'post mortem', 1392–3.

submitted their own title deeds, bonds and agreements to Chancery, where, for a fee, clerks would until 1903 make a copy on the back (dorse) of the close roll. The value of this security measure is attested by the survival of the endorsements in the public records, whereas the originals are usually lost from the family muniments. Enrolments cover genealogically productive areas, including deeds of bargain and sale, trust deeds of charity estates, bankrupts' estates, change of name, naturalisation and boundary settlements. Fine rolls (C 60) from 1199 to 1641 detail payments to the Crown for borough charters; grants of franchise over fairs, markets or free warren; privileges concerning property and the profitable wardship of minors; and matrimonial affairs with a property dimension. The series is calendared and indexed.

The Crown exercised feudal rights over the estates held by individuals directly from the monarch as tenants in chief or by giving knight service. On the death of the tenant and pending succession of an heir, during the minority or wardship of a tenant, and on marriage, the Crown drew profits from the estate. During such periods various inquisitions, surveys and extents were conducted, referring to families and their property. Inquisitions *post mortem* (C 132–41), following the deaths of tenants in chief, were surveys of lands and sub-tenants as well as genealogical investigations into the descent of heirs apparent. The Crown required official proofs of age to ensure it was not cheated out of any profits arising from wardship and minority. Until the abolition of feudal tenures in England and Wales in 1660, such documents were of importance for authenticating pedigrees. Inquisitions are available in print, calendars, lists and indexes and include parallel documentation from Exchequer (E 150) and the Court of Wards (WARD 7) for the period 1541–1660. Finding aids comprise summaries omitting details of estates and the names of jurors, which the genealogist will probably wish to research in the original records. A family's rights in markets, fairs and other profitable enterprises may be traced through inquisitions *ad quod damnum* ('to what hurt') (C 143) from the thirteenth to the fifteenth century.

The service of heirs in Scotland regulated succession to heritable property from

1545 onwards through investigation of a claimant's genealogy. The process ensured that the financial rights of feudal superiors, from common lairds to the Crown, were not neglected. The findings of inquests were returned to Chancery and are known as retours. The originals in Edinburgh from 1700 onwards are accessed through printed alphabetical indexes, arranged under surname of the heir or person served. Supplementary indexes refer to ancestors of different names. Normally, no death date appears: 'Mackenzie, Kenneth of Dundonnell, to his Father Kenneth Mackenzie of Dundonnell. heir general. Dated 22 Feb 1743, recorded 24 March 1743 Monthly no. 22'. Retours before 1700 have been summarised, mostly in Latin, in volumes entitled (shortly) *Inquisitionum Retornatarum Abbreviatio.* There is an index by county, surname and place, spelled as in the original document.

An English inquisition of 1516 (published in 1897) concerned the decay of tillage and arable husbandry and the desertion of villages since 1488 associated with the creation of deer parks and the expansion of sheep pastures. These were years of rural change when yeomen were able to buy up common land, create enclosures and act as owner-occupiers. Peasants were dispossessed, degraded to the status of agricultural labourers or forced to leave their homes and seek work in towns. This may be the earliest era to which a humble family's lineage can be certainly traced. Many family histories are brought to a halt around 1500 as the trail is lost in a trackless era of population movements and inadequate records.

Trinity College, Dublin, preserves an archive of depositions gathered from 1641 during official investigations into alleged robberies, rapes and massacres of named Protestant settlers in Ireland. Genealogists approach the records with caution, making allowances for special pleading, myth, propaganda, and falsehood arising from racial or religious prejudice:

> Alice Gregg the Relict of Richard Gregg late of Loughgall … farmer … deposeth … the Rebells … stripped att one time above 300 of them, of all their clothes & then drive them like sheep into the Church of Loughgall. And then & there the grand Rebell Doghertie publiquely sayd to his bloudy and Rebellious crew That all theis (meaning the protestants soe imprisoned) shall be putt to death … and then left them there naked … And with their skeanes sett upon this deponent and her husband & children … and gave her eight wounds in her head: and devided & cutt her soun John Gregg whilest he was alive into quarters & threw them att his fathers face … forced about fourscore protestants into the water off the bridge of Callon nere Mr Fairfax howse & there drowned them

> (21st July 1643)

In 1696, Parliament required all office holders to swear an oath of loyalty to the Crown. The resulting association oath rolls (C 213) in national and county archives contain names of civil servants, military personnel, clergy, JPs and city freemen. The rolls, arranged by regions, were partially indexed by Bernau for the Society of Genealogists.

From as early as the thirteenth century, authorities attempted to establish central registers for title deeds and other documents. In Scotland, the notary public enjoyed a lucrative business drawing up legal instruments and maintaining an archive of copies transcribed into protocol books. These volumes are now the responsibility of the National Archives in Edinburgh, though some examples are also to be found in council archives. From 1617, a particular register of sasines was inaugurated in the sheriffdoms with a general register in Edinburgh to enrol title deeds recording the transfer of land in burgh and county, 'by deliverance of earth and stone', according to the medieval ceremony of sasine. Most registers are in Edinburgh, though a few burgh series are lodged locally. There are printed indexes and calendars that may give sufficient information for simple genealogy. Scottish officials also maintained registers of various legal transactions likely to become problematical if original

(229)   Aug. 23. 1788.
WILLIAM PATERSON, son of Robert Paterson, Minister, Newapynie, John Brown, son of William Brown in Dumbarton, & Margaret Brown, spouse of Alexander Cruickshanks, Weaver, Dumbarton, as heirs to Margaret M'Kenzie, spouse of William Collie, Minister, Kinnedder, Margaret Mercer, spouse of William Brown at Dumbarton, and Hugh Mercer, son of William Mercer, M. D., Frederick Burgh, Virginia, their grandmother, mother, and uncle respectively, *Seised*, for their respective interests, Aug. 21. 1788,—in EARNSIDE & Ordies, and Mill of Earnside; Kirktown of Alves, par. Alves;—in security of 3000 Merks Scots, in Bond by John Spens of Alves Kirktown, to Hugh Anderson, Minister, Kinnedder, and spouse, Nov. 6. 1735;—on Disp. & Assig. by him to the said Margaret M'Kenzie, & Hugh, and Margaret Mercer, Oct. 30. 1740; Ret. Gen. Serv. of the said William Paterson, as heir to the said Margaret M'Kenzie, his grandmother, Jul. 3. 1788; Ret. Gen. Serv. of the said John Brown, as heir to the said Margaret Mercer, his mother, Jul. 3. 1788; & Ret. Gen. Serv. to the said John and Margaret Brown, as heirs of provision to the said Hugh Mercer, their uncle, Jul. 3. 1788.   P. R. 9. 189.

Calendar of a register of sasines showing relationships among various family members concerned in a property named Earnside, 1788.

documentation was mislaid by the parties. To protect the interests of creditors by providing a record of the outcome of the legal process of diligence, courts maintained particular registers of hornings and inhibitions. These were supplemented from 1602 by general, that is national, registers. A national register of tailzies (entails) was commenced in 1688.

Irish registration was notably comprehensive, recording titles to land and also the terms of jointures, children's portions, marriage settlements, family descents, leases for specified lives and wills, though not leases for less than twenty-one years, the sole tenure permitted to Roman Catholics.

The miscellanea of the English Chancery includes a promiscuous collection of documents accumulated from estates, families, boroughs and businesses in the course of centuries of administrative activity. There are charters; manorial records; pedigrees; coroners' inquests; surveys of Crown rights in the Channel Islands from the thirteenth century; Jews in commerce under Edward I; inquisitions on Irish manors, castles and monasteries; perambulations of forests; certificates returned by guilds and chantries under Richard II; captured Scottish public records; returns of lands in Wales; returns with oral testimonies of charitable bequests under acts of 1597 and 1601 continuing until the Charity Commission was established in 1853; and commissions to certify lunatics, a process which operated into the twentieth century.

From 1876, solicitors in England and Wales could deposit unclaimed money from Chancery for safe keeping while legatees and next of kin were traced. These dormant funds and unclaimed fortunes have inspired many a family legend and genealogical endeavour.

20
National archives: courts

A civil or criminal court case might devastate family relationships and consume the accumulated wealth of a generation, but resulting records are full of genealogical information. In England archives commence before 1200, with authority extending into Wales and Ireland with the Norman conquests. These medieval courts heard criminal and civil cases until reforms of 1873–5. Some documentation, especially up to 1300, has been transcribed and published, while cases for later centuries are variously calendared, listed and indexed. The Court of King's (or Queen's) Bench from 1194 (KB) decided questions affecting the king's (or queen's) peace, including trespass, theft and personal actions of ejectment on titles to freehold property. The Court of Common Pleas (CP) heard civil disputes that might require the production of family papers, inquisitions, marriage contracts, settlements, title deeds, pedigrees, valuations and wills. If not reclaimed when the case was over, these might be retained in court files and classified as public records. In Common Pleas, genealogical information was elicited during the process of issuing documents known as final concords and recoveries to establish clear titles to landed property. The law cases were in fact shams, pursued for the sake of a judgement, but involving actual people and property, though assisted by more or less fictitious participants. Fines are preserved for the period 1132–1838, recoveries for 1472–1837, and may be duplicated in family and estate deed bundles. As a court of common law, Exchequer specialised in personal actions of ejectment from property, church tithes and related civil disputes. Chancery also operated as a court of

Pedigree used as evidence in the Court of King's Bench, 1310.

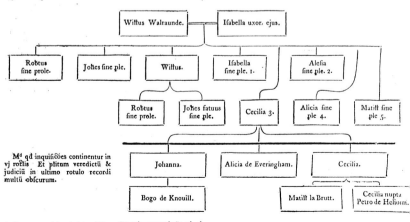

Et jur̄ dic̄ q̄d p̄dictus Wiłłus avus p̄dieti Joħes nullum aliud exitum percavit de p̄dicta Isabella uxore sua nisi tantummodo p̄fatos Wiłłm Roħtum p̄fatam Aliciam & unam aliam filiam similiter Aliciam nomine que monialis fuit & abbissa de Romesey & obiit p̄fessa & sine herede de se.

E. contra p̄dicta Alic̄ de Everingham & alii heredes dicunt q̄d p̄dictus Wiłłus nullā aliā habuit filiam nisi monialem illam . Et monstrat descensum suum hereditarium in modum sequen̄.

M̄d q̄d inquisic̄ōes continentur in vj roł̄lis Et p̄litum veredictū & judiciū in ultimo rotulo recordi multū obscurum.

Ambo petunt q̄d inquiratur p̄ p̄riam Et ambo concordarūt q̄d vic̄ Suth̄ & Glouc̄ vel̄ fac̄ xij tam milites quā at, &c. Et Joħes de Basings Joħes de Popham Ric̄us de Stratton Ric̄us de Johene Ric̄us de Tisted Joħes de Ticheburn milites de com̄ Suth̄ Joħes de Sc̄o Laudo Roħtus de Berkeley Joħes de Owlepenne Joħes de Brokencberton Wiłłus de Colewich Wiłłus atte Haye de com̄ Glouc̄ judicium redditū ex pte Alani Plukenet & alii nichil capiant.   -   roł̄ 126.

The Court of Common Pleas around 1450.

common law partly in competition with other, perhaps less expensive, jurisdictions. Chancery cases are catalogued down to the 1620s, with indexes suitable to the needs of family historians. Later cases are accessible through the original files and official finding aids.

Central courts also worked on equitable rather than common or statute law principles. Equitable jurisdiction claimed to correct or supplement the written law by the application of principles of fair play, conscience and common sense. Chancery's equity work in England originated in the fourteenth century, swelling in importance as the department's administrative role withered. Officials based their authority on the supposed inability of the common law to remedy a variety of difficulties because hampered by restrictive legislation and legal precedent. Chancery specialised in cases relating to debt, inheritance, marriage settlements, succession to property and wills. As a court proceeding by rules of equity and conscience, Chancery was notionally a refuge for poor pleaders denied a remedy through common law. From about 1410, pleas, known as bills, were submitted in English rather than Latin or Norman French. Despite good intentions, Chancery became renowned for tardy and expensive justice:

> compleyneth … Owen o Ryordan & Mahowne o Ryordan … of the Towne & lands of Bohernefoyny … that Mortagh mcBryen of Castelltowwne … disseysed your supplyants of two third parts … in as much as your supplyants are verry poore and unhable to try right vith the said mcBryen … a man of greate alyance & kinred … with whom your supplyants can hardly have anny indifferency of tryall by ordenary cowrse of common lawe … to graunt … wrytt of subpena to be dyrected unto the said mcBryen

> (National Archives of Ireland, C198 (IC.2.146), after 1604)

Chancery gained exclusive jurisdiction in respect of trusts and the rights of married women, infants and lunatics. For nineteenth-century cases the unpublished indexes are voluminous and the bundles of papers put into court enormous – a test of the genealogist's mettle, but richly rewarding perseverance. Depositions are especially significant, giving name, age, parish, occupation and, as appropriate, life history (C 21, 22 and 24). Exchequer's equity jurisdiction emerged during the sixteenth century and continued until 1841. The court was not as busy, nor as dilatory, as Chancery and its records are simpler to research. Families involved in disputes over church tithes, benefices, patronage and boundaries turned principally to Exchequer. The court's registrar, known as the King's Remembrancer, preserved legal archives as well as all manner of estate and family muniments produced in court but not subsequently reclaimed. The Privy Council spawned two further equity courts. Star Chamber (STAC), named after the room known as *camera stellata* in the Palace of Westminster in which it originally sat, heard criminal cases of abuse by landowners, or families with whom the monarch quarrelled. The Court of Requests (REQ) was notionally yet another place for poor men's civil causes concerning, for example, messuages, wills and burgages. Riot, forgery and admiralty cases were also heard. Cases are listed by names of parties, issues involved and county. Both courts were abolished at the insistence of Parliament at the start of the Civil War.

Legal proceedings associated with business failure reveal a family's commercial enterprises. Individuals include employees, shareholders, clients, customers, suppliers, sharp operators buying up a bankrupt's stock and agents taking a percentage from the sale. Genealogists search archives of the Court of **Bankruptcy**, founded in 1571, and some twenty thousand files of cases from 1710 onwards; bankruptcy records of Chancery Petty Bag Office, including original records of certain firms during the period 1774–1830; Exchequer extents and inquisitions referring to Crown debtors; published lists of bankrupts from 1772 – all supplemented by newspaper articles and official rolls detailing the sale of bankrupts' property. Dissolutions of partnerships and commissions of bankruptcy are reported in the *London Gazette*. From 1824, records relating to insolvent debtors were lodged with the clerk of the peace.

The High Court of **Admiralty** in London was concerned with piracy and spoil from the fourteenth century onwards, with an evolving umbrella of jurisdiction over shipping and merchandise around the coasts, murder and assault in maritime contexts, collision, wages, commercial disputes, insurance and salvage. Subsidiary vice-admiralty courts assisted with the workload. Records are found in both national and local archives.

In England, the Crown commissioned judges to travel on circuit to the shires. These itinerant or eyre courts originated during the twelfth century and continued until 1294. Eyre judges heard cases of murder, manslaughter, robbery, wounding and rape as well as a variety of civil disputes. From 1271, keepers of the peace travelled the country. Their gaol delivery rolls continued until 1476. From 1305, royal justices sat in shire Courts of Oyer and Terminer 'to hear and decide' criminal and civil cases. Early records have been variously listed, catalogued and printed by the PRO and county record societies.

Assize 'sitting' judges toured the country in fixed circuits before holding court in designated towns until merged with quarter sessions in 1971. The Old Bailey functioned as assize court for London from 1834, but sessions papers recording its work as the central criminal court are preserved from 1801. For the London circuit documentation dates from the sixteenth century; for the midlands only from 1818. The genealogist searches particularly for presentments by grand juries as well as indictments stating an alleged offence, perhaps with an endorsement relating to verdict and punishment. Gaol calendars provide names, ages and offences of individuals held for trial. There are also recognisances to appear in court, depositions by witnesses and official minute books of decisions and sentences. Calendars of prisoners awaiting trial or under sentence were published commercially and printed in the newspapers. Prisoners were listed in the Newgate Calendar of 1782–1853, records of the Fleet, Marshalsea and King's Bench prisons, 1685–1862, and miscellaneous criminal registers, 1791–1892, all among the public records. Assizes were a convenient repository for the records of coroners' inquests, at least from about 1487 until 1700. Assize judges decided profitable civil cases, officially the exclusive preserve of lawyers and judges at Westminster. The cases were thus known as *nisi prius*, maintaining a fiction that Westminster would have the trial 'unless' completed 'before' on circuit.

Divided between the PRO and National Library of Wales is the archive of the **Court of Great Sessions** for Wales, an itinerant court with four circuits. Legal papers, indictments, presentments, common recoveries, final concords, plans, family settlements, title deeds, inquisitions, enclosure awards, financial accounts, the muniments of the lordship of Ruthin and court minutes cover the period 1542 until 1830, when it was absorbed into the national assizes.

Scottish civil and criminal court records are the responsibility of the National Archives. The highest central court of first instance and appeal was the Court of Session, sitting in Edinburgh and hearing civil cases concerning, for example, property and debt. From the sixteenth century onwards, general and particular minute books serve as chronological indexes of cases. Detail is provided in registers of acts and decrees and especially in the bundles of relevant case papers known as processes. From 1554, personal legal documents such as title deeds, marriage and business contracts could be copied for security into registers of deeds known as books of council and session. Commissary courts from 1563 addressed executry, slander, aliment and marital causes. The Exchequer Court determined smuggling, illicit distilling and other revenue matters.

Itinerant or ayre courts circulated around the more settled regions of Scotland, records surviving for the period 1493–1575. The High Court of Justiciary in Edinburgh, with circuit courts convening in provincial centres, was the supreme

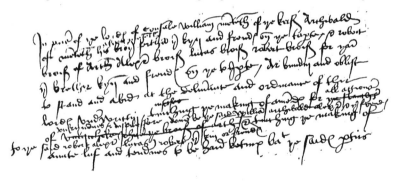

In p̄ns of þe lordꝭ of confale Williā m̄teth of þe kerß
Archibald of m̄teth his broß alexr m̄teth for thaī
þ kyn and frendꝭ oñ þe tapte / t robert broiß of
Arth Alexr broiß lucas broiß robert broiß for þaī þ
brethir kyñ and frendꝭ oñ þe toßpte / Ar bundin and
obliſt to ſtand and abid / at the deliūance and ordi-
nance of thir lordꝭ vnd°writtin / tuiching þe making

all accioñs   vnkyndnes ᴇ difpileſſore doñe be þe faid
of am̄dꝭ for þe flaucht of vmquhile Johñe þe
Williā archibald alexr ᴇ ß frende þe faid robert alexr lucas robert ß kin or frende
broiß of arth t tuiching þe making of amite luf

Original manuscript and record-type transcription of minutes of a case in the Scottish Court of Session.

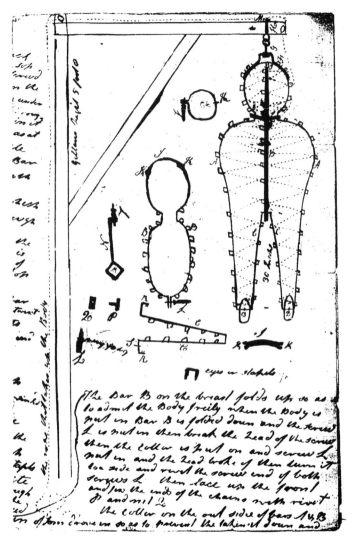

Design for chains to exhibit the body of the murderer Alexander Gillan, 1810.

criminal court. Books of adjournal and minutes with witness reports from 1812 are the principal records. In 1810 this court sentenced a slow-witted teenager, Alexander Gillan, to be hanged and hung in chains for the murder of a neighbour's daughter. Additional papers in the case file show that a few weeks later Gillan's friends stole the body from the gibbet for secret burial. The despised hangman who executed Gillan was himself killed on his way home. His two murderers, apprentices from the county town, were sentenced to transportation. Five families were thus bereft, three communities distraught. Two generations later, with memories still fresh and nerves raw, the Ordnance Survey marked the site of 'Gillan's grave' in woodland near the spot where he and his victims died. Chains allegedly from the gibbet are ghoulishly exhibited in a nearby farmhouse.

A visualisation of the execution of Alexander Gillan in 1810.

From the twelfth century, sheriffs heard civil and criminal cases, initially perambulating only lowland sheriffdoms but in the twenty-first century operating throughout Scotland. In royal burghs, courts operated with shrieval powers within urban liberties. Documents created by the courts included minutes, act books, decreets recording decisions and diet or day books of cases. The most revealing series are the processes, bundles of papers presented to the court, commencing typically with a libel or petition, continuing with replies, duplies, bills and accounts. Papers are the responsibility of the National Archives where shortage of space has demanded weeding back to 1707. Extensive collections, however, survive in Edinburgh, burgh archives and council heritage centres. Some cases raise interesting genealogical questions, depending upon which party's story we choose to believe. In 1818, the wisdom of the sheriff of Elginshire was taxed by a custody dispute with an interesting twist, whose resolution might influence the genealogist's decision to follow the male or female line of ancestors. The case was initiated by a petition from William Lewis at Drumduan:

> That it was your petitioner's misfortune ... to form an illicit connection with Ann Campbell ... his Servant and in consequence ... Ann Campbell became pregnant ... the Petitioner has repeatedly informed the said Ann Campbell Her Father John Campbell and Jane Dunbar her Mother that he is ready & willing to pay ... Inlying charges ... as also ... aliment for the child or children ... notwithstanding ... Ann Campbell is determined neither to keep nurse or care for the child ... And that [it] shall immediately after the birth be carried to the Petitioners house and there left even at the door ... as the Petitioner happens to be a married man with a family such threats have alarmed him exceedingly ... his wife from the delicate state of her health can ill put up with such a shock.

Sheriffs could impose a death sentence in criminal cases, as in this example of an incorrigible Banffshire cattle thief in 1699:

> James Gray ... commonly bruted for a loose man & common thief ... did steal ...

List of tenants to be evicted during the legal clearance of the estates of James Brodie of Brodie, 1768.

ane young Cow and did … kill her & did Eat & make use of the blood … with which Fang wholl & Inteir, Skein & birne, hyd & horne … Red hand apprehended … to be takin upon Fryday nixt … From the prison of Cullen … to the Clune hill theroff & Gibbitt standing theron, betuixt the hours of tuo & Four aclocke in the afternoon & therupon hang'd up by the neck by the hand of the Common executioner til yee be dead

Transportation, initially to the American colonies and subsequently to Australia, was available as a humane and economically productive alternative in an age of colonial expansion, as here in a case of 1721:

No.	Reign.	Plaintiffs.	Defendants.	Premises, and Matters in Dispute.	Places.	Counties.
10.	N. D.	Anthony Brown and Johan his Wife, Coufin and Heir of Sir Henry Farrington, Knight.	Robert Farrington, William Fyther, and others.	Difputed Title to Manors, Lands, and Tenements, in Breach of Decree, and after Commitment of Defendants to the Fleet Prifon.	Farrington Manor otherwife Farrington Hall. Leylande Manor. Ulnefwalton. Prefton in Amounder-nefs. Fleet Prifon.	Lancafhire. London.
11.	1 Mary.	Robert Barrett.	William Webfter.	Difputed Title to Lands and Appurtenances called Duffeyld Wood, Pymeleys, and Hayfield.	Duffelde Fryth Manor. Idrythhey. Wyrkefworth Manor.	Derbyfhire.
12.	N. D.	Thomas Bower.	Richard Grymefhay.	Difputed Title to Lands and Appurtenances.	Ayntre.	Lancafhire.
13.	N. D.	Thomas Bradyfhawe.	Adam Pendilton.	Difputed Title to a Meffuage and Appurtenances in Whitecroffe Street.	Lytherpole.	Lancafhire.
14.	N. D.	William Butler.	James Haworth and Margaret his Wife, Thomas Such, and Anthony Layton.	Difputed Title to a Meffuage and Lands.	Ormyfkyrke.	Lancafhire.
15.	N. D.	Ralph Burye.	Hamnet Stokley.	Tortious Poffeffion of a Meffuage and Lands, and Detention of Title Deeds.	Rowbyehall. Rowbye.	Lancafhire.
16.	N. D.	Richard Bold.	Sir Thomas Holt, Knight, Thomas Salter, and others.	Forcible Entry and tortious Poffeffion of Land called the Abbot's Acre.	Wydnes Lordfhip.	Lancafhire.
17.	6 Edw. 6.	Thomas Bennet, Inhabitant of Hoddifdon.	Thomas Blackborne, Bailiff of Spilfley, and Robert Bryan, Bailiff of Bolingbroke.	Difputed Claim of Exemption from Tolls of Markets and Fairs.	Hoddifdon Manor. Spilfley. Bolingbroke.	Hertfordfhire. Lincolnfhire.
18.	N. D.	Richard Buxton.	William Meyre.	Illegal Poffeffion of a Meffuage and Lands, in Breach of Decree.	Bryggynge. Duffeld Fryth Manor.	Derbyfhire.
19.	N. D.	Johan Backhoufe, Widow.	Roland Harteley, William Sawrey, and others.	Trefpafs and Dilapidation of a Tenement and Lands.	Bardfall. Urfewyke.	Lancafhire.
20.	N. D.	James Browne.	George Hefkethe and Gabriel Hefkethe.	Difputed Title to Meffuages and Lands.	Wigan.	Lancafhire.
21.	N. D.	Robert Browne.	Randall Bromefiete.	Difputed Title to a Tenement and Appurtenances, Parcel of Saint Wilfryd's Chantry.	Ryppon.	Yorkfhire.

Calendar of property disputes in the court of the Duchy of Lancaster.

James MackKenzie theiff … Did … being lodged in John Mackie his barn where his servants were lying when they were all asleep aryse under Cloud and Silence of Night and brack open ane Chist Belonging to Donald Clunes servitor [did] steall … fifty three merks … ane Coat … ane pair of Britches three gravets three necks and ane axe to be … taken to the harbour of Findhorn And there to be imbarqued on boord of the first ship going for London And from thence to be transported to Barbadoes

In 1701, a petty thief, using a name often adopted by members of the proscribed McGregor clan, got off relatively lightly:

John Donaldson alias Mugach … wes scourged within the burgh of Forres … for stealing money … Confesses … putting his hand in ane mans pockit … stealing tuo towels … to be taken to the west end of the Toun … and to be scourged to the cross where he is to be burnt on the right cheek with the letter F [for Felon] and then to be

The noted Gaelic poet and preacher Iain MacDhomnuill was born in the town of Balnabeen, Caithness, in 1779. The entire settlement was later cleared and the houses demolished, though the foundations and field boundaries of this peasant community can still be traced on the ground.

scourged to the east end of the Toun and never to be seen within the shyre ... under pain of death

Also of genealogical relevance are cases concerning probate, business contracts, debt, poinding or distraint of straying animals. Political and religious dissidents were pursued, sometimes by subtle means, occasionally more overtly. Judgements in the sheriff courts gave authority to landowners bent on the clearance of villages and the enclosure of open field landscapes from 1756 onwards. The major landowners in Moray and their factors crowded to court in the year 1766 in a flurry of legal activity that paved the way for wholesale clearance of the county over the course of the succeeding generation. Peasant tenants were ordered 'to flitt & remove themselves wives Bairns servants subtenants Cottars & hail goods & Gear Furth & from their respective possessions at the term of Whitsunday next'. Notice was given by a sheriff officer:

by delivering ... full writen Copies in their own hands ... Excepting ... Donald Grant in Mains of Relugas whose Copie I left in the Lock hole of the most patent door of his house ... because I could not personally apprehend him

A single clearance case might list a whole community of tenants, subtenants, servants and cottars. Few possessed written title in the form of a lease or tack to holdings held by customary tenure for generations. Some protested that their rental payments gave them security, but many were illiterate, and most had failed carefully to preserve at home the receipts and paperwork that might have supported their claims. An estate was therefore easily and legally cleared. Families thereafter worked as day labourers for newly established farmers or moved away to the better life of colonies and industrial towns.

Common law and equity courts of the **palatinates** of Durham, Lancaster and Chester operated independently of national courts until the nineteenth century. Law cases involving final concords and common recoveries were heard. Records of the Scottish Land Court and Crofters' Commission from 1886 relate to family tenure of crofts and smallholdings chiefly, but not exclusively, in the Highlands and Islands. Archives of the supreme Court of Judicature for England and Wales, commencing in 1876, cover probate, divorce, admiralty, appeal and bankruptcy. These are retained by the court rather than deposited in the Public Record Office and may be available to ordinary genealogical researchers if a convincing legal argument justifies access. Appeals from regional courts were directed up to Parliament, the highest court in the land, comprising senior judges of the House of Lords. Legal records are reasonably full from 1621 onwards. Recourse to the Lords was not restricted to the rich and powerful. Anyone could try.

Courts never caught up with the bigamous fugitive Horatio Mather (referred to on pages 19–21), here seen on 7th September 1885 with his new wife in a photograph from the archives of Urlin's Mammoth Art Gallery, 216 and 218 South High Street, Columbus, Ohio; 'by sending name, copies can always be obtained ... at reduced rates.'

21
National archives: administration

As an instrument of government, the English **Privy Council** emerged during the 1380s. Administrative reforms under Edward IV and Henry VII shifted considerable executive power into the hands of the monarch in council. A professional secretariat maintained a register of discussions of matters of state. Practical and detailed work was done through subsidiary committees such as councils in the Marches of Wales until 1688 and in the North down to 1642. Privy Council proceedings and ordinances from 1386 to 1631 have been edited and published. Unpublished files concerning, for example, schools, burials, public health and poor relief are approached through the List and Index Society publication number 36. Particular aspects of the council's original broad remit were subsequently hived off to dedicated boards, ministries and departments.

From the sixteenth century, **secretaries of state** took over the administrative work formerly done by the Chancellor. Their records are known as state papers. Families and individuals came into contact with the reformed administration, usually through written communication. The archive includes petitions, letters, requests for deployment of armed forces in the provinces, muster certificates relating to regional defence forces, a census of inns and alehouses (1577), financial accounts for expenses incurred on behalf of the Crown, confiscation of the estates of Roman Catholics and supporters of the royal Stuarts, and miscellaneous pleas for preferments, perquisites, privileges and pensions. Indexes and calendars of various series up to the reign of George III are available in print.

In Ireland during the sixteenth and seventeenth centuries Protestant settlers, soldiers and adventurers were planted on native baronies. Many families now resident in Ireland but of English or Scottish origin and surname date their arrival to this period. The legal process of colonisation required documentation in surveys, maps, title deeds and financial statements. Strafford's inquisition for Charles I into Irish property in the 1630s provided a model for Cromwell's comprehensive civil survey of 1654–6, based on information from jurors in each barony. The whole Irish nation was deemed to be in rebellion and all houses and industrial premises were notionally forfeited, allowing surveyors a free hand in twenty-seven counties of Connacht, Leinster, Munster and Ulster. Records in the Quit Rent Office, Dublin, have been published:

> Nicholas Fanying of Limericke Alderman Irish Papist … stone house next on the north to the former house of Andrew Creaghs … Two Cadgworke Houses thereunto adioyning … with a passadge betwixt them, with a Backside … Another House of stone and Clay … Rent to the Corporation 9d yearely
> (City of Limerick, parish of St Nicholas)

Barony maps commissioned by Parliament were surveyed and drawn under the supervision of William Petty from 1654 to 1656. Known as the *Down Survey* because it was laid *down* on paper, the maps may also be sought with the public records in Dublin and Belfast, the National Library of Ireland and Bibliothèque Nationale, Paris. Books of survey and distribution continued the record of family property transfer and confiscation under the restored monarchy from 1662 onwards.

Throughout Britain the Civil War and its aftermath may mark a watershed in a family's fortunes, for good or ill. Individuals gaining estates and houses moved across the country to enjoy and exploit their new possessions. Families who lost their property also travelled, seeking a fresh start perhaps in expanding towns or colonies. During the period 1644–57, Parliament authorised the survey of delinquents' estates. The lands of uncompromising royalists were sequestered (confiscated) in a process that created voluminous records naming owners, tenants and their family connections. Documents are scattered among estate papers, deed bundles, lawyers' accumulations, county and national archives, with a selection also available in print. Following rebellions in support of the Stuart dynasty, especially the risings of 1715 and 1745, estates of Roman Catholics and Jacobites were surveyed and annexed, that is taken temporarily under government control. Records of the Annexed Estates Commissioners after 1746, documenting the day-to-day management of estates with their resident populations, were published by the Scottish Record Office in 1973.

The **Board of Trade** originated in a Privy Council committee formed in 1621 concerned with colonial trade. Following Pitt's reforms of 1786, the Board's remit expanded to include commerce and industry, factories, joint stock companies, trade disputes, coal mines and railways. An early function was the regulation of seamen, ship owners, merchant shipping and fishing boats. Crew lists were required for British vessels from 1747. For the period 1861–1938 and from 1951 the national archives (London and Edinburgh) retained a ten per cent sample of lists and ships' logs. Remaining documents were dispersed to county record offices, the National Maritime Museum, the Memorial University of Newfoundland and, for 1939–50 and the more recent period, the General Register of Shipping and Seamen, Cardiff. The PRO holds apprenticeship records for 1824–1953, registers of seamen, masters, officers and engineers, some from 1835. The National Maritime Museum retains masters' original certificates of competency before 1900, best accessed through Lloyd's captain's registers at Guildhall Library, London, where also may be studied historical marine records of Lloyd's of London. Petitions from seamen's families seeking assistance from Trinity House, the incorporation having official regulation of shipping, may be searched at Guildhall and, in copy, at the Society of Genealogists, London. Merchant seamen on board ship figure in the national census returns from 1851 (from 1861 seamen on the high seas and in foreign ports may be specified). Seamen appear in archives of various port authorities and of ship owners (records of T. & J. Brocklebank at Merseyside Maritime Museum begin in 1809). Passenger lists of individuals arriving in or leaving Britain for points outside Europe, retained from 1890 onwards, are arranged by ports.

The fighting **Navy** was administered by boards of management. From the sixteenth century, commissioners of marine causes shared responsibility with the Admiralty. Registers, reports, correspondence, ships' log books and victualling accounts are key sources for genealogists with ancestors connected with naval bases including Chatham, Devonport, Dartmouth and Portsmouth. Lists of men serving in the Navy commence about 1660. Physical description books, pay books, medical registers and muster books setting out ships' companies from about 1690 are sometimes accompanied by a record of service. Among the most often consulted are passing out certificates, 1691–1902. Information on pensions to seamen, civilian officials, coastguards, artificers, labourers and their families may be found in the records of Greenwich Hospital, chiefly from the eighteenth century onwards. Apprenticeship registers for the hospital for 1808–38 are among Admiralty archives (ADM 73). Other apprentices are traced in the series ADM 1 and 106. Examination results for dockyard artificers and apprentices, recorded from 1876, are among Civil Service Commission archives (CSC 10). Royal Marines are documented in War Office and Admiralty archives. Description books from about 1750, arranged by companies, giving name, age, birthplace and physical description, are supported by attestation forms from 1790 arranged by date of discharge, correspondence, minutes and registers.

The **army** is referred to in archives of the Board of Ordnance from 1570, Secretary-at-War from 1661, Commander-in-Chief from 1765, Secretary for War from 1794, Judge Advocate General, Commissary General, Board of General Officers and Adjutant General. The archives refer to military personnel and civilian support staff in an array of different establishments, for example powder mills at Ballincollig, County Cork, the musketry school at Pendine, Carmarthenshire, the depot at Lymington and the royal hospitals at Chelsea and Kilmainham. Military archives are relevant for the history of civilian families, including contractors, garrison town prostitutes, Chartists, Sinn Feiners, strikers and households dispossessed for a fort or camp. Pre-1660 records of soldiers may be traced in Exchequer and state papers. From the middle of the eighteenth century, War Office and Paymaster General's archives include attestation papers, muster books, pay lists, monthly returns, description books, medal rolls, pension accounts, casualty returns, lists of deserters and discharge papers. These are filed in the series WO 10–12, 14–15, 17, 25, 67, 71–3, 81–93, 97 and 121. Surveys of full- and half-pay officers, conducted 1828–9 and 1847, returned biographical information. Research into soldier ancestors usually begins with finding out the name of his unit from family sources because documents are arranged by regiment from 1760 to 1873 and only thereafter by surname. Regimental records also are generally retained in army museums. Ongoing indexing programmes are likely to remedy this difficulty.

Gibraltar 28th November 1856
REGIMENTAL BOARD … for the purpose of verifying … the Services, Conduct, Character … of … No. *3367 Private Hugh Gillen …*
Age   *24⁷/₁₂,*
Height *5* Feet *4* Inches
Hair   *Light Brown*
Trade *Labourer*
Intended Place of Residence *Glasgow*

Official schedule N containing a description of George Cormack, deserter from the 2nd Battalion, Royal Regiment of Artillery, 1822.

Deserted 2d June ... 1855 ... Sentenced 84 days Imprisonment ... Not in possession of Good Conduct Badge
MEDICAL REPORT. – ... *suffers from secondary Syphilitic Symptoms which render him unable to perform his duty*

Venereal diseases, endemic from the mid sixteenth century, were epidemic during some generations and in certain localities, professions and social groups.

Personal records of men serving in the First World War are at the Army Records Office of the Ministry of Defence, Bourne Avenue, Hayes, Middlesex. Microfilms may be available at the PRO. Many files were destroyed by enemy bombing during the Second World War. For war graves and memorials, researchers contact the Commonwealth War Graves Commission, 2 Marlow Road, Maidenhead, Berkshire.

From the seventeenth century onwards, the government expected adult males to serve militarily in their own localities to keep the peace or repel invaders. Records of the volunteers, fencibles, territorials, Home Guard and other militia forces were haphazardly made and preserved by officials even after the definitive Militia Act of 1757. Some ten departments were involved, none with overall responsibility, hence the complexity of archival arrangements. Scottish militia apportionments for each county from 1798 are relatively uncomplicated of access among Privy Council archives.

The **Air Department** of the Admiralty, formed in 1910, expanded during the war of 1914–18 into an independent flying service under the Air Ministry. Air Force personnel are documented in defence department files at the PRO and the Ministry of Defence air historical branch, with notable additional sources at the Imperial War Museum, London, National Maritime Museum, Greenwich, National Army Museum, Chelsea, and Royal Air Force Museum, Hendon. The loss of Whitley bomber N1440 over the town of Forres in November 1940 was reported in two top-secret RAF documents: a casualty list and an accident record. (Testimony of an eye-witness has been quoted on page 14.) The crash widowed Marion Gilchrist, a civilian clerkess at RAF Kinloss. She was married again in 1941, to an American pilot from San Antonio. The couple drifted apart before the birth of their daughter Patricia. Marion married again. Her child, adopted and renamed Alice, grew up not knowing her own father, mother, surname or given name. The eventually successful search for her roots involved RAF files, American consulates, the US Air Force and social work agencies in the USA. Alice's researches were helpful also to a relative of another of the Whitley crew. The wife of the distinguished wildlife artist David Shepherd had been informed, quite correctly, by a council official 'that there is no reference to the air crash in the official records'. Through genealogical networking, Mrs Shepherd, the daughter of Sergeant H. D. Gaywood (born 1908), was able at last to know the story, sadly accepting the 'seemingly needless' death of her father.

Boards of management were a popular means of managing the economy. Scottish economic development, for instance in the linen industry, was fostered by the Board of Manufactures of 1727–1927. A main role of the Scottish Board of Excise was the prosecution of the illegal *uisgebeatha* (whisky) industry. The organised traffic in illicit whisky was a profitable business defended with violence and murder. The full potential of the law was seldom exercised and distillers seem to have accepted prosecution almost with equanimity, as a kind of oblique taxation: 'William Leslie, Neither ley Rothes, Moray ... Discovered By T. Stephen ... Distilling privately & seized at Work one still, Penalty £500 ... Fines awarded 10s 6d' (1816). Several individuals prosecuted for illegal whisky trafficking reappeared after reform of excise laws in 1825 as respectable businessmen operating legal distilleries such as the famous Cardow on Speyside.

Administrative reform in 1782 created the **Home Office**, concerned with internal security, political dissent, militia, police, transport, agriculture and industry. The Home Secretary liaised with county magistrates, government spies and politicians in respect of political dissidents, trade unionists and prisoners in gaols. The umbrella of control extended over town government, markets, burial grounds, lunacy, mines, fisheries and bomb damage during the World Wars. Files of incoming papers are classified HO 42 and 44, books of outgoing letter books HO 43. From the mid nineteenth century, documentation may be found in single-subject files, some internally indexed.

In Ireland, the **Chief Secretary** created copious and genealogically productive documentation during the period 1778–1924. The secretary was greatly exercised over internal security. State papers from 1778 offer an intriguing confection of outrages, arson, boycotting, riots and strikes arising from economic distress, nationalist agitation and sectarian prejudice. Outrage papers highlight popular unrest during the period 1832–52, here documented in a report from the Chief Constable of Dublin in 1838:

> as the fair of Killsalaghan was drawing to a close, a fight commenced between two Parties, one calling themselves *Sackmen*, and the other *'Billysmiths'* … I charged the mob and made four of the ringleaders prisoners, the principal ringleader … who resides generally at Swords and who is a very noted character … Escaped

Records from 1878 refer to nationalist movements such as the Fenians, Land League and National League. The following report concerns a typical episode in this conflict:

> In the month of March 1884 Henry Young and his son Denis Young, of Glin, took a farm of seven acres at Tullyglass, near Glin, from which the former tenant, Stackpool, was evicted by the Knight of Glin for non-payment of rent … On the 11th May 1884 … notices were posted … calling on the people to boycott the Youngs … viz. :–
> *Henry … professes the faith of Luther. He says he will swim in a flood*
> *of butchered papist crimson blood …*
> *Upon some poachers he did swear,*
> *to see them start and kill a hare …*
> *By perjury did clinch the nail at the sessions in Rathkeal …*
> *But the time of our release is near …*
> *Then all such grabbing creatures … Shall be driven from Ireland's shore*
> the house of Denis Young was attacked … a cow … was killed … In February 1886 Denis Young surrendered the farm … was then admitted a member of the Glin branch of the Irish National League. His customers returned to him, and he is now working at his trade as boot and shoe maker

The Valuation Office survey of Ireland began in 1809, permitting officials to assign values for rating purposes to domestic, commercial, industrial and agricultural properties. Valuators drew up maps depicting houses and landscapes a generation before the Ordnance Survey. House books describe family homes and business premises with comments on the state of trade:

> Wibrants Olphirt Esq. Flax Mill Length 22ft 6in Breadth 18–0 Water Wheel Diameter 13–0 Fall of Water 7 0 No. of Buckets 48 … Has water & Employment for 9 Months in Each year at 12 Hours per day
>
> (Ballyness, County Donegal, 1855)

> Revd. Mr Stewart, Muff Lodge: House Basement Story Stable Offices Open Sheds & privy … a nice situation. a good distance from the road. Small yard well enclosed
>
> (Innishowen West, County Donegal, 1839)

Field books indicated land use, while record of tenure books specified acreage, rental, tenure, occupier and immediate lessor:

> Townland under ejectment but 6 months given to Mr McCarty to redeem, the Tenants
> were let on those Conditions ...
> Mortimer Curtin Land 42. 2. 0 £55. 10. 0 No Lease 1848
> Morty Curtin Hotel Offices & Land £12. 10. 0 Lease of 3 lives & 31 years 1824
> Saml Huchings Esq holds this mountain ... for the purpose of Planting
> Mary Kenney House No Rent No Title ...
> Mary Murphy House Yard & Garden £1. 0. 0 Yearly 1849
> (Grenagh, barony of Barretts, County Cork, 1849)

Commissioner Richard Griffith's valuation of 1847–65 was printed for wide circulation showing lessors and values. Agricultural crises in Ireland from 1815 onwards highlighted problems arising from restrictive entails and family settlements. The Landed Estates Court from 1849 assisted the sale of encumbered estates through publication of descriptions and plans of property. The Irish Land Commission of 1881 acquired and documented land redistributed among smallholders. The Congested Districts Board from 1891 to 1923 assisted families in western counties to acquire viable holdings or disperse through emigration.

A national system of **education** developed from around 1830, ultimately affecting the children of every family in Britain and Ireland. Commissioners were appointed in Ireland in 1831, where their one-roomed national schools are a feature of rural communities. Expenditure on parish schools in England and Wales is documented in reports and minutes of a Privy Council committee. From 1870 (1872 in Scotland), a national system of compulsory, and later free, education was established.

Archives of the **Local Government** Board concern that ponderous body's implementation of national policies in respect of poor relief, public health and groups deemed problematical, such as single parents and the disabled. Ministry of Housing and Local Government files complement town and county archives in explaining a family's housing and working conditions.

The **Post Office** employed people directly or by contract. Registers of appointments, salary accounts and establishment books are among the most comprehensive of government staff records, including name, age, birthplace, previous occupation, names of referees, place of appointment and nature of post. Pension documentation is especially productive of biographical data, including name, rank, date of birth, residence, service record and wages. Archives at Post Office Heritage, Freeling House, Phoenix Place, London, trace the service and its staff from 1635 onwards. Postmen travelled far from their native parishes and might otherwise be difficult to follow in the usual genealogical records. A telegraph service was established under acts of 1868 and 1870. Private and municipal telephone companies flourished from 1877. Telephone directories from 1880 onwards, photographs and staffing records are located on the Internet at the PRO on-line catalogue and by a personal visit to British Telecom Archives, London WC1.

The **civil service** has been among the largest of employers since the 1830s, as well as creating more information on ordinary families than any other organisation. Both types of documentation are among the public records. Individual servants may be named from the thirteenth century onwards. Chancery clerks doodled their names in the corners of documents and are further documented in the correspondence they signed, in the reports of their supervisors and in salary records. The following staffing memoranda concern the career of the famous palaeographer Charles Trice Martin, a clerk, and later assistant keeper, at the PRO:

> for that portion of the work ... materials for the History of Great Britain & Ireland ...
> which has been finished – £15 (1893) Mr Martin has always discharged his duties

with diligence and fidelity to the entire satisfaction of myself and my predecessors –
The retirement of so highly qualified an Officer will in fact be a distinct loss to the
Department in which he has served so many years   (1906)

Administration of railways, canals and other **industries** by the state has created
bulky files on employees for purposes of wages, pensions, health care and
discipline. The Forestry Commission was appointed from 1919 to regenerate forests
and timber production denuded during the First World War. The commission
inherited the archives of forests, some dating back to the seventeenth century. Estate
muniments, perhaps dating from the Middle Ages, were also transferred when land
was purchased for planting. The commission is thus an example of a relatively
modern body offering medieval archival sources. The archive of the Department of
Agriculture and Fisheries for Scotland includes records of the Fishery Board from
1809; agricultural statistics from 1866 to date; returns of names of crofters and
cottars for the Highlands and Islands Commission from 1883.

Office for the Herring Fishery
Edinr, 31st. October 1821

Sir
It likewise appearing from the Reports … several of the Officers hold shares of
Vessels and rent small pieces of Land for the grazing of a cow and for raising
Vegetables for the use of their families, that some of them hold Farms … that one acts
as an agent for an Insurance Company and another as Cashier for a Coal work … one
officer allows his wife to keep a shop for the sale of Medicines and Tea
　　Mr Thos McDonald　　　　Officer of the Fishery Findhorn

Some records of nationalised industries such as gas, water, rivers, harbours,
docks, canals and railways are found in national and county archives as well as
lawyers' offices. Coal and steel established dedicated archives and research centres.
Archives of predecessor companies were taken over, though some dispersal has
followed subsequent privatisation.

From time to time the government responded to public concern by means of a
royal commission, public or judicial inquiry. During the nineteenth century these
inquiries and other official documents might be published, typically in distinctively
coloured paper covers popularly termed 'Blue Books'. Unpublished records may be
among the public records, perhaps preserving the authentic voices of witnesses who
gave evidence on a diverse range of concerns, for example the work of the climbing
boys and master sweeps who cleaned the nation's chimneys until the later nineteenth
century; the living conditions of the urban poor in slums known as rookeries; the
impact upon families and individuals of industrial calamities and natural disasters.

Family histories are sometimes traced through public records created in the
regions. Orkney and Shetland were administered until 1494 from Scandinavia,
where documentation can now be discovered. In the western counties of Ireland,
administration was the responsibility of native chiefs whose wise men, known in the
vernacular as sennachies, preserved histories and genealogies orally through the
generations, perhaps finally committing the information to writing only during the
degenerate twilight of their influence. Chester with Flintshire, Durham and
Lancashire were autonomous palatinates, entitled to administer their territories
largely independent of central government. Palatinate archives, organised on the
same general lines as national records, offer genealogists charters, manor court
rolls, testaments, financial accounts, court records, rentals, leases, surveys, maps,
plans and inquisitions. The Duchy of Lancaster included the honours of
Bolingbroke, Clare, Leicester, Mandeville, Pontefract and Tutbury as well as estates
in Essex, Herefordshire, London and Wales. Duchy and palatinate records, much

The Board of Trade regulated railways, whose construction and operation kept many families on the move and in employment from the 1830s, as here on the main London–Newcastle line over the river Wear.

weeded and fragmented, are now at the PRO. Portions of the Durham archive rejected by government archivists in 1912 were rescued through community pressure for preservation in Gateshead Public Library. The Crown's Duchy of Cornwall remains a going concern, with archives accessible to researchers in the London office.

Royal commissions were concerned during the later nineteenth century at the depopulation of rural areas for hunting and fishing.

Burgeoning enthusiasm for history and genealogy resulted in the dedication of palatial repositories for the public records.

183

Further reading

The first edition is given here unless there is a substantially revised later edition. In libraries and bookshops it is advisable to look for the latest available edition containing the most recent information, particularly of the standard and continually updated archival guides issued by the Federation of Family History Societies (FFHS) and reference works on computer research. The place of publication is London unless otherwise stated.

Archives: books about various national and local documents

Alcock, N. W. *Old Title Deeds*. Phillimore, Chichester, 1986.

Arkell, T., Evans, N., and Goose, N. (editors). *When Death Do Us Part. Understanding and Interpreting the Probate Records of Early Modern England.* Leopard's Head Press, Oxford, 2000.

Bailey, R. M. *Scottish Architects' Papers*. Rutland Press, Edinburgh, 1996.

Bouens, B. G. *Wills and Their Whereabouts*. Lund Humphries, 1939, revised by A. Camp for Society of Genealogists, 1963, and periodically revised.

Chapman, C. R. *Ecclesiastical Courts, Their Officials and Their Records*. Lochin, Dursley, 1992.

Chapman, C. R. *The Growth of British Education and Its Records*. Lochin, Dursley, 1991.

Chapman, C. R. *Pre-1841 Censuses and Population Listings in the British Isles*. Lochin, Dursley, 1990.

Cole, A. *An Introduction to Poor Law Documents before 1834*. FFHS, 1993.

Cornwall, J. *How to Read Old Title Deeds XVI–XIX Centuries*. Birmingham University, 1964.

Cox, J. *Affection Defying the Power of Death: Wills, Probate and Death Duty Records*. FFHS, 1993.

Dibben, A. A. *Title Deeds, 13th–19th Centuries*. Historical Association, 1968.

Emmison, F. G. *Archives and Local History*. Methuen, 1966.

Emmison, F. G. *Introduction to Archives*. BBC, 1964.

Emmison, F. G., and Gray, I. *County Records*. Historical Association, revised edition, 1973.

Fowler, S. *Using Poor Law Records.* Public Record Office, Richmond, 2001.

Gibson, J. S. W. *Bishops' Transcripts and Marriage Licences, Bonds and Allegations: a Guide to Their Location and Indexes*. FFHS, 1981.

Gibson, J. S. W. *Census Returns*. FFHS, 1979.

Gibson, J. S. W. *The Hearth Tax, Other Later Stuart Tax Lists and the Association Oath Rolls*. FFHS, 1985.

Gibson, J. S. W. *Quarter Sessions Records for Family Historians: a Select List*. FFHS, 1982.

Gibson, J. S. W. *Wills and Where to Find Them*. Phillimore, Chichester, 1974, revised as *A Simplified Guide to Probate Jurisdictions* and then as *Probate Jurisdictions*. Gulliver Press and FFHS, 1994.

Gibson, J. S. W., and Creaton, H. *Lists of Londoners*. FFHS, 1992.

Gibson, J. S. W., and Dell, A. *Tudor and Stuart Muster Rolls*. FFHS, 1989.

Gibson, J. S. W., and Hampson, E. *Marriage, Census and Other Indexes for Family Historians*. FFHS, 1984.

Gibson, J. S. W., and Hampson, E. *Specialist Indexes for Family Historians*. FFHS, 1998.

Gibson, J. S. W., and Hunter, J. *Victuallers' Licences*. FFHS, 1994.

Gibson, J. S. W., and Medlycott, M. *Local Census Listings, 1522–1930: Holdings in the British Isles*. FFHS, 1992.

Gibson, J. S. W., and Medlycott, M. *Militia Lists and Musters, 1757–1876*. FFHS, 1989.

Gibson, J. S. W., Medlycott, M., and Mills, D. *Land and Window Tax Assessments*. FFHS, 1993.

Gibson, J. S. W., and Rogers, C. D. *Coroners' Records in England and Wales*. FFHS, 1988.

Gibson, J. S. W., and Rogers, C. D. *Electoral Registers since 1832; and Burgess Rolls*. FFHS, 1989.

Gibson, J. S. W., and Rogers, C. D. *Poll Books c.1696–1872*. FFHS, 1989.

Gibson, J. S. W., and Rogers, C. D. *Poor Law Union Records*. FFHS, 1993.

Hogg, P. L. *Basic Facts about Using Merchant Ship Records for Family Historians*. FFHS, 1997.

Holding, N. *The Location of British Army Records 1914–18*. FFHS, 1984, revised by I. Swinnerton,1999.

Holding, N. *World War I Army Ancestry*. FFHS, 1982.

Humphery-Smith, C. R. *Marriage Licences, Bonds and Allegations*. Institute of Genealogical and Heraldic Studies, Canterbury, 1967.

Humphery-Smith, C. R. *Phillimore Atlas and Index of Parish Registers*. Phillimore, Chichester, 1984.

Iredale, D. *Enjoying Archives*. Phillimore, Chichester, second edition, 1985.

Iredale, D., and Barrett, J. *Discovering Your Old House*. Shire, Princes Risborough, fourth edition, 2002.

Leadam, I. S. *The Domesday of Inclosures*. Historical Society of Great Britain, 1897.

Leeson, F. *A Guide to the Records of the British State Tontines and Life Annuities of the 17th and 18th Centuries*. Pinhorns, Shalfleet, Isle of Wight, 1968.

Lumas, S. *An Introduction to the Census Returns of England and Wales*. FFHS, 1992.

Lumas, S. *Making Use of the Census*. PRO guide 1, 1993.

MacFarlane, A. *A Guide to English Historical Records*. Cambridge University Press, 1983.

McLaughlin, E. *Wills before 1858*. E. McLaughlin, Haddenham, 1979, reissued by FFHS.

Moody, D. *Scottish Family History*. Batsford, 1988.

Mullins, E. L. C. (editor). *Texts and Calendars*. Royal Historical Society, 1958 and 1983.

Owen, D. M. *The Records of the Established Church in England Excluding Parochial Records*. British Records Association, 1970.

Palgrave-Moore, P. *How to Locate and Use Manorial Records*. Elvery Dowers, 1985.

Palgrave-Moore, P. *Understanding the History and Records of Non-conformity*. Elvery Dowers, 1987.

Pols, R. *Looking at Old Photographs*. FFHS, 1998.

Probert, E. *Company and Business Records for Family Historians*. FFHS, 1994.

Richards, T. *Was Your Grandfather a Railwayman?* FFHS, 1988.

Rodger, N. A. M. *Naval Records for Genealogists*. PRO guide 22, 1984.

Smith, K. J., Watts, C. T., and Watts, M. J. *Records of Merchant Shipping and Seamen*. PRO guide 20, 1998.

Spencer, W. *Air Force Records for Family Historians*. PRO guide 21, 2000.

Stafford, G. *Where to Find Adoption Records*. British Agencies for Adoption and Fostering, 1985.

Steel, D. J. (editor). *National Index of Parish Registers*. Society of Genealogists, 1973–86.

Swinnerton, I. *The British Army: Its History, Tradition and Records*. FFHS, 1996.

Tate, W. E. *The Parish Chest*. Cambridge University Press, 1969.

Thomas, G. *Records of the Militia from 1757*. PRO guide 3, 1993.

West, J. *Town Records*. Phillimore, Chichester, 1983.

West, J. *Village Records*. Macmillan, 1962.

Whiteman, A. (editor). *The Compton Census of 1676: a Critical Edition*. Oxford University Press for British Academy, 1986.

Wilson, E. *The Records of the Royal Air Force*. FFHS, 1991.

Wood, T. *An Introduction to Civil Registration*. FFHS, 1994.

Archives: principal repositories and their collections

The Acts of the Parliaments of Scotland (APS). Record Commission, 1814–75.

Analytical Table of Private Statutes. 1813 and 1835.

Bardon, J. *A Guide to Local History Sources in the Public Record Office of Northern Ireland.* Blackstaff Press, Belfast, 2000.

Bevan, A. (editor). *Tracing Your Ancestors in the Public Record Office.* Fifth edition of J. Cox and T. Padfield's 1981 guide, Public Record Office, 1999.

Bond, M. F. *Guide to the Records of Parliament.* HMSO, 1971.

Boyle, L. E. *A Survey of the Vatican Archives and of Its Medieval Holdings.* Pontifical Institute of Mediaeval Studies, Toronto, 1972.

Calendars of Scottish Supplications to Rome. Scottish History Society, 1934 (in progress).

Chronological Table of Local Legislation. From 1797.

Chronological Table of the Statutes, 1235–. HMSO, 1870–.

Colwell, S. *Dictionary of Genealogical Sources in the PRO.* Weidenfeld & Nicolson, 1992.

Cox, J., and Padfield, T. See Bevan, A.

Devine, R. *Index to Local and Personal Acts.* From 1797.

Ford, P. and G. *Select List of British Parliamentary Papers 1833–1899.* Irish University Press, Shannon, 1969.

Foster, J., and Sheppard, J. *British Archives: a Guide to Archive Resources in the United Kingdom.* Palgrave, Basingstoke, fourth edition, 2002.

Galbraith, V. H. *An Introduction to the Use of Public Records.* Oxford University Press, 1934.

Gibson, J. S. W., and Peskett, P. *Record Offices: How to Find Them.* FFHS, 1998.

Guide to the Contents of the Public Record Office. 1963–8.

Guide to the National Archives of Scotland. 1996.

Hansard, L. *Catalogue and Breviate of Parliamentary Papers 1696–1834.* Irish University Press, Shannon, 1969.

Helferty, S., and Refaussé, R. *Directory of Irish Archives.* Four Courts Press, Dublin, third edition, 1999.

Historical Manuscripts Commission. *Record Repositories in Great Britain.* HMSO, 1999.

Index of Manuscripts in the British Library. British Library, 1984.

Index to Local and Personal Acts. From 1801.

Index to Statutes in Force. HMSO.

National Library of Wales. *Guide to the Department of Manuscripts and Records.* 1994.

Nickson, M. A. E. *The British Library: Guide to the Catalogues and Indexes of the Department of Manuscripts.* The British Library, 1978.

Nicolas, H., *et al.* (editors). *Proceedings and Ordinances of the Privy Council of England.* Record Commission and Public Record Office, 1834–1964.

Public Record Office. *Calendars of Entries in the Papal Registers Relating to Great Britain and Ireland.* 1893 (in progress), by Irish Manuscripts Commission, from 1961.

Riden, P. *Record Sources for Local History.* (PRO) Batsford, 1987.

Sinclair, C. *Jock Tamson's Bairns: a History of the Records of the General Register Office for Scotland.* General Register Office, Edinburgh, 2000.

Sinclair, C. *Tracing Your Scottish Ancestors: a Guide to Ancestry Research in the Scottish Record Office.* HMSO, Edinburgh, 1990.

Statutes of the Realm (Statutes at Large). Record Commission, 1810–28.

Chronology

Blackburn, R., and Holford-Strevens, L. *The Oxford Companion to the Year.* Oxford University Press, 1999.

Cheney, C. R. *Handbook of Dates.* Royal Historical Society, 1945.

Dunbar, A. *Scottish Kings.* David Douglas, Edinburgh, 1899.

Fryde, E. B., *et al.* (editors). *Handbook of British Chronology.* Royal Historical

Society, third edition, 1986.

Nicolas, H. *The Chronology of History*. Longman, 1833.

Computers and the Internet

Bradley, A. *A Family History on Your PC: a Book for Beginners*. Sigma Press, Wilmslow, 1996.

Christian, P. *The Genealogist's Internet*. Public Record Office, 2001.

Christian, P. *Web Publishing for Genealogy*. David Hawgood, second edition, 1999.

Crowe, E. P. *Genealogy Online: Researching Your Roots*. McGraw-Hill, New York, 1996.

Gormley, M. V. *Prima's Official Companion to Family Tree Maker Version 5*. Prima Publishing, Rocklin, California, 1988.

Hawgood, D. *Computers for Family History*. Hawgood Computing, 1985.

Hawgood, D. *Family Search on the Internet*. FFHS and Hawgood, 1999.

Hawgood, D. *Genealogy Computer Packages*. Hawgood Computing, 1993.

Hawgood, D. *GENUKI. U.K. & Ireland Genealogy on Internet*. FFHS and Hawgood, 2000.

Hawgood, D. *Internet for Genealogy*. Hawgood Computing, 1996.

Helm, M. L. and A. L. *Family Tree Maker for Dummies*. IDG Books, Foster City, California, 2000.

Helm, M. L. and A. L. *Genealogy Online for Dummies*. IDG Books, Foster City, California, 1998.

Howells, C. *Cyndi's List: a Comprehensive List of 40,000 Genealogy Sites on the Internet*. Genealogical Publishing Company, Baltimore, Maryland, 1999.

Mawdsley, E., and Munck, T. *Computing for Historians: an Introductory Guide*. Manchester University Press, 1993.

Public Record Office. *Census Online: 1901 Census Online User Guide*. PRO and Qinetiq, Richmond, 2001.

Rose, C., and Ingalls, K. G. *The Complete Idiot's Guide to Genealogy*. Alpha Books, New York, 1997.

Shea, V. *Netiquette*. Albion Books, San Francisco, 1994.

Wilson, R. S. *Publishing Your Family History on the Internet*. Writers Digest Books, 1999.

Dictionaries: biography

Colvin, H. *A Biographical Dictionary of British Architects*. John Murray, 1978.

Dictionary of Business Biography. Butterworths, 1984–.

Dictionary of Labour Biography, edited by J. M. Bellamy and J. Saville. Macmillan, 1972–2000.

Dictionary of Labour Biography, edited by G. Rosen, Politico's, 2001.

Dictionary of National Biography. Oxford University Press, 1917–.

Who's Who. A. & C. Black, 1849–.

Who Was Who from 1897. A. & C. Black, 1920–.

Dictionaries: language

Craigie, W. A. *Dictionary of the Older Scottish Tongue from the Twelfth Century to the End of the Seventeenth*. Oxford University Press, 1937–2002.

Dónaill, N. *Ó Fóclóir Gaeilge-Béarla*. Oifig an tSoláthair, Dublin, 1977.

Dwelly, E. *The Illustrated Gaelic–English Dictionary*. Gairm Publications, Glasgow, eighth edition, 1973.

Geiriadur Prifysgol Cymru. University of Wales, 1950 (in progress).

Gooder, E. A. *Latin for Local History*. Longman, second edition, 1978.

Kelham, K. *A Dictionary of the Norman or Old French Language*. Edwards Brooke, 1779, reprinted Tabard Press, East Ardsley, 1978.

Latham, R. E. *Revised Medieval Latin Word-List*. British Academy/Oxford University Press, 1965.

Middle English Dictionary. University of Michigan, 1952 (in progress).

Oxford English Dictionary (OED). Oxford University Press, 1989.

Partridge. E. *A Dictionary of Slang and Unconventional English*. 1937, abridged by J. Simpson as *The Penguin Dictionary of Historical Slang*, 1972.
Scottish National Dictionary. 1931–76.
Stratmann, F. H. *A Middle English Dictionary*. Revised by H. Bradley. Oxford University Press, 1891.
Wright, J. *The English Dialect Dictionary*. Henry Frowde, 1896–1905.

Directories
Atkins, P. J. *The Directories of London 1677–1977*. Mansell, 1990.
Lloyd's Casualty Returns. Lloyd's of London, 1890–.
Lloyd's List. Lloyd's of London, 1740–.
Lloyd's Register of Shipping. Lloyd's of London, 1764–.
Mercantile Navy List. General Register and Record Office of Shipping and Seamen, 1850–.
Norton, J. E. *Guide to the National and Provincial Directories of England and Wales ... before 1856*. Royal Historical Society, 1950.
Shaw, G., and Tipper, A. *British Directories: a Bibliography and Guide to Directories Published in England and Wales (1850–1950) and Scotland (1773–1950)*. Leicester University Press, 1989.

Family histories and pedigrees: guides and catalogues
Barrow, G. B. *The Genealogist's Guide: an Index to Printed British Pedigrees and Family Histories 1950–1975*. Research Publishing Company, 1977.
Ferguson, J. P. S. *Scottish Family Histories Held in Scottish Libraries*. Scottish Central Library, Edinburgh, 1960.
Marshall, G. W. *The Genealogist's Guide to Printed Pedigrees*. London, 1879.
Montgomery-Massingberd, H. *Burke's Family Index*. Burke's Peerage, 1976.
Raymond, S. *British Genealogical Periodicals: a Bibliography of their Contents*. FFHS, 1991.
Thomson, T. R. *A Catalogue of British Family Histories*. John Murray, 1928.
Whitmore, J. B. *A Genealogical Guide: an Index to British Pedigrees in Continuation of Marshall's Genealogist's Guide*. London, 1953.

Family tree research: general guides
Buckley, K. A. *Ancestry Tracing*. K. A. Buckley, Birmingham, 1978.
Burns, N. *Family Tree*. Faber, 1962.
Camp, A. J. *First Steps in Family History*. Society of Genealogists, third edition, 1998.
Camp, A. J. *Tracing Your Ancestors*. John Giffard, 1972.
Catlett, E. *Track Down Your Ancestors: Draw Up Your Family Tree*. Elliot Right Way Books, Tadworth, Surrey, 1995.
Chapman, C. R. *Tracing Your British Ancestors*. Lochin, Dursley, 1993.
Cole, J. A., and Armstrong, M. *Tracing Your Family Tree*. Equation (Thorsons), Wellingborough, 1988.
Collins, R. P. *A Journey in Ancestry*. Alan Sutton, Stroud, 1984.
Collins, R. P. *Forward to the Past: Another Journey in Ancestry*. Alan Sutton, Stroud, 1995.
Colwell, S. *The Family History Book*. Phaidon Press, Oxford, 1980.
Colwell, S. *Tracing Your Family Tree*. Faber, 1984.
Croom, E. A. *The Genealogist's Companion and Sourcebook*. Betterway Books, Cincinnati, Ohio, 1994.
Crush, M. *Trace Your Family Tree*. Granada, 1983.
Currer-Briggs, N., and Gambier, R. *Debrett's Family Historian*. Debrett/Webb & Bower, 1981.
Dixon, J. T., and Flack, D. D. *Preserving Your Past: a Painless Guide to Writing Your Autobiography and Family History*. Doubleday, 1977.
Field, D. M. *Step-by-Step Guide to Tracing Your Ancestors*. Hamlyn, 1982.
Fitzhugh, T. V. H. *The Dictionary of Genealogy*. Alphabooks, Sherborne, 1985.

Fitzhugh, T. V. H. *How to Write a Family History: the Lives and Times of Our Ancestors*. Alphabooks, Sherborne, 1988.
Galford, E. *The Essential Guide to Genealogy*. Reader's Digest, 2001.
Gandy, M. *Tracing Catholic Ancestors*. Public Record Office, Richmond, 2001.
Gandy, M. *Tracing Nonconformist Ancestors*. Public Record Office, Richmond, 2001.
Gardner, D. E., and Smith, F. *Genealogical Research in England and Wales*. Bookcraft, Salt Lake City, 1956–64.
Hamilton-Edwards, G. K. *In Search of Ancestry*. Michael Joseph, 1966.
Herber, M. D. *Ancestral Trails*. Sutton Publishing, Stroud, 1997.
Hey, D. *Family History and Local History in England*. Longman, 1987.
Hey, D. *The Oxford Companion to Local and Family History*. Oxford University Press, 1996.
Hey, D. *The Oxford Dictionary of Local and Family History*. Oxford University Press, 1997.
Hey, D. *The Oxford Guide to Family History*. Oxford University Press, 1993.
Humphery-Smith, C. R. *A Genealogist's Bibliography*. Phillimore, Chichester, 1976.
Mander, M. *Tracing Your Ancestors*. David & Charles, Newton Abbot, 1976. (Republished as *How to Trace Your Ancestors*. Granada, 1977.)
Matthews, C. M. *Your Family Tree: and How to Discover it*. Lutterworth, Guildford, 1976.
McLaughlin, E. *Laying Out a Pedigree*. FFHS, 1988.
Palgrave-Moore, P. *How to Record Your Family Tree*. Elvery Dowers, Norwich, 1979.
Pelling, G. *Beginning Your Family History*. FFHS, 1980.
Pine, L. G. *The Genealogist's Encyclopedia*. David & Charles, Newton Abbot, 1969.
Pine, L. G. *Trace Your Ancestors*. Evans, 1954.
Reader's Digest. *Explore Your Family's Past*. Reader's Digest, 2000.
Rogers, C. D. *The Family Tree Detective: a Manual for Analysing and Solving Genealogical Problems in England and Wales, 1538 to the Present Day*. Manchester University Press, 1983.
Rogers, C. D., and Smith, J. H. *Local Family History in England*. Manchester University Press, 1991.
Saul, P., and Markwell, F. C. *The Family Historian's Enquire Within*. Countryside Books, Newbury, and FFHS, 1985.
Steel, D. J. *Discovering Your Family History*. BBC, 1984.
Steel, D. J., and Taylor, L. *The Steels*. Nelson, Walton-on-Thames, 1976.
Titford, J. *Succeeding in Family History*. Countryside Books, Newbury, 2001.
Titford, J. *Writing and Publishing Your Family History*. Countryside Books, 1996.
Unett, J. *Making a Pedigree*. David & Charles, Newton Abbot, second edition, 1971.
Willis, A. J. *Genealogy for Beginners*. Ernest Benn, 1955.
Yurdan, M. *Tracing Your Ancestors*. David & Charles, Newton Abbot, 1988.

Family tree research: regional guides

Baxter, A. *In Search of Your European Roots: a Complete Guide to Tracing Your Ancestors in Every Country in Europe*. Genealogical Publishing Co Inc, Baltimore, 1985.
Begley, D. F. *Irish Genealogy: a Record Finder*. Heraldic Arts, Dublin, 1981.
Bigwood, R. *Tracing Scottish Ancestors*. HarperCollins, Glasgow, 1999.
Black, J. A. *Your Irish Ancestors: an Illustrated History of Irish Families and Their Origins*. Paddington Press, 1974.
Clare, W. *A Simple Guide to Irish Genealogy*. Third edition by R. Ffolliott, Irish Genealogical Research Society, London, 1966.
Cory, K. B. *Tracing Your Scottish Ancestry*. Polygon, Edinburgh, second edition, 1996.
Currer-Briggs, N., and Gambier, R. *In Search of Huguenot Ancestry*. Phillimore, Chichester, 1985.

Davis, B. *An Introduction to Irish Research*. FFHS, 1992.
Family Care. Birthlink Adoption Counselling Centre. *Search Guide for Adopted People in Scotland*. HMSO, 1997.
Fowler, S. *Tracing Irish Ancestors*. Public Record Office, Richmond, 2001.
Fowler, S. *Tracing Scottish Ancestors*. Public Record Office, 2001.
Grenham, J. *Tracing Your Irish Ancestors*. Gill & Macmillan, Dublin, 1992.
Hamilton-Edwards, G. *In Search of Scottish Ancestry*. Phillimore, Chichester, 1972.
Hamilton-Edwards, G. *In Search of Welsh Ancestry*. Phillimore, Chichester, 1985.
Hotten, J. *The Original Lists of Persons of Quality ... Who Went from Great Britain to the American Plantations 1600–1700*. Chatto & Windus, 1874.
James, A. *Scottish Roots: a Step-by-Step Guide for Ancestor-Hunters in Scotland and Overseas*. Macdonald, Loanhead, 1981.
Kinealy, C. *Tracing Your Irish Roots*. Appletree Press, Belfast, 1991.
Mac Conghail, M., and Gorry, P. *Tracing Irish Ancestors*. HarperCollins, Glasgow, 1997.
Neill, K. *How to Trace Family History in Northern Ireland*. Irish Heritage Association, Belfast, 1986.
O'Connor, M. H. *A Guide to Tracing Your Kerry Ancestors*. Flyleaf Press, Glenageary, 1990.
Rowlands, J. and S. (editors). *Welsh Family History*. FFHS, 1993.
Wagner, A. R. *English Ancestry*. Oxford University Press, 1961.
Wagner, A. R. *English Genealogy*. Clarendon Press, Oxford, 1960.
Way, G., and Squire, R. *Scottish Clan and Family Encyclopaedia*. HarperCollins, Glasgow, 1994.
Whyte, D. *Introducing Scottish Genealogical Research*. Scottish Genealogy Society, Edinburgh, 1960.
Yurdan, M. *Irish Family History*. Batsford, 1990.

Handwriting, old (palaeography)
Barrett, J., and Iredale, D. *Discovering Old Handwriting*. Shire, Princes Risborough, 1995.
Cameron, E. *An Introduction to Graphology*. Collins, 1989.
Cappelli, A. *Dizionario di Abbreviature Latine ed Italiane*. Ulrico Hoepli, Milan, 1899.
Dawson, G. E., and Kennedy-Skipton, L. *Elizabethan Handwriting 1500–1650: a Guide to the Reading of Documents and Manuscripts*. Faber, 1968.
Denholm-Young, N. *Handwriting in England and Wales*. University of Wales Press, Cardiff, second edition, 1964.
Emmison, F. G. *How to Read Local Archives 1550–1700*. Historical Association, 1967.
Grieve, H. E. P. *Examples of English Handwriting 1150–1750*. Essex Education Committee, Chelmsford, 1954.
Hector, L. C. *The Handwriting of English Documents*. Edward Arnold, 1958.
Jackson, D. *The Story of Writing*. Cassell, Studio Vista, 1981.
Jenkinson, H. *The Later Court Hands in England from the Fifteenth to the Seventeenth Century*. Cambridge University Press, 1927.
Johnson, C., and Jenkinson, H. *English Court Hand A.D. 1066 to 1500*. Clarendon Press, Oxford, 1915.
Martin, C. T. *The Record Interpreter*. 1892; Phillimore, Chichester, fourth edition, 1982.
Newton, K. C. *Medieval Local Records: a Reading Aid*. Historical Association, 1971.
Simpson, G. G. *Scottish Handwriting 1150–1650*. Bratton, Edinburgh, 1973.
Whalley, J. I. *English Handwriting 1540–1853*. HMSO, 1969.

Heraldry
Brooke-Little, J. P. *Heraldry*. Blackwell, Oxford, 1975.
Burke, J. B. *The General Armory of England, Scotland, Ireland and Wales*. Harrison, 1878.

Elvin, C. N. *A Dictionary of Heraldry.* Kent & Co, 1889.
Elvin, C. N. *A Hand-book of Mottoes.* 1860, reprinted by Heraldry Today, 1963.
Fairbairn, J. *Book of Crests of the Families of Great Britain and Ireland.* T. C. & E. C. Jack, revised edition, 1892.
Fearn, J. *Discovering Heraldry.* Shire Publications, Princes Risborough, 1980.
Fox-Davies, A. C. *Armorial Families: a Complete Peerage, Baronetage and Knightage, and a Directory of some Gentlemen of Coat-Armour, and being the First Attempt to Show which Arms in Use at the Moment are Borne by Legal Authority.* T. C. & E. C. Jack, Edinburgh, 1895.
Fox-Davies, A. C. *The Art of Heraldry.* T. C. & E. C. Jack, 1904. (Translation of H. G Ströhl's *Heraldischer Atlas,* 1899, reprinted by Bloomsbury Books in 1986.)
Fox-Davies, A. C. *A Complete Guide to Heraldry.* T. C. & E. C. Jack, 1909.
Fox-Davies, A. C. *Heraldry Explained.* T. C. & E. C. Jack, 1907. Second edition of 1925, reprinted, David & Charles, Newton Abbot, 1971.
Friar, S. *Heraldry for the Local Historian and Genealogist.* Sutton Publishing, Stroud, 1992.
Friar, S., and Ferguson, J. *Basic Heraldry.* Herbert Press, 1993.
Innes, T. *Scots Heraldry.* Oliver & Boyd, 1934.
Mackinnon, C. *The Observer's Book of Heraldry.* Frederick Warne, 1966.
Moncrieffe, I., and Pottinger, D. *Simple Heraldry Cheerfully Illustrated.* John Bartholomew, second edition, 1978.
Neubecker, O. *A Guide to Heraldry.* McGraw-Hill & Cassell, 1979.
Papworth, J. W. *An Alphabetical Dictionary of Coats of Arms Belonging to Families in Great Britain and Ireland forming an Extensive Ordinary of British Armorials; upon an Entirely New Plan, in which Arms are Systematically Subdivided Throughout, and so Arranged in Alphabetical Order, that the Names of Families whose Shields are Found on Buildings, Monuments, Seals, Paintings, Plate, etc., whether Mediaeval or Modern, can be Readily Ascertained.* T. Richards, 1874.
Pine, L. G. *Teach Yourself Heraldry and Genealogy.* English Universities Press, 1957.
Ralphs, D. H. *A First Look at Heraldry.* Franklin Watts, 1973.
Rogers, H. C. B. *The Pageant of Heraldry.* Seeley Service, 1957.
Scott-Giles, C. W., and Brooke-Little, J. P. *Boutell's Heraldry.* 1863, Frederick Warne, revised edition, 1950.
Summers, P. G. *Hatchments in Britain.* Phillimore, 1974–94.
Summers, P. *How to Read a Coat of Arms.* National Council for Social Service for Standing Conference for Local History, 1967.
Woodcock, T., and Robinson, J. M. *The Oxford Guide to Heraldry.* Oxford University Press, 1988.

Oral history

Evans, G. E. *The Days That We Have Seen.* Faber, 1975.
Evans, G. E. *From Mouths of Men.* Faber, 1976.
Evans, G. E. *Where Beards Wag All: the Relevance of Oral Tradition.* Faber, 1970.
Thompson, P. *The Voice of the Past.* Oxford University Press, 1978.
Vansina, J. *Oral Tradition: a Study in Historical Methodology.* Routledge & Kegan Paul, 1965.

Peerage, baronetage and landed gentry

Burke, J. *A Genealogical and Heraldic Dictionary of the Peerages of England, Ireland and Scotland, Extinct, Dormant and in Abeyance.* Second edition, H. Colburn, 1840.
Burke, J. *A Genealogical and Heraldic History of the Commoners of Great Britain and Ireland, Enjoying Territorial Possessions, or High Official Rank.* For Henry Colburn by R. Bentley, 1833–8. (Ancestor of Burke's *Landed Gentry.*)
Burke, J. *A Genealogical and Heraldic History of the Extinct and Dormant Baronetcies of England.* H. Colburn, 1838.

Burke, J. *Peerage and Baronetage*. H. Colburn, 1826–37.

Cokayne, G. E. *A Complete Baronetage*. W. Pollard, 1900–6.

Cokayne, G. E. *The Complete Peerage of England, Scotland, Ireland, Great Britain and the United Kingdom, Extant, Extinct or Dormant*. St Catherine's Press, 1887–98.

Debrett, J. *The Baronetage of England*. F. C. & J. Rivington, 1808.

Debrett, J. *Debrett's Peerage of England, Scotland, and Ireland*. J. Debrett, 1802.

Paul, J. B. *The Scots Peerage*. David Douglas, Edinburgh, 1904–14.

Surnames and given (Christian) names

Bardsley, C. W. *A Dictionary of English and Welsh Surnames with Special American Instances*. 1901; reprinted Genealogical Publishing Company, Baltimore, 1980.

Bell, R. *The Book of Ulster Surnames*. Blackstaff Press, Belfast, 1988.

Black, G. F. *The Surnames of Scotland: Their Origin, Meaning and History*. New York Public Library, 1946.

Cottle, B. *The Penguin Dictionary of Surnames*. Penguin, Harmondsworth, second edition, 1978.

Dorward, D. *Scottish Surnames*. HarperCollins, 1995.

Fry, E. A., and Phillimore, W. P. W. *An Index to Changes of Name under Authority of Act of Parliament or Royal Licence, and including Irregular Changes ... 1760–1901*. Phillimore, 1905.

Hanks, P., and Hodges, F. *A Dictionary of Surnames*. Oxford University Press, 1988.

Hassall, W. O. *History Through Surnames*. Pergamon, Oxford, 1967.

Hey, D. *Family Names and Family History*. Hambledon Press, 2000.

MacLysaght, E. *Irish Families*. Hodges Figgis, Dublin, 1957.

MacLysaght, E. *More Irish Families*. Irish Academic Press, Black Rock, new edition, 1982.

MacLysaght, E. *The Surnames of Ireland*. Irish Academic Press, Dublin, fifth edition, 1980.

Matthews, C. M. *English Surnames*. Weidenfeld & Nicolson, 1996.

Matthews, C. M. *How Surnames Began*. Lutterworth, 1967.

McKinley, R. *A History of British Surnames*. Longman, 1990.

McKinley, R. *Norfolk and Suffolk Surnames in the Middle Ages*. Phillimore, Chichester, 1975.

Morgan, T. J. and P. *Welsh Surnames*. University of Wales, Cardiff, 1985.

Ó Corrain, D., and Maguire, F. *Irish Names*. Academy Press, Dublin, 1981.

Pine, L. G. *The Story of Surnames*. Country Life, 1965.

Pine, L. G. *They Came with the Conqueror*. Evans, 1954.

Reaney, P. H. *A Dictionary of British Surnames*. Routledge & Kegan Paul, 1958.

Reaney, P. H. *The Origin of British Surnames*. Routledge & Kegan Paul, 1967.

Redmonds, G. *Yorkshire, West Riding*. Phillimore, Chichester, 1973.

Verstappen, P. *The Book of Surnames*. Pelham, 1980.

Whyte, D. *Scottish Forenames*. Birlinn, Edinburgh, 1996.

Whyte, D. *Scottish Surnames*. Birlinn, Edinburgh, 1996.

Withycombe, E. G. *Oxford Dictionary of English Christian Names*. Clarendon Press, Oxford, 1945.

Useful addresses

This select list of addresses and websites in Britain, Ireland and elsewhere is arranged alphabetically usually according to the organisation title (so East Sussex, not Sussex, East). *FHSoc* denotes Family History Society, Group or other association concerned with genealogy and normally a member of the Federation of Family History Societies; email addresses and websites are given if available. *FHCen* (LDS) denotes Family History Centre of the Church of Jesus Christ of Latter-Day Saints (Mormons); these are libraries where the public are welcomed to conduct genealogical research but are not staffed to answer postal enquiries. Under local government websites, find archives by A–Z search of services

Aberdeen and North East Scotland FHSoc, Family History Shop, 164 King Street, Aberdeen AB24 5BD. Email: enquiries@anesfhs.org.uk; website: www.anesfhs.org.uk

Aberdeen City Archives, Town House, Broad Street, Aberdeen AB10 1AQ. Website: www.aberdeencity.gov.uk

Aberdeen FHCen (LDS), North Anderson Drive, Aberdeen AB2 6DD.

Aberdeen University Library, Department of Special Collections and Archives, King's College, Aberdeen AB24 3SW.

Aerial Photography for England, Central Registry, Ordnance Survey, Romsey Road, Maybush, Southampton SO9 4DH.

Aerofilms Ltd, Gate Studios, Station Road, Boreham Wood, Hertfordshire WD6 1EJ.

Air Historical Branch, Ministry of Defence, Lacon House, Theobalds Road, London WC1X 8RY.

Air Photographs, Central Register of, Welsh Office, Crown Offices, Cathays Park, Cardiff CF1 3NQ.

Air Photographs Unit, Scottish Development Department, New St Andrew's House, St James Centre, Edinburgh EH1 3SZ.

Aldershot FHCen (LDS), LDS Chapel, St Georges Road, Aldershot, Hampshire.

Alloway & Southern Ayrshire FHSoc, Alloway Library, Doonholm Road, Ayr KA7 4QQ.

American Archive, Albert F. Simpson Historical Research Centre, USAAF Maxwell Air Force Base, Alabama 36112.

Ancient Monuments Society, St Ann's Vestry Hall, 2 Church Entry, Queen Victoria Street, London EC4V 5HB.

Anglesey County Record Office, Shire Hall, Glanhwfa Road, Llangefni LL77 7TW. Website: www.anglesey.gov.uk

Anglo Scottish FHSoc, see Manchester and Lancashire FHSoc.

Angus Archives, Montrose Library, 214 High Street, Montrose, Angus DD10 8HE. Website: www.angus.gov.uk/history

Archbishop Marsh's Library, St Patrick's Close, Dublin 8.

Argyll and Bute Council Archives, Manse Brae, Lochgilphead, Argyll PA31 8QU. Website: www.argyll-bute.gov.uk

Army Records Centre, Bourne Avenue, Hayes, Middlesex UB3 1RF. Website: www.mod.uk/contacts/records-army.htm

Arts Council of Great Britain, 105 Piccadilly, London W1V 9FN.

Ashton FHCen (LDS), Patterdale Road, Ashton under Lyne, Lancashire OL7 9JA.

Association for Industrial Archaeology, The Wharfage, Ironbridge, Telford, Shropshire TF8 7AW.

Association of Family History Societies of Wales, Geoff Riggs, Peacehaven, Badgers Meadow, Pwllmeyric, Chepstow, Monmouthsire NP16 6UE. Website: www.fhswales.info

Association of Genealogists and Researchers in Archives, 29 Badgers Close, Horsham, West Sussex RH12 5RU. Website: www.agra.org.uk

Association of Scottish Genealogists and Record Agents, 51/3 Mortonhall Road, Edinburgh EH9 2HN. Website: www.asgra.co.uk

Australian Institute of Genealogical Studies, PO Box 339, Blackburn, Victoria 3130.

Ayrshire Archives, Craigie Estate, Ayr KA8 0SS. Website: www.south-ayrshire.gov.uk/archives

Barking and Dagenham Public Libraries, Valence House Museum, Becontree Avenue, Dagenham, Essex RM8 3HT. Website: www.barking-dagenham.gov.uk

Barnet Archives and Local Studies Department, Hendon Catholic Social Centre, Chapel Walk, Egerton Gardens, Hendon, London NW4 4BE; correspondence to Hendon Library, The Burroughs, NW4 4BQ. Website: www.barnet.gov.uk

Barnsley FHSoc, Mrs K. Wright, 58A High Street, Royston, Barnsley S71 4RN. Email: kath@barnsleyfhs.freeserve.co.uk; website: www.barnsleyfhs.co.uk

Barnsley Libraries, Archives and Local Studies Department, Central Library, Shambles Street, Barnsley S70 2JF. Email: archives@barnsley.gov.uk

Barrow FHCen (LDS), Abbey Road, Barrow in Furness, Cumbria LA14.

Bath and North East Somerset Record Office, Guildhall, Bath BA1 5AW. Website: www.bathnes.gov.uk

Bedfordshire and Luton Archives and Record Service, Record Office, County Hall, Bedford MK42 9AP. Website: www.bedfordshire.gov.uk

Bedfordshire FHSoc, Mrs Pauline Redpath, PO Box 214, Bedford MK42 9RX. Email: bfhs@bfhs.org.uk; website: www.bfhs.org.uk

Belfast Central Library, Royal Avenue, Belfast BT1 1EA.

Belfast FHCen (LDS), 403 Holywood Road, Belfast BT4 2GU.

Berkshire FHSoc, J. Gurnett, 5 Wren Close, Burghfield Common, Berkshire RG7 3PF. Email: secretary@berksfhs.org.uk; website: www.berksfhs.org.uk

Berkshire Record Office, 9 Coley Avenue, Reading RG1 6AF. Email: arch@reading.gov.uk; website: www.bracknell-forest.gov.uk/leisure

Berwick-upon-Tweed Record Office, Council Offices, Wallace Green, Berwick upon Tweed TD15 1ED. Email: lb@berwick-upon-tweed.gov.uk

Bexley Local Studies and Archive Centre, Central Library, Townley Road, Bexleyheath, Kent DA6 7HT. Email: archives@bexleycouncil.freeserve.co.uk

Billingham FHCen (LDS), The Linkway, Billingham, Cleveland TS23 3HJ.

Birkenhead Central Library, Borough Road, Birkenhead, Wirral CH41 2XB. Email: birkenhead.ref@wirral-library.net; website: www.wirral-libraries.net

Birkenhead FHCen (LDS), Prenton Lane/Reservoir Road, Prenton, Birkenhead CH42.

Birmingham and Midland Institute and *Priestley Library*, 3 Margaret Street, Birmingham B3 3BS. Email: admin@bmi.org.uk; website: www.bmi.org.uk

Birmingham and Midland Society for Genealogy and Heraldry, Mrs Olive Price, 9 Claydon Grove, Yardley Wood, Birmingham B14 4NB. Email: gensec@bmsgh.org; website: www.bmsgh.org

Birmingham and Midlands FHSoc, 111 Kenilworth Court, Coventry CV3 6JD.

Birmingham City Archives, Central Library, Chamberlain Square, Birmingham B3 3HQ. Email: archives@birmingham.gov.uk; website: www.birmingham.gov.uk

Birmingham University Information Services, Special Collections Department, Main Library, Edgbaston, Birmingham B15 2TT.

Blackpool FHCen (LDS), LDS Chapel, Warren Drive, Thornton Cleveleys, Blackpool FY5.

Bolton Archive and Local Studies Service, Central Library, Civic Centre, Le Mans Crescent, Bolton BL1 1SE. Email: archive.library@bolton.gov.uk; website: bold.bolton.gov.uk/library

Borders FHSoc, Mrs Carol Trotter, 'Pentennen', 15 Edinburgh Road, Greenlaw, Berwickshire TD10 6XF. Website: www.vivdunstan.clara.net

Borthwick Institute of Historical Research, University of York, St Anthony's Hall, Peasholme Green, York YO1 7PW. Website: www.york.ac.uk

Bradford District Archives, 15 Canal Road, Bradford BD1 4AT. Email: bradford@wyjs.org.uk; website: www.archives.wyjs.org.uk (See also West Yorkshire)

Bradford FHSoc, Mr Dennis Flaxington, 2 Leaventhorpe Grove, Thornton, Bradford BD13 3BN. Email: dflax@aol.com; website: www.genuki.org.uk/big/eng/YKS

Brent Community History Library and Archive, Cricklewood Library, 152 Olive Road, Cricklewood, London NW2 6UY. Email: archive@brent.gov.uk; website: www.brent.gov.uk

Bristol and Avon FHSoc, Mrs Audrey Lovell, 784 Muller Road, Eastville, Bristol BS5 6XA. Website: www.bafhs.org.uk

Bristol FHCen (LDS), 721 Wells Road, Whitchurch, Bristol BS14 9HU.

Bristol Record Office, 'B' Bond Warehouse, Smeaton Road, Bristol BS1 6XN. Website: www.bristol-city.gov.uk

British Academy, 10 Carlton House Terrace, London SW1Y 5AH. Email: secretary@britac.ac.uk; website: www.britac.ac.uk

British and Foreign Bible Society, Stonehill Green, Westlea, Swindon, Wiltshire SN5 7DG.

British Archaeological Association, 1 Priory Gardens, Bedford Park, London W4 1TT.

British Architectural Library, Drawings Collection, 21 Portman Square, London W1H 9HF, and Manuscripts and Archives Collection, 66 Portland Square, London W1N 4AD. (Royal Institute of British Architects)

British Association for Local History, 24 Lower Street, Harnham, Salisbury, Wiltshire SP2 8EY.

British Broadcasting Corporation, Written Archives Centre, Caversham Park, Reading RG4 8TZ.

British Library, Department of Manuscripts, 96 Euston Road, St Pancras, London NW1 2DB. Email: mss@bl.uk; website: www.bl.uk/collections

The British Museum, Great Russell Street, London WC1B 3DG.

British Record Society Ltd, College of Arms, Queen Victoria Street, London EC4V 4BT.

British Records Association, London Metropolitan Archives, 40 Northampton Road, London EC1R 0HB.

British Steel, Records Services, see Warwick University, Modern Records Centre. Website: www.uksteel.org.uk

British Telecom Archives, 3rd Floor, Holborn Telephone Exchange, 268–70 High Holborn, London WC1V 7EE. Email: archives@bt.com; website: www.groupbt.com/archives

Bromley Public Libraries, Archives Section, Central Library, High Street, Bromley, Kent BR1 1EX.

Buckinghamshire Archaeological Society, County Museum, Church Street, Aylesbury HP20 2QP.

Buckinghamshire FHSoc, PO Box 403, Aylesbury, Buckinghamshire HP21 7GU. Website: www.bucksfhs.org.uk

Buckinghamshire Records and Local Studies Service, County Hall, Aylesbury HP20 1UU. Website: www.buckscc.gov.uk/archives

Burnham and Highbridge FHSoc, 1 Greenwood Close, West Huntspill, Somerset TA1 4TR.

Burton-upon-Trent Archives, Public Library, Riverside, High Street, Burton-upon-Trent, Staffordshire DE14 1AH. Email: burton.library@staffordshire.gov.uk; website: www.staffordshire.gov.uk/archives (See also Staffordshire and Stoke-on-Trent Archive Service)

Bury Archive Service, Derby Hall Annexe, Edwin Street, off Crompton Street, Bury BL9 0AS. Website: www.bury.gov.uk

Bury St Edmunds Branch (Suffolk Record Office), 77 Raingate Street, Bury St Edmunds, Suffolk IP33 2AR. Email: bury.ro@libher.suffolk.gov.uk; website: www.suffolkcc.gov.uk

Business Archives Council, The Clove Building, 4 Maguire Street, London SE1 2NQ.

Business Archives Council of Scotland, Glasgow University Archives, 13 Thurso Street, Glasgow G11 6PE.

Business Statistics Office Library, Cardiff Road, Newport NP9 1XG.

Caernarfonshire, see Gwynedd.

Caithness FHSoc, Belmont, Willowbank, Wick, KW1 4NZ.

Calderdale District Archives, Central Library, Northgate House, Northgate, Halifax HX1 1UN. Email: calderdale@wyjs.org.uk; website: www.archives.wyjs.org.uk (See also West Yorkshire)

Calderdale FHSoc (incorporating Halifax and District), Mrs M. Walker, 61 Gleanings Avenue, Norton Tower, Halifax HX2 0NU. Email: mail@cfhsweb.co.uk; website: www.cfhsweb.co.uk

Cambrian Archaeological Association, The Laurels, Westfield Road, Newport NP9 4ND.

Cambridge FHCen (LDS), 670 Cherry Hinton Road, Cambridge CB1 4DR.

Cambridge Group for the History of Population and Social Structure, Department of Geography, University of Cambridge, Downing Place, Cambridge CB2 3EN. Website: www.geog.cam.ac.uk

Cambridge University Committee for Aerial Photography, Mond Building, Free School Lane, Cambridge CB2 3RF.

Cambridge University, Department of Manuscripts *and* University Archives, University Library, West Road, Cambridge CB3 9DR. Website: www.lib.cam.ac.uk/mss

Cambridge University Heraldry and Genealogy Society, Crossfield House, Dale Road, Stanton, Bury St Edmunds, Suffolk IP31 2DY. Email: njb25@hermes.cam.ac.uk;

website: www.cam.ac.uk/societies

Cambridgeshire County Record Office, Shire Hall, Castle Hill, Cambridge CB3 0AP *and* Grammar School Walk, Huntingdon PE18 6LF. Website: www.camcnty.gov.uk

Cambridgeshire FHSoc, Mrs Ann Thompson, 2 Offa Lea, Newton, Cambridge CB2 5PW. Email: michaelandann@offalea.fsnet.co.uk; website: www.cfhs.org.uk

Camden Local Studies and Archives Centre, Holborn Library, 32–8 Theobalds Road, London WC1X 8PA. Website: www.camden.gov.uk

Canterbury Cathedral Archives, The Precincts, Canterbury CT1 2EH.

Canterbury FHCen (LDS), LDS Chapel, Forty Acres Road, Canterbury CT2 7HJ.

Cardiff FHCen (LDS), Heol-y-Deri, Rhiwbina, Cardiff CF4 6UH.

Cardiganshire FHSoc, Mrs S. Martin, Trebrysg, Tregaron, Ceredigion SY25 6HL. Website: www.heaton.celtic.co.uk/cgnfhs (See also Ceredigion)

Carlisle FHCen (LDS), Langrigg Road, Morton Park, Carlisle, Cumbria CA2 5HT.

Carmarthenshire Archive Service, Parc Myrddin, Richmond Terrace, Carmarthen SA31 1DS. Website: www.llgc.org.uk/cac

Catholic Archives Society, Innyngs House, Hatfield Park, Hatfield, Hertfordshire AL9 5PL. Website: www.catholic-history.org.uk

Catholic Central Library, 47 Francis Street, London SW1P 1DN.

Catholic FHSoc, Mr and Mrs T. Goggin, 45 Gates Green Road, West Wickham, Kent BR4 9DE. Website: www.catholic-history.org.uk

Catholic Record Society, 12 Melbourne Place, Wolsingham, County Durham DL13 3EH. Website: www.catholic-history.org.uk

Central Scotland FHSoc, 4 Fir Lane, Larbert, Stirlingshire FK5 3LW. Website: www.csfhs.org.uk

Centre for Kentish Studies, Sessions House, County Hall, Maidstone ME14 1XQ. Website: www.kent.gov.uk (See also East Kent)

Centre for Scottish Studies, University of Aberdeen, Taylor Building, King's College, Old Aberdeen AB9 2UB.

Ceredigion Archives, Swyddfa'r Sir, Glan-u-mor, Aberystwyth SY23 2DE. Email: archives@ceredigion.gov.uk; website: www.llgc.org.uk/cac (See also Cardiganshire)

Channel Islands FHSoc, Mrs S. Payn, PO Box 507, St Helier, Jersey JE4 5TN. Website: user.itl.net/~glen

Channel Islands, see also Guernsey *and* Jersey.

Charity Commission for England and Wales, St Albans House, 57–60 Haymarket, London SW1V 4QX.

Chartered Institute of Library and Information Professionals, 7 Ridgmount Street, London WC1E 7AE. Email: info@cilip.org.uk; website: www.cilip.org.uk

Cheltenham FHCen (LDS), Thirlestaine Road, Cheltenham, Gloucestershire GL53 7AS.

Cheshire and Chester Archives and Local Studies, Duke Street, Chester CH1 1RL. Website: www.cheshire.gov.uk/recoff

Cheshire FHSoc, Mrs H. Massey, 101 Irby Road, Heswall, Wirral L61 6UZ. Email: info@fhsc.org.uk; website: www.fhsc.org.uk

Cheshire, see also North *and* South.

Chester Archives, Town Hall, Chester CH1 2HJ.

Chester FHCen (LDS), 50 Clifton Drive, Blacon, Chester CH1 5LT.

Chesterfield and District FHSoc, Ms Joanna Frazer, Skerries, 485 Newbold Road, Upper Newbold, Chesterfield S41 8AE. Email: cadfhs@mcmail.com

Chetham's Library, Long Millgate, Manchester M3 1SB.

Chief Herald of Ireland, Genealogical Office, The Castle, Dublin 2. Website: www.nli.ie

Chorley FHCen (LDS), Reception Building, Temple Way, Chorley, Lancashire PR6 7EQ.

Church Commissioners, 1 Millbank, London SW1P 3JZ.

Church Distribution Centre (LDS), 399 Garretts Green Lane, Sheldon, Birmingham B33 0UH. Website: lds.org.uk

Church Monuments Society, Royal Armouries, Tower of London EC3N 4AB.

Church of England Record Centre, 15 Galleywall Road, South Bermondsey, London SE16 3PB. Website: cofe.anglican.org

Church of Jesus Christ of Latter-day Saints, Branch Library, Hyde Park Chapel, 64 Exhibition Road, London SW7 2PA.

Churchill Archives Centre, Churchill College, Cambridge CB3 0DS.

City of Westminster Archives Centre, 10 St Ann's Street, London SW1P 2XR. Website:

www.westminster.gov.uk/archives

Civic Trust, 17 Carlton House Terrace, London SW1Y 5AH.

Clackmannanshire Council Archives, 26–8 Drysdale Street, Alloa FK10 1JL. Website: www.clacksweb.org.uk

Clare County Archives Service, Local Studies Centre, Clare County Library, The Manse, Harmony Row, Ennis. Email: jhayes@clarecoco.ie; website: www.clarelibrary.ie

Cleveland, North Yorkshire and South Durham FHSoc, Mr A. Sampson, 1 Oxgang Close, Redcar TS10 4ND. Website: website.lineone.net/~pjoiner

Clwyd FHSoc, Mrs A. Anderson, The Laurels, Dolydd Road, Cefn Mawr, Wrexham, LL14 3NH. Website: www.clwydfhs.org.uk

Coal see Mining Records Office.

College of Arms, Queen Victoria Street, London EC4V 4BT. Website: www.college-of-arms.gov.uk

Commons, Open Spaces and Footpaths Preservation Society (Open Spaces Society), 25A Bell Street, Henley-on-Thames, Oxfordshire RG9 2BA.

Commonwealth War Graves Commission, 2 Marlow Road, Maidenhead, Berkshire SL6 7DX. Website: www.cwgc.org

Conwy Archive Service, Old Board School, Lloyd Street, Llandudno LL30 2YG. Email: archifau.archives@conwy.gov.uk; website:www.conwy.gov.uk

Cork Archives Institute, Christ Church, South Main Street, Cork. Website: www.corkcorp.ie

Cork FHCen (LDS), Scarsfield Road, Wilton, Cork.

Cornwall FHSoc, The Administrator, 5 Victoria Square, Truro, Cornwall TR1 2RS. Email: secretary@cornwallfhs.com; website: www.cornwallfhs.com

Cornwall Record Office, County Hall, Truro TR1 3AY. Website: www.cornwall.gov.uk

Corporation of London Records Office, PO Box 270, Guildhall, London EC2P 2EJ. Email: clro@corpoflondon.gov.uk; website: www.cityoflondon.gov.uk (See also Guildhall *and* London)

Corus, Records Services. See Warwick University, Modern Records Centre. Website: www.uksteel.org.uk

Council for British Archaeology, Bowes Morrell House, 111 Walmgate, York YO1 2UA.

Court of the Lord Lyon, HM General Register House, Edinburgh EH1 3YT.

Coventry City Archives, Mandela House, Bayley Lane, Coventry CV1 5RG. Email: coventryarchives@discover.uk.com; website: www.coventry-city.co.uk/archives

Coventry FHCen (LDS), Riverside Close, Whitley, Coventry CV3 4AT.

Coventry FHSoc, PO Box 2746, Coventry CV5 7YD. Website: www.covfhs.demon.co.uk

Crawley FHCen (LDS), Old Horsham Road, Crawley, Sussex RH11 8PD.

Croydon Archives Service, Central Library, Croydon Clocktower, Katharine Street, Croydon CR9 1ET.

Cumberland and Westmorland Antiquarian and Archaeological Society, 2 High Tenterfell, Kendal LA9 4PG.

Cumbria FHSoc, Mrs M. Russell, 32 Granada Road, Denton, Manchester M34 2IJ. Website: www.genuki.org.uk/big

Cumbria Record Office, The Castle, Carlisle CA3 8UR *and* 140 Duke Street, Barrow-in-Furness LA14 1XW *and* County Offices, Kendal LA9 4RQ *and* Scotch Street, Whitehaven CA28 7BJ. Website: www.cumbria.gov.uk/archives

Customs and Excise, New King's Beam House, 22 Upper Ground, London SE1 9PJ.

Denbighshire Record Office, The Old Jail, 42 Clwyd Street, Ruthin, Denbighshire LL15 1HP. Email: archives@denbighshire.gov.uk; website: www.denbighshire.gov.uk

Derbyshire FHSoc, Mr G. Wells, Bridge Chapel House, St Mary's Bridge, Sowter Road, Derby DE1 3AT. Website: www.dfhs.org.uk

Derbyshire Record Office, New Street, with correspondence to County Offices, Matlock DE4 3AG. Website: www.derbyshire.gov.uk

Devon FHSoc, PO Box 9, Exeter Devon EX2 6YP. Email: secretary@devonfhs.org.uk; website: www.devonfhs.org.uk

Devon Record Office, Castle Street, Exeter EX4 3PU. Website: www.devon.gov.uk (See also North Devon)

Doctor (Dr) Williams's Library, 14 Gordon Square, London WC1H 0AG. Email: enquiries@DWLib.co.uk

Doncaster and District FHSoc, Mr J. Staniforth, 125 The Grove, Wheatley Hills, Doncaster DN2 5SN. Email: TonyJuneS@aol.com; website: www.doncasterfhs.freeserve.co.uk

Doncaster Archives Department, King Edward Road, Balby, Doncaster DN4 ONA. Website: www.doncaster.gov.uk/education/document.asp?WSDOCID=413

Donegal County Archives, Three Rivers Centre, Lifford. Email: nbrennan@donegalcoco.ie; website: www.donegal.ie

Dorset FHSoc, Mrs Debbie Winter, 131 Lynwood Drive, Merley, Wimborne, Dorset BH21 1UU. Email: contact@Dorsetfhs.freeserve.co.uk; website: www.dorsetfhs.freeserve.co.uk

Dorset Record Office, Bridport Road, Dorchester DT1 1RP. Email: archives@dorset-cc.gov.uk; website: www.dorset-cc.gov.uk/archives

Douglas FHCen (LDS), Woodside, Woodburn Road, Isle of Man.

Dublin City Archives, City Assembly House, 58 South William Street, Dublin 2. Email: cityarchives@dublincorp.ie; website: www.dublincorp.ie

Dublin FHCen (LDS), The Willows, Finglas Road, Dublin 11.

Dublin, University College, Archives, 82 St Stephen's Green, Dublin 2.

Dublin, University College, Department of Irish Folklore, Belfield, Dublin 4.

Dublin University, Trinity College Library, College Street, Dublin 2.

Duchy of Cornwall, 10 Buckingham Gate, London SW1E 6LA.

Duchy of Lancaster, Lancaster Place, Strand, London WC2E 7ED.

Dudley Archives and Local History Service, Mount Pleasant Street, Coseley, West Midlands WV14 9JR. Website: www.dudley.gov.uk

Dumfries and Galloway Archives, Archive Centre, 33 Burns Street, Dumfries DG1 2PS. Website: www.dumgal.gov.uk

Dumfries and Galloway FHSoc, 9 Glasgow Street, Dumfries DG2 9AF. Email: enquiries@dgfhs.org.uk; website: www.dgfhs.org.uk

Dumfries FHCen (LDS), 36 Edinburgh Road, Albanybank, Dumfries DG1 1JQ.

Dun Laoghaire Genealogical Society, 14 Rochestown Park, Dun Laoghaire, County Dublin.

Dundee City Archives, 1 Shore Terrace, with correspondence to 21 City Square, Dundee DD1 3BY.

Dundee FHCen (LDS), Bingham Terrace, Dundee DD2 4TJ.

Dundee University Library, Department of Archives and Manuscripts, Tower Building, Dundee DD1 4HN.

Durham County Record Office, County Hall, Durham DH1 5UL. Email: archives@dorset-cc.gov.uk; website: www.durham.gov.uk/recordoffice

Durham Dean and Chapter Library, The College, Durham DH1 3EH. Website: www.dur.ac.uk/library/asc

Durham University Library, Archives and Special Collections, Palace Green, Durham DH1 3RN. Email: pg.library@durham.ac.uk; website: www.dur.ac.uk/library/asc

Dyfed FHSoc, John James, 38 Brynmelyn Avenue, Llanelli, Carmarthenshire SA15 3RT. Email: secretary@dyfedfhs.org.uk; website: www.dyfedfhs.org.uk

Ealing Local History Library, Central Library, 103 Ealing Broadway Centre, London W5 5JY.

East Ayrshire FHSoc, The Dick Institute, Elmbank Avenue, Kilmarnock KA1 3BU. Website: www.eastayrshirefhs.org.uk

East Kent Archive Centre, Enterprise Business Park, Honeywood Road, Whitfield, Dover CT16 3EH. Website: www.kent.gov.uk (See also Centre for Kentish Studies)

East of London FHSoc, Mrs Judith Taylor, 42 Alwen Grove, South Ockendon, Essex RM15 5DW. Website: eolfhs.rootsweb.com

East Riding of Yorkshire Archives and Records Service, The Chapel, Lord Roberts Road, Beverley, with correspondence to County Hall, Beverley HU17 9BA. Website: www.eastriding.gov.uk

East Surrey FHSoc, Mrs Marion Brackpool, 370 Chipstead Valley Road, Coulsdon, Surrey CR5 3BF. Website: www.eastsurreyfhs.org.uk

East Sussex Record Office, The Maltings, Castle Precincts, Lewes BN7 1YT. Email: archives@eastsussexcc.gov.uk; website: www.eastsussexcc.gov.uk

East Yorkshire FHSoc, Mrs M. S. Oliver, 12 Carlton Drive, Aldbrough, East Yorkshire HU11 4SF. Website: www.eyfhs.org.uk

Eastbourne and District FHSoc, Mrs Sarah Slaughter, 94 Northbourne Road, Eastbourne, East Sussex BN22 8QP. Email: sarahlslaughter@madasafish.com

Ecclesiastical History Society, Department of Medieval History, University of Glasgow, Glasgow G12 8QQ.

Edinburgh City Archives, City Chambers, High Street, Edinburgh EH1 1YJ. Website:

www.edinburgh.gov.uk

Edinburgh FHCen (LDS), 30A Colinton Road, Edinburgh EH10 5DQ.

Edinburgh University Library, Special Collections Department, 30 George Square, Edinburgh EH8 9LJ.

Elgin FHCen (LDS), Pansport Road, Elgin IV30 1HE.

Enfield Local History Unit, Southgate Town Hall, Green Lanes, Palmers Green, London N13 4XD. Website: www.enfield.gov.uk

English Folk Dance and Song Society, Cecil Sharp House, 2 Regent's Park Road, London NW1 7AY.

English Heritage, see Historic Buildings.

English Place-Name Survey, Grey College, Durham DH1 3LG.

Essex FHSoc, Mrs A. Church, Windyridge, 32 Parsons Heath, Colchester, Essex CO4 3HX. Email: secretary@esfh.org.uk; website: www.esfh.org.uk

Essex Record Office, Wharf Road, Chelmsford CM2 6YT *and* Colchester and North-East Essex Branch, Stanwell House, Stanwell Street, Colchester CO2 7DL *and* Southend Branch, Central Library, Victoria Avenue, Southend-on-Sea SS2 6EX. Email: ero.enquiry@essexcc.gov.uk; website: www.essexcc.gov.uk/ero

Essex Society for Archaeology and History, Hollytrees Museum, High Street, Colchester CO1 1UG.

Exeter Cathedral Library and Archives, Bishop's Palace, Exeter EX1 1HX.

Exeter FHCen (LDS), Wonford Road, off Barrack Road, Exeter EX2.

Exeter University Library, Stocker Road, Exeter EX4 4PT.

Falkirk Council Archives, History Research Centre, Falkirk Museum, Callender House, Falkirk FK1 1YR. Website: www.falkirkmuseum.demon.co.uk

Family History Library, 35 North West Temple Street, Salt Lake City, Utah 84150. Website: www.familysearch.org

Family History Societies of Wales, Association of, Geoff Riggs, Peacehaven, Badgers Meadow, Pwllmeyric, Chepstow, Monmouthshire NP16 6UE. Website: www.fhswales.info

Family Records Centre, 1 Myddelton Street, London EC1R 1UW. Email: enquiry@pro.gov.uk; website: www.familyrecords.gov.uk

Federation of Family History Societies, PO Box 2425, Coventry CV5 6YX. Email: info@ffhs.org.uk; website: www.ffhs.org.uk

Felixstowe FHSoc, Mrs J. S. Campbell, 7 Victoria Road, Felixstowe, Suffolk IP11 7PT. Website: www.btinternet.com/~woodsbj/ffhs

Field Studies Council, Preston Montford, Montford Bridge, Shrewsbury, Shropshire SY4 1HW.

Fife Council Archives Centre, Carleton House, Balgonie Road, North Street, Markinch KY7 6AH.

Fife FHSoc, 28 Craigearn Avenue, Kirkcaldy, Fife KY2 6YS. Email: fife@ffhsoc.freeserve.co.uk; website: www.fifefhs.pwp.blueyonder.co.uk

Finsbury Library, 245 St John Street, London EC1V 4NB.

Flannery Clan FHSoc, Dr L. J. O'Flannery, 81 Woodford Drive, Clondakin, Dublin 22, Ireland. Email: oflannery@eircom.net; website: www.flanneryclan.ie

Flintshire Record Office, The Old Rectory, Hawarden CH5 3NR. Website: www.llgc.org.uk/cac

Folkestone and District FHSoc, Mrs Levina B. Jones, Brickwall Farmhouse, Bengemarsh Road, Lydd, Kent TN29 9JH. Email: levina.jones@virgin.net; website: freespace.virgin.net/jennifer.killick

Folklore Society, University College, Gower Street, London WC1E 6BT.

Forest of Dean FHCen (LDS), Wynols Hill, Queensway, Coleford, Gloucestershire GL16 5SX.

Francis Frith Collection, Charlton Road, Andover, Hampshire SP10 3LE.

Furness FHSoc, Miss J. Fairbairn, 64 Cowlarns Road, Barrow-in-Furness, Cumbria LA14 4HJ. Email: julia.fairbairn@virgin.net; website: members.aol.com/FurnessFHS/fpw.htm

Gaerwen FHCen (LDS), Holyhead Road, Gaerwen, Anglesey LL60.

Gateshead Central Library, Prince Consort Road, Gateshead NE8 4LN. Website: www.gateshead.gov.uk

Genealogical Society of Ireland, Mr Michael Merrigan, Hon. Secretary, 11 Desmond Avenue, Dun Laoghaire, Co. Dublin, Ireland. Email: GenSocIreland@iol.ie; website: welcome.to/GenealogyIreland

Genealogical Society of Utah, Family History Library, 35 North West Temple Street, Salt Lake City, Utah 84150. Website: www.familysearch.org

Genealogical Society of Utah (UK), Mr G. D. Mawlam, 185 Penns Lane, Sutton Coldfield B76 1JU.

Genealogists, Society of, 14 Charterhouse Buildings, Goswell Road, London EC1M 7BA. Email: info@sog.org.uk; website: www.sog.org.uk

General Register and Record Office of Shipping and Seamen, Anchor House, Cheviot Chase, Parc Ty Glas, Llanishen, Cardiff CF4 5JA.

General Register Office (birth, marriage, death):

England and Wales, PO Box 2, Smedley Hydro, Trafalgar Road, Birkdale, Southport PR8 2HH.

Guernsey, Royal Court House, St Peter Port, Guernsey GY1 2PB. Email: ken.tough@gov.gg

Ireland, Joyce House, 8/11 Lombard Street East, Dublin 2.

Isle of Man, Registries Building, Deemster's Walk, Buck's Road, Douglas, Isle of Man IM1 3AR. Email: civil@registry.gov.uk

Jersey, 10 Royal Square, St Helier, Jersey JE2 4WA. Email: jgreffe@psilink.co.je; website: www.judicialgreffe.gov.je

Northern Ireland, Oxford House, 49–55 Chichester Street, Belfast BT1 4HL. Website: www.nisra.gov.uk/gro

Scotland, New Register House, Edinburgh EH1 3YT. Website: www.open.gov.uk/gros/groshome.htm

Genuki, David Hawgood, 26 Cloister Road, Acton, London W3 0DE.

Georgian Group, 6 Fitzroy Square, London W1P 6DX.

Gillingham FHCen (LDS), 2 Twydall Lane, Gillingham, Kent ME8.

Glamorgan FHSoc, Mrs Janet Thomas, Hampton House, 86 Penprysg Road, Pencoed, Bridgend CF35 6SF. Email: secretary@glamfhs.org; website: www.glamfhs.org

Glamorgan Record Office, Glamorgan Building, King Edward VII Avenue, Cathays Park, Cardiff CF1 3NE. Email: glamro@cardiff.ac.uk; website: www.glamro.gov.uk (See also West Glamorgan)

Glasgow and West of Scotland FHSoc, Unit 5, 22 Mansfield Street, Glasgow G11 5QP. Website: www.gwsfhs.org.uk

Glasgow City Archives, Mitchell Library, 201 North Street, Glasgow G3 7DN. Website: www.mitchelllibrary.org

Glasgow FHCen (LDS), 35 Julian Avenue, Glasgow G12 0RB.

Glasgow University Archives and Business Record Centre, 13 Thurso Street, Glasgow G11 6PE.

Glasgow University Library, Department of Special Collections, Hillhead Street, Glasgow G12 8QE.

Gloucestershire FHSoc, Mrs Sue Stafford, 4 Twyver Close, Upton St Leonards, Gloucestershire GL4 8EF. Email: glosearch@hotmail.com; website: www.cix.co.uk/~rd/GENUKI/gfhs.htm

Gloucestershire Record Office, Clarence Row, off Alvin Street, Gloucester GL1 3DW. Website: www.gloscc.gov.uk

Greater Manchester County Record Office, 56 Marshall Street, New Cross, Ancoats, Manchester M4 5FU. Website: www.gmcro.co.uk

Greater Manchester Museum of Science and Industry, Liverpool Road, Castlefield, Manchester M3 4JP.

Greenwich Local History Library, Woodlands, 90 Mycenae Road, Blackheath, London SE3 7SE. Email: local.history@greenwich.gov.uk; website: www.greenwich.gov.uk

Grimsby FHCen (LDS), Grimsby Ward Chapel, Linwood Avenue/Waltham Road, Grimsby DN33 2NL.

Guernsey: Greffe, Royal Court House, St Peter Port GY1 2PB.

Guernsey: La Société Guernesiaise, FHS, Secretary, PO Box 314, Candie, St Peter Port, Guernsey GY1 3TG. Website: www.societe.org.gg

Guernsey: States of Guernsey Island Archives Service, 29 Victoria Road, St Peter Port, Guernsey GY1 1HU. Website: user.itl.net/~glen/archgsy

Guild of One-name Studies, 14 Charterhouse Buildings, Goswell Road, London EC1M 7BA. Website: www.one-name.org

Guildhall Library, Aldermanbury, London EC2P 2EJ. Email: manuscripts.guildhall@corpoflondon.gov.uk; website: www.cityoflondon.gov.uk (See also Corporation *and* London)

Gwent FHSoc, 11 Rosser Street, Wainfelin, Pontypool NP4 6EA. Email: secretary@gwentfhs.info; website: www.gwentfhs.info

Gwent Record Office, County Hall, Cwmbran NP44 2XH. Website: www.llgc.org.uk/cac

Gwynedd Archives Service, Gwynedd Council, Shirehall Street, Caernarfon LL55 1SH *and* Meirionydd Archives, Cae Penarlâg, Dolgellau LL40 2YB. Email: archives@gwynedd.gov.uk; website: www.gwynedd.gov.uk

Gwynedd FHSoc, Ms Yvonne Edwards, 36 Y Wern, Port Dinorwic, Gwynedd LL56 4TX. Email: Gwynedd.Roots@tesco.net; website: www.gwynedd.fsbusiness.co.uk

Hackney Archives Department, 43 De Beauvoir Road, London N1 5SQ. Website: www.hackney.gov.uk

Halifax, see Calderdale.

Hammersmith and Fulham Archives and Local History Centre, the Lilla Huset, 191 Talgarth Road, London W6 8BJ. Email: lbhfarchives@hotmail.com; website:www.lbhf.gov.uk

Hampshire Genealogical Society, Mrs Sue Smith, Oakbourne, Uplands Road, Denmead, Hampshire PO7 6HE. Email: secretary@hgs-online.org.uk; website: www.hgs-online.org.uk

Hampshire Record Office, Sussex Street, Winchester SO23 8TH. Email: enquiries.archives@hants.gov.uk; website: www.hants.gov.uk

Harborne FHCen (LDS), 38 Lordswood Road, Harborne, Birmingham B17 9QS.

Haringey Archive Service, Bruce Castle Museum, Lordship Lane, London N17 8NU. Website: www.brucecastlemuseum.org.uk

Harrow Reference Library, PO Box 4, Civic Centre, Station Road, Harrow HA1 2UU.

Hastings and Rother FHSoc, Miss Christine Heywood, Flat 22, The Cloisters, St Leonards-on-Sea, East Sussex TN37 6JT. Website: www.hrfhs.org.uk

Hastings FHCen (LDS), 2 Ledsham Avenue, St Leonards-on-Sea, East Sussex TN37 7LE.

Helston FHCen (LDS), Clodgey Lane, Helston, Cornwall TR13 8PJ.

Heraldry Society, PO Box 32, Maidenhead, Berkshire SL6 3FD. Website: www.kwtelecom.com/heraldry

Heraldry Society of Scotland, 2/6 Huntingdon Place, Edinburgh EH7 4AT.

Hereford FHCen (LDS), 262 Kings Acre Road, Hereford HR4 0SD.

Hereford Record Office, The Old Barracks, Harold Street, Hereford HR1 2QX. Email: shubbard@herefordshire.gov.uk; website: www.herefordshire.gov.uk

Herefordshire FHSoc, Mr Brian Prosser, 6 Birch Meadow, Gosmore Road, Clehonger, Hereford HR2 9RH. Email: prosser_brian@hotmail.com; website: www.rootsweb.com

Hertfordshire Archives and Local Studies, County Hall, Hertford SG13 8EJ. Website: www.hertsdirect.org

Hertfordshire Family and Population HSoc, Mr Ken Garner, 2 Mayfair Close, St Albans, Hertfordshire AL4 9TN. Email: secretary@hertsfhs.org.uk; website: www.hertsfhs.org.uk

High Wycombe FHCen (LDS), 743 London Road, High Wycombe, Buckinghamshire HP11 1HD.

Highland Council Archive, Inverness Library, Farraline Park, Inverness IV1 1NH. Website: www.highland.gov.uk (See also North Highland)

Highland FHSoc, Public Library, Farraline Park, Inverness IV1 INH. Website: www.genuki.org.uk

Hillingdon FHSoc, Mrs G. May, 20 Moreland Drive, Gerrards Cross, Buckinghamshire SL9 8BB. Email: gillmay@dial.pipex.com; website: rootsweb.com/~enghfhs

Hillingdon Local Heritage Service, Central Library, 14–15 High Street, Uxbridge UB8 1HD. Email: ccotton@hillingdon.gov.uk; website: www.hillingdon.gov.uk

Historic Buildings and Monuments Commission for England (English Heritage), Fortress House, 23 Savile Row, London W1X 1AB.

Historic Buildings Council for Scotland, Longmore House, Salisbury Place, Edinburgh EH9 1SH.

Historic Buildings Council for Wales, Crown Building, Cathays Park, Cardiff CF1 3NQ.

Historic Monuments and Buildings Branch, Department of the Environment for Northern Ireland, Commonwealth House, Castle Street, Belfast BT1 1GU.

Historic Society of Lancashire and Cheshire, Southport Reference Library, Lord Street, Southport, Lancashire PR8 1DJ.

Historical Association, 59A Kennington Park Road, London SE11 4JH.

Historical Association of Ireland, Department of History, University College, Belfield,

Dublin 4.

Historical Manuscripts Commission, Quality House, Quality Court, Chancery Lane, London WC2A 1HP. Website: www.hmc.gov.uk

Honourable Society of Cymmrodorion, 30 Eastcastle Street, London W1N 7PD.

Honourable the Irish Society, 214 Carey Lane, London EC2V 8AA.

Hounslow Local History Collection, Local Studies Department, Hounslow Library, 24 Treaty Centre, Hounslow TW3 1ES.

House of Lords Record Office, House of Lords, London SW1A 0PW. Website: www.parliament.uk

Huddersfield and District FHSoc, Mrs Eileen Bass, 292 Thornhills Lane, Clifton, Brighouse, West Yorkshire HD6 4JQ. Email: secretary@hdfhs.org.uk; website: www.hdfhs.org.uk

Huddersfield FHCen (LDS), 12 Halifax Road, Dewsbury, West Yorkshire WF13 4JD.

Huddersfield, see also Kirklees.

Huguenot Library, University College, Gower Street, London WC1E 6BT.

Hull City Archives, 79 Lowgate, Kingston upon Hull HU1 1HN. Website: www.hullcc.gov.uk

Hull FHCen (LDS), 725 Holderness Road, Hull HU8 9AN.

Hull University, Brynmor Jones Library, Cottingham Road, Hull HU6 7RX.

Huntingdon FHSoc, Mrs C. Kesseler, 42 Crowhill, Godmanchester, Huntingdon, Cambridgeshire PE29 2NR. Email: huntsec@ckesseler.freeserve.co.uk; website: www.genuki.org.uk

Hyde Park FHCen (LDS), 64/8 Exhibition Road, South Kensington, London SW7 2PA.

Imperial War Museum, Department of Documents, Lambeth Road, London SE1 6HZ. Website: www.iwm.org.uk

Industrial Archaeology, Association for, The Wharfage, Ironbridge, Telford, Shropshire TF8 7AW.

Institute of Field Archaeologists, University of Manchester, Oxford Road, Manchester M13 9PL.

Institute of Heraldic and Genealogical Studies, Mr J. Palmer, 79–82 Northgate, Canterbury, Kent CT1 1BA. Email: ihgs@ihgs.ac.uk; website: www.ihgs.ac.uk

Institute of Historical Research, School of Advanced Study, University of London, Senate House, Malet Street, London WC1E 7HU.

Institute of Irish Studies, Queen's University of Belfast, 8 Fitzwilliam Street, Belfast BT9 6AW.

Institution of Civil Engineers, 1–7 Great George Street, London SW1P 3AA.

International Society for British Genealogy and Family History, PO Box 3115, Salt Lake City, Utah 84110. Website: www.genealogysourcecatalog.com

Inverness FHCen (LDS), 13 Ness Walk, Inverness IV3 5SQ.

Ipswich FHCen (LDS), 42 Sidegate Lane West, Ipswich, Suffolk IP1 3DB.

Ipswich Branch (Suffolk Record Office), Gatacre Road, Ipswich, Suffolk IP1 2PQ. Email: ipswich.ro@libher.suffolk.gov.uk; website: www.suffolkcc.gov.uk

Irish Architectural Archive, 63 Merrion Square, Dublin 2.

Irish Family History Forum, PO Box 67, Plainview, NY 11803-0067, USA. Email: ifhf@ifhf.org; website: www.ifhf.org

Irish Family History Foundation, website: www.irishroots.net

Irish FHSoc, PO Box 36, Naas, Co. Kildare, Ireland. Email: ifhs@eircom.net; website: homepage.eircom.net/~ifhs

Irish Genealogical Association, 164 Kingsway, Dunmurry, Belfast BT17 9AD.

Irish Genealogical Research Society, Mr R. Findlay, The Irish Club, 82 Eaton Square, London SW1W 9AJ.

Irish Genealogical Society International, PO Box 16585, St Paul, Minnesota 55116-0585, USA. Website: www.rootsweb.com

Irish Manuscripts Commission, 73 Merrion Square, Dublin 2.

Ironbridge Gorge Museum, Library and Archives, The Wharfage, Telford, Shropshire TF8 7AW.

Isle of Axholme FHSoc, A. B. Wise, Alwinton, 51 Mill Road, Crowle, Isle of Axholme, North Lincolnshire DN17 4LW. Email: alwinton51@btinternet.com; website: www.linktop.demon.co.uk/axholme

Isle of Man Civil Registry, Registries Building, Buck's Road, Douglas IM1 3AR. Email: civil@registry.gov.im

Isle of Man FHSoc, Mr E. W. Q. Cleator, 5 Selborne Drive, Douglas, Isle of Man.

Isle of Man FHSoc Library, 13 Michael Street, Peel, Isle of Man IM5 1HB. Website: www.isle-of-man.com

Isle of Man Manx National Heritage Library, Manx Museum and National Trust, Douglas IM1 3LY.

Isle of Man Public Record Office, Unit 3, Spring Valley Industrial Estate, Braddan, Douglas IM2 2QR. Email: public.records@registry.gov.im; website: www.gov.im

Isle of Wight County Record Office, 26 Hillside, Newport PO30 2EB. Email: record.office@iow.gov.uk; website: www.iwight.com

Isle of Wight: Newport FHCen (LDS), Chestnut Close, Shide Road, Newport PO30 1YE.

Isle of Wight FHSoc, Mrs Betty Dhillon, Spindrift, 3 Milne Way, Newport PO30 1YF. Email: betty.dhillon@btinternet.com; website: www.dina.clara.net/iowfhs

Islington Archives, Central Reference Library, 2 Fieldway Crescent, London N5 1PF. Email: is.osc.his.@dial.pipex.com; website: www.islington.gov.uk

Jersey Archive and *Heritage Trust*, Clarence Road, St Helier, Jersey JE2 4JY. Email: archives@jerseyheritagetrust.org; website: www.jerseyheritagetrust.org

Jersey: Channel Islands FHSoc, PO Box 507, St Helier, Jersey JE4 5TN.

Jersey: Judicial Greffe, Morier House, Halkett Place, St Helier JE1 1DD. Email: jgreffe@psilink.co.je; website: www.judicialgreffe.gov.je

Jersey: La Société Jersiaise, 7 Pier Road, St Helier JE2 4XW.

Jersey: St Helier FHCen (LDS), Rue de la Vallée, St Mary, Jersey.

Jersey: Superintendant Registrar, 10 Royal Square, St Helier, Jersey JE2 4WA.

Jewish Genealogical Society of Great Britain, Mr A. Winner, PO Box 13288, London N3 3WD. Email: jgsgb@ort.org; website: www.jgsgb.ort.org

Jewish Historical Society of England, 33 Seymour Place, London W1H 5AP.

John Rylands University Library of Manchester, 150 Deansgate, Manchester M3 3EH. Email: j.r.hodgson@man.ac.uk; website: rylibweb.man.ac.uk

Keighley and District FHSoc, Mrs S. Daynes, 2 The Hallowes, Shann Park, Keighley, West Yorkshire BD20 6HY. Website: www.ffhs.org.uk/members/keighley.htm

Kensington and Chelsea Libraries and Arts Service, Central Library, Phillimore Walk, London W8 7RX.

Kent Archaeological Society, Three Elms, Woodlands Lane, Shorne, Gravesend DA12 3HH.

Kent FHSoc, Mrs Kristin Slater, Bullockstone Farm, Bullockstone Road, Herne, Kent CT6 7NL. Email: kristn@globalnet.co.uk; website: www.kfhs.org.uk

Kent, see also Centre for Kentish Studies *and* East Kent *and* North West Kent.

Kilmarnock FHCen (LDS), 1 Whatriggs Road, Kilmarnock, Ayrshire KA1 3QY.

King's Lynn FHCen (LDS), Reffley Lane, King's Lynn, Norfolk PE30 3EQ.

Kingston Museum and Heritage Service, North Kingston Centre, Richmond Road, Kingston upon Thames KT2 5PE.

Kirkcaldy FHCen (LDS), Winifred Crescent, Forth Park, Kirkcaldy, Fife KY2 5SX.

Kirklees District Archives, Central Library, Princess Alexandra Walk, Huddersfield HD1 2SU. Email: kirklees@wyjs.org.uk; website: www.archives.wyjs.org.uk (See also West Yorkshire)

Lambeth Archives Department, Minet Library, 52 Knatchbull Road, London SE5 9QY. Website: www.lambeth.gov.uk

Lambeth Palace Library, London SE1 7JU. Website: www.lambethpalacelibrary.org

Lanarkshire FHSoc, Hamilton Central Library, 98 Cadzow Street, Hamilton ML3 6HQ. Email: infoFHS@aol.com; website: www.lanarkshirefhs.org.uk

Lancashire FHSoc, Mrs J Huntingdon, 15 Christ Church Street, Accrington, Lancashire BB5 2LZ. Email: jehuntingdon@08002go.com; website: www.lancashire-fhhs.org.uk

Lancashire Parish Register Society, Mr Tom O'Brien, 188 Greenwood Crescent, Houghton Green, Warrington WA2 0EG. Email: tom_OBrien@bigfoot.com; website: www.genuki.org.uk

Lancashire Record Office, Bow Lane, Preston PR1 8ND. Website: www.lancashire.gov.uk

Lancaster FHCen (LDS), Lancaster Ward House, Overangle Road, Morecambe LA15.

Lancaster FHSoc, Mrs M. Wilmshurst, 94 Croston Road, Garstang, Preston PR3 1HR.

Largs and North Ayrshire FHSoc, 12 Kelvin Gardens, Largs, Ayrshire KA30 3SX. Website: www.freeyellow.com/members7/lnafhs

Latter-Day Saints, Church Distribution Centre, 399 Garretts Green Lane, Sheldon, Birmingham B33 0UH. Website: lds.org.uk

Leeds District Archives, Chapeltown Road, Sheepscar, Leeds LS7 3AP. Email: leeds@wyjs.org.uk; website: www.archives.wyjs.org.uk (See also West Yorkshire)

Leeds FHCen (LDS), Vesper Road, Leeds LS5 3QT.

Leeds University, Brotherton Library, Leeds LS2 9JT.

Leicester FHCen (LDS), Wakerley Road, Leicester LE5 4WD.

Leicester University, Department of English Local History, University Road, Leicester LE1 7RH.

Leicestershire and Rutland FHSoc, Ray Broad, 11 Spring Lane, Wymondham, Leicestershire LE14 2AY. Email: ray.broad@ntlworld.com; website: lrfhs.org.uk

Leicestershire, Leicester and Rutland Record Office, Long Street, Wigston Magna, Leicester LE18 2AH. Email: recordoffice@leics.gov.uk; website: www.leics.gov.uk

Lerwick FHCen (LDS), South Road, Lerwick ZE1 0RB.

Letchworth and District FHSoc, Mrs D. M. Paterson, 84 Kings Hedges, Hitchin, Hertfordshire SG5 2QE. Website: www.hertsdirect.org

Lewisham Local Studies Centre, Lewisham Library, 199–201 Lewisham High Street, London SE13 6LG. Website: www.lewisham.gov.uk

Library Association, now Chartered Institute of Library and Information Professionals, 7 Ridgmount Street, London WC1E 7AE. Email: info@cilip.org.uk; website: www.cilip.org.uk

Library of Congress, Washington, DC 20540-4840.

Lichfield FHCen (LDS), Purcell Avenue, Lichfield, Staffordshire.

Lichfield Record Office, Lichfield Library, The Friary, Lichfield WS13 6QG. Email: lichfield.record.office@staffordshire.gov.uk; website: www.staffordshire.gov.uk (See also Staffordshire and Stoke-on-Trent Archive Service)

Limerick FHCen (LDS), Doraddoyle Road, Limerick.

Limerick Regional Archives, Michael Street, Limerick.

Lincoln FHCen (LDS), Skellingthorpe Road, Lincoln LN6 0PB.

Lincolnshire Archives, St Rumbold Street, Lincoln LN2 5AB. Website: www.lincolnshire.gov.uk (See also North East Lincolnshire)

Lincolnshire FHSoc, Colin E. Baslington, 1 Pennygate Gardens, Spalding, Lincolnshire PE11 1XJ. Email: LINfhsSec@aol.com; website: www.genuki.org.uk

Linnean Society of London, Burlington House, Piccadilly, London W1V 0LQ.

Liverpool and South-west Lancashire FHSoc, Mr David Guiver, 11 Bushbys Lane, Formby, Liverpool L37 2DX. Website: www.liverpool-genealogy.org.uk

Liverpool FHCen (LDS), 4 Mill Bank, Liverpool L13 0BW.

Liverpool Record Office and Local History Service, Central Library, William Brown Street, Liverpool L3 8EW. Email: recoffice.central.library@liverpool.gov.uk; website: www.liverpool.gov.uk

Liverpool University, Department of Special Collections and Archives, PO Box 123, Liverpool L69 3DA.

Local Population Studies Society, 78 Harlow Terrace, Harrogate HG2 8AW.

London and North Middlesex FHSoc (including *Westminster & Central Middlesex FHS*), Mrs S. Lumas, 7 Mount Pleasant Road, New Malden, Surrey KT3 3JZ. Website: www.lnmfhs.dircon.co.uk

London: Hyde Park FHCen (LDS), 64/8 Exhibition Road, South Kensington, London SW7 2PA.

London Library, 14 St James's Square, London SW1Y 4LG.

London Metropolitan Archives, 40 Northampton Road, London EC1R 0HB. Email: ask.lma@corpoflondon.gov.uk; website: www.cityoflondon.gov.uk (See also Corporation *and* Guildhall)

London: Museum of London, 150 London Wall, London EC2Y 5HN.

London, University College, Manuscripts Room, DMS Watson Library, Gower Street, London WC1E 6BT.

London University Library, Palaeography Room, Senate House, Malet Street, London WC1E 7HU.

Londonderry FHCen (LDS), Racecourse Road, Belmont Estate, Londonderry BT48.

Lothian FHSoc, Lasswade High School Centre, Eskdale Drive, Bonnyrigg, Midlothian EH19 2LA. Email: anne_agnew@online.rednet.co.uk; website: www.lothianfhs.org.uk

Lowestoft FHCen (LDS), 165 Yarmouth Road, Lowestoft, Suffolk NR32 4AF.

Lowestoft Branch (Suffolk Record Office), Central Library, Clapham Road, Lowestoft, Suffolk NR32 1DR. Email: lowestoft.ro@libher.suffolk.gov.uk; website: www.suffolkcc.gov.uk

Lyon: Court of the Lord Lyon, HM General Register House, Edinburgh EH1 3YT.

Maidstone FHCen (LDS), 76B London Road, Maidstone, Kent ME16 0DR.

Malvern FHSoc, Roy Daughtree, D'Haute Rive, 37 Tennyson Drive, St James Park, Malvern, Worcestershire WR14 2TQ. Website: www.mfhg.org.uk

Manchester and Lancashire FHSoc, Clayton House, 59 Piccadilly, Manchester M1 2AQ. Email: office@mlfhs.demon.co.uk; website: www.mlfhs.demon.co.uk

Manchester FHCen (LDS), Altrincham Road, Wythenshawe, Manchester M22 4BJ.

Manchester Local Studies Unit, Archives, Central Library, St Peter's Square, Manchester M2 5PD. Website: www.manchester.gov.uk

Manchester University, John Rylands Library, 150 Deansgate, Manchester M3 3EH. Website: rylibweb.man.ac.uk

Mansfield and District FHSoc, Miss B. E. Flintham, 15 Cranmer Grove, Mansfield, Nottinghamshire NG19 7JR.

Mansfield FHCen (LDS), Southridge Drive, Mansfield, Nottinghamshire NG18 4RT.

Medieval Settlement Research Group, Planning Department, County Hall, Bedford MK42 9AP.

Meirionydd Archives, Cae Penarlâg, Dolgellau LL40 2YB. Website: www.gwynedd.gov.uk/archives/archivesframeset.htm

Merseyside Maritime Museum, Albert Dock, Liverpool L3 4AA. Website: www.nmgm.org.uk

Merseyside Record Office, Central Library, William Brown Street, Liverpool L3 8EW, with correspondence to Liverpool Record Office and Local History Service. Email: recoffice.central.library@liverpool.gov.uk; website: www.liverpool.gov.uk

Merthyr Tydfil FHCen (LDS), Nantygwenith Street, George Town, Merthyr Tydfil, Glamorgan CF48 1DE.

Methodist Archives and Research Centre, John Rylands Library, 150 Deansgate, Manchester M3 3EH. Website: rylibweb.man.ac.uk

Midlothian Council Archives, Library Headquarters, 2 Clerk Street, Loanhead, Midlothian EH20 9DR. Website: www.midlothian.gov.uk

Mid-Norfolk FHS, Mrs Melanie Donnelly, Codgers Cottage, 6 Hale Road, Bradenham, Thetford, Norfolk IP25 7RA. Email: melaniedonnelly@codgerscottage.fsnet.co.uk; website: www.uea.ac.uk/~s300/genuki/NFK/organisations/midnfhs

Mid-West Regional Development Organisation, 104 Henry Street, Limerick.

Military Historical Society, National Army Museum, Royal Hospital Road, Chelsea, London SW3 4HT. Website: www.national-army-museum.ac.uk

Mining Records Office (Coal Authority), 200 Lichfield Lane, Mansfield, Nottinghamshire NG18 4RG. Website: www.coal.gov.uk

Modern Records Centre, University of Warwick Library, Coventry CV4 7AL. Email: archives@warwick.ac.uk; website: www.warwick.ac.uk

Montgomeryshire Genealogical Society (FHSoc), Mr D. Pugh, Rhoswen, Bryn Street, Newtown, Powys SY16 2HW. Email: montgensoc@freeuk.com; website: home.freeuk.net/montgensoc

Monumental Brass Society, Lowe Hill House, Stratford St Mary, Colchester, Essex CO7 6JX.

Moray Council Heritage Centre, Grant Lodge Local Heritage Centre, Cooper Park, Elgin IV30 1HS. Email: libstock@moray.gov.uk; website: www.moray.org

Morley and District FHSoc, Mrs B. Moxon, 26 Wynyard Drive, Morley, Leeds LS27 9NA. Email: secretary@morleyfhg.co.uk; website: www.morleyfhg.co.uk

Morpeth Record Centre, The Kylins, Loansdean, Morpeth NE61 2EQ, with correspondence to Northumberland Record Office. Website: www.swinhope.demon.co.uk/NRO

Museum of London Library, 150 London Wall, London EC2Y 5HN.

Museum of Welsh Life, St Fagan's, Cardiff CF5 6XB.

Museums Association, 42 Clerkenwell Close, London EC1R 0PA.

National Archives and Records Administration, National Archives Building, 8th Street at Pennsylvania Avenue, NW, Washington DC 20408, USA.

National Archives, Cartographic and Architectural Branch, 8601 Adelphi Road, College Park, ND 20740-6001, USA.

National Archives of Ireland, Bishop Street, Dublin 8. Email: mail@nationalarchives.ie; website: www.nationalarchives.ie

National Archives of Scotland and *National Register of Archives*, PO Box 36, HM General Register House, Edinburgh EH1 3YY *and* West Register House, Charlotte

Square, Edinburgh EH2 4DF. Email: enquiries@nas.gov.uk; website: www.nas.gov.uk

National Army Museum, Department of Archives, Royal Hospital Road, Chelsea, London SW3 4HT. Email: amassie@national-army-museum.ac.uk; website: www.national-army-museum.ac.uk

National Art Library, Archive of Art and Design, Blythe House, 23 Blythe Road, London W14 0QF.

National Council for Voluntary Organizations, Regents Wharf, 8 All Saints Street, London N1 9RL.

National Film and Television Archive, British Film Institute, 21 Stephen Street, London W1P 2LN.

National Genealogical Society (USA), 4527 17th Street North, Arlington, Virginia 22207-2399. Website: www.ngsgenealogy.org

National Library of Ireland, Kildare Street, Dublin 2.

National Library of Scotland, Department of Manuscripts, George IV Bridge, Edinburgh EH1 1EW. Websites: www.nls.uk

National Library of Wales, Department of Manuscripts and Records, Aberystwyth SY23 3BU. Website: www.llgc.org.uk

National Maritime Museum, Manuscripts Section, Greenwich, London SE10 9NF. Email: jf48@dial.pipex.com; website: www.nmm.ac.uk

National Monuments Record, see Royal Commission.

National Museum of Labour History, 103 Princess Street, Manchester M1 6DD.

National Museum of Photography, Film and Television, Prince's View, Bradford BD5 0TR.

National Museums and Galleries of Wales, Cathays Park, Cardiff CF1 3NP.

National Museums and Galleries on Merseyside, Maritime Archives and Library, Albert Dock, Liverpool L3 4AQ. Email: maritime@nmgmnh1.demon.co.uk; website: www.nmgm.org.uk

National Museums of Scotland, Chambers Street, Edinburgh EH1 1JF.

National Railway Museum Reading Room, Leeman Road, York YO2 4XJ. (Science Museum)

National Register of Archives, Quality House, Quality Court, Chancery Lane, London WC2A 1HP. Website: www.hmc.gov.uk (See also National Archives of Scotland)

National Sound Archive, 29 Exhibition Road, London SW7 2AS.

National Trust for Places of Historical Interest or Natural Beauty, 36 Queen Anne's Gate, London SW1H 9AS.

National Trust for Scotland, 5 Charlotte Square, Edinburgh EH2 4DU.

Natural History Museum, Cromwell Road, London SW7 5BD.

New Zealand FHSoc Inc, PO Box 13301, Armagh, Christchurch, New Zealand.

New Zealand, Genealogical Research Institute, PO Box 36-107, Moera, Lower Hutt, Wellington.

Newcastle Emlyn FHCen (LDS), Cardigan Road, Newcastle Emlyn, Dyfed SA38 9RD.

Newcastle-under-Lyme FHCen (LDS), PO Box 457, The Brampton, Newcastle-under-Lyme, Staffordshire ST5 0TD.

Newcastle upon Tyne University, Robinson Library, Newcastle upon Tyne NE2 4HQ.

Newcomen Society for the Study of the History of Engineering and Technology, Science Museum, Imperial College Road, South Kensington, London SW7 2DD.

Newham Local Studies Library, Stratford Library, Water Lane, London E15 4NJ. Email: r.durack@newham.gov.uk

Newport FHCen (LDS), Chestnut Close, Shide Road, Newport, Isle of Wight PO30 1YE.

Norfolk FHSoc, Mrs Rhona Kerswell, Kirby Hall, 70 St Giles Street, Norwich NR2 1LS. Email: nfhs@paston.co.uk; website: www.uea.ac.uk/~s300/genuki/NFK/organisations/nfhs

Norfolk Record Office, Gildengate House, Anglia Square, Upper Green Lane, Norwich NR3 1AX. Website: www.archives.norfolk.gov.uk

Norfolk, see also Mid-Norfolk,

North Cheshire FHSoc, Mrs Rhoda Clarke, 2 Denham Drive, Bramhall, Stockport, Cheshire SK7 2AT. Website: www.genuki.org.uk

North Devon Record Office, Tuly Street, Barnstaple EX31 1EL. Website: www.devon.gov.uk (See also Devon)

North East Lincolnshire Archives, Town Hall, Town Hall Square, Grimsby DN31 1HX. Website: www.nelincs.gov.uk (See also Lincolnshire)

North Highland Archive, Wick Library, Sinclair Terrace, Wick, Caithness KW1 5AB. Email: brenda.lees@highland.gov.uk; website: www.highland.gov.uk (See also Highland)

North Lanarkshire Archives, 10 Kelvin Road, Lenziemill, Cumbernauld G67 2BA.

North Meols FHSoc, Mrs Nadine Taylor, 9 The Paddock, Ainsdale, Southport, Lancashire PR8 3PT. Website: www.users.zetnet.co.uk/nmfhs

North of Ireland FHSoc, Ms R. Sibbett, School of Education, Queen's University of Belfast, 69 University Street, Belfast BT7 1HL. Email: r.sibbett@tesco.net; website: www.nifhs.org

North West Kent FHSoc, Mrs S. Rhys, 6 Windermere Road, Barnehurst, Bexleyheath, Kent DA7 6PW. Email: secretary@nwkfhs.org.uk; website: www.nwkfhs.org.uk

North Yorkshire County Record Office, Malpas Road, with correspondence to County Hall, Northallerton DL7 8AF. Website: www.northyorks.gov.uk

Northampton FHCen (LDS), 137 Harlestone Road, Northampton NN5 6AA.

Northamptonshire FHSoc, Mrs Lynn Rawling, The Old Bakehouse, Achurch, Near Oundle, Peterborough PE8 5SL. Website: www.fugazi.demon.co.uk

Northamptonshire Record Office, Wootton Hall Park, Northampton NN4 8BQ. Website: www.nro.northamptonshire.gov.uk

Northumberland and Durham FHSoc, Mrs Frances Norman, 23 Monkton Avenue, Simonside, South Shields NE34 9RX. Email: frances@fnorman.fsnet.co.uk; website: www.ndfhs.org.uk

Northumberland Record Office, Melton Park, North Gosforth, Newcastle upon Tyne NE3 5QX. Website: www.swinhope.demon.co.uk/NRO (See also Morpeth)

Norwich FHCen (LDS), 19 Greenways, Eaton, Norwich, Norfolk NR4 6PA.

Nottingham FHCen (LDS), Stanhome Square, Nottingham NG22 7GF.

Nottingham University Library, Manuscripts Department, Hallward Library, University Park, Nottingham NG7 2RD.

Nottinghamshire Archives, Castle Meadow Road, Nottingham NG2 1AG. Email: archives@nottscc.gov.uk; website: www.nottscc.gov.uk

Nottinghamshire FHSoc, Geoff Harrington, 15 Holme Close, Woodborough, Nottingham NG14 6EX. Email: tracy.dodds@tesco.net; website: www.nottsfhs.org.uk

Nuneaton and North Warwickshire FHSoc, Leigh Riddell, General Secretary, 14 Amos Avenue, Nuneaton, Warwickshire CV10 7BD. Email: secretary@nnwfhs.org.uk; website: www.nnwfhs.org.uk

Oldham Archives Service, Local Studies Library, 84 Union Street, Oldham OL1 1DN. Email: archives@oldham.gov.uk; website: www.oldham.gov.uk

Oral History Society, Sociology Department, Essex University, Colchester CO4 3SQ.

Ordnance Survey, Phoenix Park, Dublin 7.

Ordnance Survey, Romsey Road, Maybush, Southampton SO9 4DH.

Orkney Archives, Orkney Library, Laing Street, Kirkwall KW15 1NW.

Orkney FHSoc, Strynd Community Room, Kirkwall KW15 1HG.

Ormskirk and District FHSoc, Avril Freemain, Ormskirk College, Hants Lane, Ormskirk, Lancashire L39 1PX.

Orpington FHCen (LDS), Station Approach, Orpington, Kent BR6 0ST.

Oxford University, Bodleian Library, Department of Western Manuscripts, Broad Street, Oxford OX1 3BG. Email: western.manuscript@bodley.ox.ac.uk

Oxfordshire FHSoc, Mrs J. Kennedy, 19 Mavor Close, Woodstock, Oxford OX20 1YL. Email: secretary@ofhs.org.uk; website: www.ofhs.org.uk

Oxfordshire Record Office, St Luke's Church, Temple Road, Cowley, Oxford OX4 2EX. Email: archives@oxfordshire.gov.uk; website: www.oxfordshire.gov.uk

Paisley FHCen (LDS), Glenburn Road, Paisley PA2.

Pembrokeshire Record Office, The Castle, Haverfordwest SA61 2EF.

Perth and Kinross Council Archive, AK Bell Library, 2–8 York Place, Perth PH2 8EP. Email: archives@pkc.gov.uk; website: www.pkc.gov.uk

Peterborough and District FHSoc, Mrs Pauline Kennelly, 33 Farleigh Fields, Orton Wistow, Peterborough PE2 6YB.

Peterborough Central Library, Broadway, Peterborough PE1 1RX.

Peterborough FHCen (LDS), Cottesmore Close, off Atherstone Avenue, Netherton Estate, Peterborough.

Plymouth and West Devon Area Record Office, Unit 3, Clare Place, Coxside, Plymouth PL4 0JW. Website: www.plymouth.gov.uk

Plymouth FHCen (LDS), Hartley Chapel, Mannamead Road, Plymouth, Devon PL3 5QJ.

Pontefract and District FHSoc, Mrs V. Teasdale, 62 Wheatfield Avenue, Oakes, Huddersfield HD3 4FR. Website: freespace.virgin.net/richard.lockwood

Pontefract FHCen (LDS), Park Villas Drive, Pontefract WF8 4QF.

Poole FHCen (LDS), 8 Mount Road, Parkstone, Poole, Dorset BH14 0QW.

Portsmouth City Museums and Records Service, 3 Museum Road, Portsmouth PO1 2LJ. Email: dgregg@portsmouthcc.gov.uk; website: www.portsmouthmuseums.co.uk

Portsmouth FHCen (LDS), Kingston Crescent, Portsmouth, Hampshire PO2 8QL.

Post Office Archives, Heritage Services, Freeling House, Phoenix Place, London WC1X 0DL.

Powys County Archives, County Hall, Llandrindod Wells LD1 5LG. Email: archives@powys.gov.uk; website: archives.powys.gov.uk

Powys FHSoc, Mrs Vera Brown, Oakers Lodge, The Vineyards, Winforton, Herefordshire HR3 6EA. Email: verabrown1@cs.com; website: www.rootsweb.com/~wlspfhs

Presbyterian Historical Society of Ireland, Church House, Fisherwick Place, Belfast BT1 6DW.

Principal Probate Registry, Postal Searches, York Probate Sub-Registry, Duncombe Place, York YO1 2EA.

Principal Registry of the Family Division, First Avenue House, 42–49 High Holborn, London WC1.

Public Record Office, Ruskin Avenue, Kew, Richmond, Surrey TW9 4DU. Website: www.pro.gov.uk

Public Record Office of Northern Ireland, 66 Balmoral Avenue, Belfast BT9 6NY. Email: proni@dcalni.gov.uk; website: proni.nics.gov.uk

Quaker FHSoc, 5 Rad Valley Gardens, Shrewsbury SY3 8AW.

Quaker see also Religious Society of Friends.

Railway and Canal Historical Society, 17 Clumber Crescent North, The Park, Nottingham NG7 1EY.

Rawtenstall FHCen (LDS), Haslingden Road, Rawtenstall, Rossendale, Lancashire BB4.

Reading FHCen (LDS), 280 The Meadway, Tilehurst, Reading, Berkshire RG3 4PG.

Reading University Library, PO Box 223, Whiteknights, Reading, Berkshire RG6 6AE.

Reading University Rural History Centre, PO Box 229, Whiteknights, Reading, Berkshire RG6 6AG.

Redbridge Central Library, Local History Room, Clements Road, Ilford, Essex IG1 1EA.

Redditch FHCen (LDS), 321 Evesham Road, Crabbs Cross, Redditch, Worcestershire B97 5JA.

Registrar General (birth, marriage, death):
England and Wales, PO Box 2, Smedley Hydro, Trafalgar Road, Birkdale, Southport PR8 2HH.
Guernsey, Royal Court House, St Peter Port, Guernsey GY1 2PB. Email: ken.tough@gov.gg
Ireland, Joyce House, 8/11 Lombard Street East, Dublin 2.
Isle of Man, Registries Building, Deemster's Walk, Buck's Road, Douglas, Isle of Man IM1 3AR. Email: civil@registry.gov.uk
Jersey, 10 Royal Square, St Helier, Jersey JE2 4WA. Email: jgreffe@psilink.co.je; website: judicialgreffe.gov.je
Northern Ireland, Oxford House, 49–55 Chichester Street, Belfast BT1 4HL. Website: www.nisra.gov.uk/gro
Scotland, New Register House, Edinburgh EH1 3YT. Website: www.open.gov.uk/gros/groshome.htm

Registry of Shipping and Seamen, Anchor House, Cheviot Close, Parc Ty Glas, Llanishen, Cardiff CF4 5JA.

Religious Society of Friends Library, Friends House, 173–7 Euston Road, London NW1 2BJ. Website: www.quaker.org.uk

Renfrewshire FHSoc, Paisley Museum and Art Galleries, High Street, Paisley PA1 2BA. Website: www.renfrewshirefhs.org.uk

Representative Church Body Library, Braemor Park, Churchtown, Dublin 14. Email: library@ireland.anglican.com; website: www.ireland.anglican.org

Rhyl FHCen (LDS), Rhuddlan Road, Rhyl LL18.

Ripon, Harrogate and District FHSoc, Mrs W. A. Symington, 18 Aspin Drive, Knaresborough, North Yorkshire HG5 8HH. Website: www.users.globalnet.co.uk/~gdl

Rochdale Local Studies Library, 3rd Floor, Champness Hall, Drake Street, Rochdale

OL16 1PB. Website: www.gmcro.co.uk/guides/gmguide/reposit.htm

Rochester upon Medway Studies Centre, Civic Centre, Strood, Rochester ME2 4AW.

Romford FHCen (LDS), 64 Butts Green Road, Hornchurch, Essex RM11 2JJ.

Rotherham Metropolitan Borough, Archives and Local Studies Section, Brian O'Malley Central Library, Walker Place, Rotherham S65 1JH. Email: archives@rotherham.gov.uk

Royal Agricultural Society of England, National Agricultural Centre, Stoneleigh Park, Kenilworth, Warwickshire CV8 2LZ.

Royal Air Force Museum, Research and Information Services, Grahame Park Way, Hendon, London NW9 5LL. Email: info@rafmuseum.com; website: rafmuseum.com

Royal Archives, Windsor Castle, Berkshire SL4 1NJ.

Royal Botanic Gardens, Library and Archives, Kew, Richmond, Surrey TW9 3AB.

Royal College of Physicians of London, 11 St Andrew's Place, Regent's Park, London NW1 4LE.

Royal College of Surgeons of England, 35–43 Lincoln's Inn Fields, London WC2A 3PN. Website: www.rcseng.ac.uk

Royal Commission on Historical Manuscripts and *National Register of Archives*, Quality House, Quality Court, Chancery Lane, London WC2A 1HP. Website: www.hmc.gov.uk

Royal Commission on the Ancient and Historical Monuments of Scotland and *National Monuments Record*, John Sinclair House, 16 Bernard Terrace, Edinburgh EH8 9NX.

Royal Commission on the Ancient and Historical Monuments of Wales and *National Monuments Record*, Crown Building, Plas Crug, Aberystwyth SY23 1NJ.

Royal Commission on the Historical Monuments of England, National Monuments Record Centre, Kemble Drive, Swindon, Wiltshire SN2 2GZ *and* London Search Room, 55 Blandford Street, London W1H 3AF. Email: info@rchme.gov.uk; website: www.english-heritage.org.uk

Royal Historical Society, University College, Gower Street, London WC1E 6BT.

Royal Institute of British Architects, see British Architectural Library.

Royal Institution of Cornwall, Courtney Library, River Street, Truro TR1 2SJ.

Royal Institution of Great Britain, 21 Albemarle Street, London W1X 4BS.

Royal Irish Academy, 19 Dawson Street, Dublin 2.

Royal Mail Group, Heritage Services, Freeling House, Phoenix Place, London WC1X 0DL.

Royal Society Library, 6 Carlton House Terrace, London SW1Y 5AG.

Royal Society of Antiquaries of Ireland, 63 Merrion Square, Dublin 2.

Royston and District FHSoc, Mrs Joyce Hellier, 60 Heathfield, Royston, Hertfordshire SG8 5BN. Website: www.hertsdirect.org/infoadvice

Rugby FHSoc, Mr John A. Chard, Springfields, Rocheberie Way, Rugby CV22 6EG. Email: j.chard@ntlworld.com

St Albans FHCen (LDS), London Road at Cutenhoe Road, Luton, Bedfordshire.

St Andrews University, Archives, North Street, St Andrews, Fife KY16 9TR.

St Austell FHCen (LDS), Kingfisher Drive, St Austell, Cornwall PL25 3AZ.

St Helens Local History and Archives Library, Central Library, Gamble Institute, Victoria Square, St Helens WA10 1DY. Website: www.sthelens.gov.uk

St Helier FHCen (LDS), Rue de la Vallée, St Mary, Jersey, Channel Islands.

St Patrick's College Library, Maynooth, County Kildare.

Salford Archives Centre, Salford Museum and Art Gallery, Peel Park, The Crescent, Salford M5 4WU. Website: www.gmcro.co.uk/guides/gmguide/reposit.htm

Sandwell Community History and Archives Service, Smethwick Library, High Street, Smethwick, Warley B66 1AB. Website: www.lea.sandwell.gov.uk

Scarborough FHCen (LDS), Stepney Drive/Whitby Road, Scarborough YO12 5DP.

School of Scottish Studies, 27–8 George Square, Edinburgh EH8 9LD.

Science Museum Library, Imperial College Road, South Kensington, London SW7 5NH *and* National Railway Museum Reading Room, Leeman Road, York YO2 4XJ.

Scots Ancestry Research Society, 29B Albany Street, Edinburgh EH1 3QN. Website: www.royalmile.com/scotsancestry

Scottish Archive Network (SCAN), website: www.scan.org.uk

Scottish Association of Family History Societies, 51–3 Morton Hall Road, Edinburgh EH9 2HN. Website: www.safhs.org.uk

Scottish Borders Archive and Local History Centre, Library Headquarters, St Mary's

Mill, Selkirk TD7 5EW.
Scottish Catholic Archives, Columba House, 16 Drummond Place, Edinburgh EH3 6PL.
Scottish Genealogy Society, Library and Family History Centre, 15 Victoria Terrace, Edinburgh EH1 2JL. Email: sales@scotsgenealogy.com; website: www.scotsgenealogy.com
Scottish History Society, Department of Scottish History, University of Edinburgh, 17 Buccleuch Place, Edinburgh EH8 9LN.
Scottish Record Office, see National Archives of Scotland.
Scottish Record Society, Department of Scottish History, University of Glasgow G12 8QH.
Scottish Records Association, Glasgow City Archives, Mitchell Library, 201 North Street, Glasgow G3 7DN.
Seamen. See General Register and Record Office.
Selden Society, Faculty of Laws, Queen Mary College, Mile End Road, London E1 4NS.
Shakespeare Birthplace Trust Records Office, Shakespeare Centre, Henley Street, Stratford-upon-Avon, Warwickshire CV37 6QW. Email: records@shakespeare.org.uk
Sheffield and District FHSoc, Mrs J. Pitchforth, 10 Hallam Grange Road, Sheffield S10 4BJ. Email: secretary@sheffieldfhs.org.uk; website: www.sheffieldfhs.org.uk
Sheffield Archives, 52 Shoreham Street, Sheffield S1 4SP. Email: sheffield.archives@dial.pipex.com
Sheffield FHCen (LDS), Wheel Lane, Grenoside, Sheffield S30 3RL.
Sheffield University Library, Archives, Western Bank, Sheffield S10 2TN.
Shetland Archives, 44 King Harold Street, Lerwick, Shetland ZE1 0EQ. Website: www.shetland.gov.uk
Shetland FHSoc, 6 Hillhead, Lerwick, Shetland ZE1 0EJ. Email: shetland.fhs@zetnet.co.uk; website: www.users.zetnet.co.uk/shetland-fhs
Shipping. See General Register and Record Office.
Shropshire FHSoc, Mrs D. Hills, Redhillside, Ludlow Road, Church Stretton, Shropshire SY6 6AD. Email: secretary@sfhs.org.uk; website: www.sfhs.org.uk
Shropshire Records and Research Centre, Castle Gates, Shrewsbury SY1 2AS. Email: research@shropshire-cc.gov.uk; website: www.shropshire-cc.gov.uk
Society for Medieval Archaeology, Archaeology Unit, Winston Churchill Building, Radbrook Centre, Radbrook Road, Shrewsbury SY3 9BJ.
Society for Post-Medieval Archaeology, Department of Medieval and Latin Antiquities, The British Museum, London WC1B 3DG.
Society for Promoting Christian Knowledge, Holy Trinity Church, Marylebone Road, London NW1 4DU. Archives at Cambridge University Library.
Society for the Protection of Ancient Buildings, 37 Spital Square, London E1 6DY.
Society of Antiquaries of London, Burlington House, Piccadilly, London W1V 0HS.
Society of Antiquaries of Scotland, Royal Museums of Scotland, Chambers Street, Edinburgh EH1 1JF.
Society of Genealogists, 14 Charterhouse Buildings, Goswell Road, London EC1M 7BA. Email: info@sog.org.uk; website: www.sog.org.uk
Soil Survey and Land Research Centre (Soil Survey of England and Wales), Silsoe Campus, Silsoe, Bedford MK45 4DT.
Somerset and Dorset FHSoc, The Secretary, PO Box 4502, Sherborne DT9 6YL. Email: society@sdfhs.org; website: www.sdfhs.org
Somerset Archive and Record Service, Obridge Road, Taunton TA2 7PU. Email: archives@somerset.gov.uk; website: www.somerset.gov.uk
South Cheshire FHSoc, PO Box 1990, Crewe, Cheshire CW2 6FF. Website: www.scfhs.org.uk
South Lanarkshire Archives and Information Management Service, 30 Hawbank Road, College Milton, East Kilbride G74 5EX. Website: www.southlanarkshire.gov.uk
Southampton Archives Service, Civic Centre, Southampton SO14 7LY. Website: www.southampton.gov.uk
Southampton University Library, Highfield, Southampton SO17 1BJ.
Southwark Local Studies Library, 211 Borough High Street, London SE1 1JA.
Staffordshire and Stoke-on-Trent Archive Service, William Salt Library, Eastgate Street, Stafford ST16 2LZ. Email: william.salt.library@staffordshire.gov.uk; website: www.staffordshire.gov.uk
Staines FHCen (LDS), 41 Kingston Road, Staines, Middlesex TW18 4LH.
State Paper Office, Dublin Castle, Dublin 2.

Steel, Records Services. See Warwick University, Modern Records Centre. Website: www.uksteel.org.uk

Stevenage FHCen (LDS), Latter-Day Saints Chapel, Buckthorn Avenue, Stevenage, Hertfordshire SG1 1TU.

Stirling Council Archives, Unit 6, Burghmuir Industrial Estate, Stirling FK7 7PY.

Stockport Archive Service, Central Library, Wellington Road South, Stockport SK1 3RS. Website: www.gmcro.co.uk/guides/gmguide/reposit.htm

Stockport Heritage Services, Woodbank Hall, Woodbank Park, Turncroft Lane, Offerton, Stockport SK1 4JR.

Stoke-on-Trent City Archives, Hanley Library, Bethesda Street, Hanley, Stoke-on-Trent ST1 3RS. Email: stoke.archives@stoke.gov.uk; website: www.staffordshire.gov.uk (See also Staffordshire and Stoke-on-Trent Archive Service)

Suffolk FHSoc, Mrs P. Turner, 48 Princethorpe Road, Ipswich IP3 8NX. Email: bridgessuffolk@lineone.net; website: www.genuki.org.uk/big/eng/SFK/sfhs

Suffolk Record Office, Bury St Edmunds Branch, Raingate Street, Bury St Edmunds IP33 2AR *and* Ipswich Branch, Gatacre Road, Ipswich IP1 2LQ *and* Lowestoft Branch, Central Library, Clapham Road, Lowestoft NR32 1DR. Website: www.suffolkcc.gov.uk

Sunderland FHCen (LDS), Linden Road, Queen Alexandra Road, Sunderland SR2 9AU.

Surrey History Centre, 130 Goldsworth Road, Woking GU21 1ND. Email: shs@surreycc.gov.uk; website: shs.surreycc.gov.uk

Sussex FHSoc, Mrs J. E. Chamberlain Hare, 7 Tower View, Manor Park, Uckfield, East Sussex TN22 1SB. Email: secretary@sfhg.org.uk; website: www.sfhg.org.uk

Sussex University Library, Manuscript Collections, Falmer, Brighton, East Sussex BN1 9QL.

Sussex, see also East *and* West Sussex.

Sutton Coldfield FHCen (LDS), 185 Penns Lane, Sutton Coldfield B76 1JU.

Sutton (London Borough) Heritage Services, Archive Section, Central Library, St Nicholas Way, Sutton SM1 1EA. Email: local.studies@sutton.gov.uk; website: www.sutton.gov.uk

Swansea FHCen (LDS), Cockett Road, Swansea, West Glamorgan SA2 0FH.

Tameside Archive Service, Local Studies Library, Astley Cheetham Public Library, Trinity Street, Stalybridge SK15 2BN. Email: localstudies.library@mail.tameside.gov.uk; website: www.tameside.gov.uk

Tay Valley FHSoc (covering Angus, Fife, Kinross and Perth), Research Centre, 179–181 Princes Street, Dundee DD4 6DQ. Email: tvfhs@tayvalleyfhs.org.uk; website: www.tayvalleyfhs.org.uk

Teesside Archives, Exchange House, 6 Martin Road, Middlesbrough TS1 1DB. Email: teesside_archives@middlesbrough.gov.uk; website: www.middlesbrough.gov.uk

Telford FHCen (LDS), 72 Glebe Street, Wellington, Shropshire TF1 1JY.

Thetford FHCen (LDS), Station Road, Thetford, Norfolk IP24 1AH.

Tower Hamlets Local History Library and Archives, Bancroft Library, 277 Bancroft Road, London E1 4DG. Website: www.towerhamlets.gov.uk

Trafford Local Studies Centre, Sale Library, Tatton Road, Sale, Manchester M33 1YH. Website: www.trafford.gov.uk/libraries/local.htm

Trinity College Library, College Street, Dublin 2.

Troon and Ayrshire FHSoc, M. E. R. C., Troon Public Library, South Beach, Troon, Ayrshire KA10 6EF. Website: www.troonayrshirefhs.org.uk

Trowbridge FHCen (LDS), Brook Road, Trowbridge, Wiltshire BA14.

Tunbridge Wells FHSoc, Mrs Oxenbury, The Old Cottage, Langton Road, Tunbridge Wells, Kent TN3 0BA. Email: brian@kcckal.demon.co.uk; website: www.kcckal.demon.co.uk/twfhsmain.htm

Tyne and Wear Archives Service, Blandford House, Blandford Square, Newcastle upon Tyne NE1 4JA. Email: twas@dial.pipex.com; website: www.thenortheast.com/archives

Ulster Folk and Transport Museum, Cultra Manor, Holywood, Belfast BT18 0EU *and* Witham Street, Newtownards, Belfast BT4 1HP.

Ulster Historical Foundation, Balmoral Buildings, 12 College Square East, Belfast BT1 6DD.

Ulster Local Studies, Federation for, Institute for Ulster Local Studies, 8 Fitzwilliam Street, Belfast BT9 6AW.

Ulster Museum, Botanic Gardens, Belfast BT9 5AB.

University of Wales, Bangor, Department of Manuscripts, Bangor LL57 2DG.

Valuation Office, 6 Ely Place, Dublin 2.

Vernacular Architecture Group, 16 Falna Crescent, Coton Green, Tamworth, Staffordshire B79 8JS.

Victoria and Albert Museum, Cromwell Road, South Kensington, London SW7 2RL.

Victoria and Albert Museum, National Art Library, Archive of Art and Design, Blythe House, 23 Blythe Road, London W14 0QF.

Victorian Society, 1 Priory Gardens, Bedford Park, London W4 1TT.

Wakefield and District FHSoc, Mrs Jean Howgate, 11 Waterton Close, Walton, Wakefield, West Yorkshire WF2 6JT. Email: general.secretary@virgin.net; website: www.wdfhs.co.uk

Wakefield Headquarters, West Yorkshire Archive Service, Registry of Deeds, Newstead Road, Wakefield WF1 2DE. Email: wakefield@wyjs.org.uk; website: www.archives.wyjs.org.uk (See also West Yorkshire)

Walsall Archives Service, Local History Centre, Essex Street, Walsall WS2 7AS. Website: www.walsall.gov.uk

Waltham Forest Archives and Local History Library, Vestry House Museum, Vestry Road, Walthamstow, London E17 9NH. Email: vestry.house@al.lbwf.gov.uk; website: www.lbwf.gov.uk

Waltham Forest FHSoc, Mr B. F. Burton, 49 Sky Peals Road, Woodford Green, Essex IG8 9NE.

Wandsworth FHCen (LDS), 149 Nightingale Lane, Balham, London SW12 8NG.

Wandsworth Local History Collection, Battersea Library, 265 Lavender Hill, London SW11 1JB.

Warrington Library, Museum Street, Warrington WA1 1JB.

Warwick University, Modern Records Centre, University Library, Coventry CV4 7AL. Email: archives@warwick.ac.uk; website: www.warwick.ac.uk

Warwickshire FHSoc, 7 Mersey Road, Bulkington, Warwickshire CV12 9QB. Email: n.wetton@virgin.net; website: www.wfhs.org.uk

Warwickshire County Record Office, Priory Park, Cape Road, Warwick CV34 4JS. Email: recordoffice@warwickshire.gov.uk; website: www.warwickshire.gov.uk

Watford FHCen (LDS), Hempstead Road, Watford, Hertfordshire WD1.

Wednesfield FHCen (LDS), Linthouse Lane, Wednesfield, West Midlands WV11.

Wellcome Institute for the History of Medicine, 183 Euston Road, London NW1 2BE.

Welsh Folk Museum, St Fagans, Cardiff CF5 6XB.

West Glamorgan Archive Service, County Hall, Oystermouth Road, Swansea SA1 3SN. Email: archives@swansea.gov.uk; website: www.swansea.gov.uk (See also Glamorgan)

West Lothian Council Archives, 7 Rutherford Square, Brucefield Industrial Estate, Livingston, West Lothian EH54 9BU. Website: www.westlothian.gov.uk

West Middlesex FHSoc, Mrs Mavis Burton, 10 West Way, Heston, Middlesex TW5 0JF. Website: www.west-middlesex-fhs.org.uk

West Surrey FHSoc, Mrs S. McQuire, Deer Dell, Botany Hill, Sands, Farnham, Surrey GU10 1LZ. Email: sylviamcq@onetel.net.uk; website: www.wsfhs.org

West Sussex Record Office, Sherburne House, 3 Orchard Street, with correspondence to County Hall, West Street, Chichester PO19 1RN. Email: records.office@westsussex.gov.uk; website: www.westsussex.gov.uk

West Yorkshire Archive Service, Wakefield Headquarters, Registry of Deeds, Newstead Road, Wakefield WF1 2DE. Email: wakefield@wyjs.org.uk; website: www.archives.wyjs.org.uk (See also Bradford, Calderdale, Kirklees, Leeds, Wakefield, Yorkshire)

Westminster Abbey Muniment Room and Library, London SW1P 3PA.

Westminster and Central Middlesex FHSoc, see London and North Middlesex FHSoc.

Westminster: City of Westminster Archives Centre, 10 St Ann's Street, London SW1P 2XR. Website: www.westminster.gov.uk

Westminster Diocesan Archives, 16a Abingdon Road, London W8 6AF.

Weston-super-Mare FHSoc, Kerry James, 32 Marconi Close, Weston-super-Mare BS23 3HH. Email: kes.jack@virgin.net; website: www.wsmfhs.org.uk

Wharfedale FHSoc, Mrs Susan Hartley, 1 West View Court, Yeadon, Leeds LS19 7HX. Website: www.users.globalnet.co.uk/~gdl/wfhg1.htm

Wigan Archives Service, Town Hall, Leigh WN7 2DY. Website: www.wiganmbc.gov.uk

Wigan FHSoc, Brian Fairhurst, 615 Wigan Road, Bryn, Wigan, Lancashire WN4 0BY.

William Salt Library, Eastgate Street, Stafford ST16 2LZ.

Wiltshire and Swindon Record Office, Libraries and Heritage Headquarters, County Hall, Bythesea Road, Trowbridge BA14 8BS. Email: wsro@wiltshire.gov.uk; website: www.wiltshire.gov.uk

Wiltshire FHSoc, Secretary, 10 Castle Lane, Devizes, Wiltshire SN10 1HJ. Website: www.genuki.org.uk/big/eng/WIL/WFHS

Wirral Archives, Wirral Museum, Town Hall, Hamilton Street, Birkenhead CH41 5BR. Email: archives@wirral-libraries.net; website: www.wirral-libraries.net

Wolverhampton Archives and Local Studies, 42–50 Snow Hill, Wolverhampton WV2 4AG. Website: www.wolverhampton.gov.uk

Woolwich and District FHSoc, Mrs Edna Reynolds, 54 Parkhill Road, Bexley, Kent DA5 1HY.

Worcestershire Record Office, City Centre Branch, Worcestershire Library and History Centre, Trinity Street, Worcester WR1 2PW. Email: wlhc@worcestershire.gov.uk; website: www.worcestershire.gov.uk

Worcestershire Record Office, County Hall Branch, County Hall, Spetchley Road, Worcester WR5 2NP. Email: recordoffice@worcestershire.gov.uk; website: www.worcestershire.gov.uk

Working Class Movement Library, Jubilee House, 51 The Crescent, Salford, Manchester M5 4WX. Email: enquiries@wcml.org.uk; website: www.wcml.org.uk

Worthing FHCen (LDS), Goring Street, Goring-by-Sea, West Sussex BN12 5AR.

Wrexham Archives Service, County Buildings, Regent Street, Wrexham LL11 1RB. Email: archives@wrexham.gov.uk; website: www.wrexham.gov.uk

Yate FHCen (LDS), Wellington Road, Yate, South Gloucestershire BS37 5UY.

Yeovil FHCen (LDS), Latter-Day Saints Chapel, Forest Hill, Yeovil, Somerset BA20 2PH.

York City and District FHSoc, Mrs Carol Mennell, 4 Orchard Close, Dringhouses, York YO2 2NX. Website: www.yorkfamilyhistory.org.uk

York City Archives Department, Art Gallery Building, Exhibition Square, York YO1 2EW. Website: www.york.gov.uk

York FHCen (LDS), West Bank, Acomb, York YO2 4ES.

York Minster Archives, Minster Library, Dean's Park, York YO1 2JD.

York University, Borthwick Institute of Historical Research, St Anthony's Hall, Peasholme Green, York YO1 2PW. Website: www.york.ac.uk

Yorkshire Archaeological Society, Archives, Claremont, 23 Clarendon Road, Leeds LS2 9NZ. Email: archives@wyjs.org.uk; website: www.archives.wyjs.org.uk (See also West Yorkshire)

Yorkshire Archaeological Society, FHSection, Miss Lynda Raistrick, 23 Clarendon Road, Leeds, LS2 9NZ. Email: lynda@raistrickl.freeserve.co.uk; website: www.users.globalnet.co.uk/~gdl/yasfhs.htm

Index